The Dangerous Rise of Therapeutic Education

The silent ascendancy of a therapeutic ethos across the education system and into the workplace demands a book that serves as a wake up call to everyone.

Kathryn Ecclestone and Dennis Hayes' controversial and compelling book uses a wealth of examples across the education system, from primary schools to university, and the workplace to show how therapeutic education is turning children, young people and adults into anxious and self-preoccupied individuals rather than aspiring, optimistic and resilient learners who want to know everything about the world.

The chapters address a variety of thought-provoking themes, including:

- how therapeutic ideas from popular culture dominate social thought and social policies and offer a diminished view of human potential
- how schools undermine parental confidence and authority by fostering dependence and compulsory participation in therapeutic activities based on disclosing emotions to others
- how higher education has adopted therapeutic forms of teacher training because many academics have lost faith in the pursuit of knowledge
- how such developments are propelled by a deluge of political initiatives in areas such as emotional literacy, emotional well-being and the 'soft outcomes' of learning.

The Dangerous Rise of Therapeutic Education is eye-opening reading for every teacher, student teacher and parent who retains any belief in the power of knowledge to transform people's lives. Its insistent call for a serious public debate about the emotional state of education should also be at the forefront of the minds of every agent of change within society … from parent to policy maker.

Kathryn Ecclestone is Professor of Post-Compulsory Education at Oxford Brookes University. She has written two best selling books on assessment, and is a member of the Assessment Reform Group and the editorial board for the *Journal of Further and Higher Education*.

Dennis Hayes is Visiting Professor in the Westminster Institute of Education, Oxford Brookes University. He is the editor and author of several books including *The RoutledgeFalmer Guide to Key Debates in Education* (2004).

The Dangerous Rise of Therapeutic Education

Kathryn Ecclestone and
Dennis Hayes

Routledge
Taylor & Francis Group

LONDON AND NEW YORK

First published 2009
by Routledge
2 Park Square, Milton Park, Abingdon, Oxon OX14 4RN

Simultaneously published in the USA and Canada
by Routledge
270 Madison Ave, New York, NY 10016

Routledge is an imprint of the Taylor & Francis Group, an informa business

© 2009 Kathryn Ecclestone and Dennis Hayes

Typeset in Garamond by
HWA Text and Data Management, London
Printed and bound in Great Britain by
TJ International Ltd, Padstow, Cornwall

British Library Cataloguing in Publication Data
A catalogue record for this book is available from the British Library

Library of Congress Cataloging-in-Publication Data
Ecclestone, Kathryn.
  The dangerous rise of therapeutic education /
Kathryn Ecclestone and Dennis Hayes.
    p. cm.
  Includes bibliographical references and index.
  1. Education – Aims and objectives – Great Britain. 2. School psychology – Great Britain. I. Hayes, Dennis, 1950- II. Title.
  LA632.E22 2009
  370.941--dc22   2007050914

ISBN10: 0-415-39700-6 (hbk)
ISBN10: 0-415-39701-4 (pbk)

ISBN13: 978-0-415-39700-1 (hbk)
ISBN13: 978-0-415-39701-8 (pbk)

Contents

Foreword

In recent decades the crisis of education has come to haunt public life. Throughout Europe the education of children in Europe has turned into a constant source of concern to policy makers and the media. Never has so much significance been attached to the role of education as in the early twenty-first century. Nobody complained when former Prime Minister Tony Blair told the 1996 Labour Party conference that his three top priorities on coming to office were 'education, education and education'. Four years later he still felt the need to constantly repeat the word 'education' when he promised that his 'government's passion' would be 'education, education, education'. Such zealous commitment to the cause of education is also constantly repeated in policy documents throughout Europe. A historian looking back on our time a couple of centuries from now may well infer that education was a dominant faith that inspired the European cultural elite in the twenty-first century.

And yet it seems that education does not work. Why else do we talk about it all the time? How do we account for the constant tendency to reorganise schooling and to introduce one reform after another? Why are examinations a permanent focus for debate? Why has the curriculum become a political football that is always chopped and changed? Why are we so worried that the pressure experienced by children is likely to increase their mental health problems? And why are so many parents so obsessed about getting their children into the 'right' school?

One possible reason why the public has so much difficulty making sense of the problems associated with education is that its intellectual energies are focused on symptoms of the crisis. Usually arguments are initiated by a report that purports to measure the achievements of students or the success and failure of schools. But too often such statistics have a nasty habit of contradicting one another. Moreover surveys that claim massive improvements in children's achievements one year come up with a more downbeat assessment a few years later. Unfortunately, we rarely pause and ask the obvious question of just what it is we are measuring. Or more specifically we rarely have a grown up discussion about what education is for.

The principal problem addressed by this book is the difficulty that contemporary society has in giving meaning to education. A sense of disorientation about the purpose of education coincides with confusion about what society ought to expect of its children. The downsizing of children's potential has been one of the outcomes of this confusion. Children are now systematically represented as 'vulnerable' and 'at risk'. Many educators believe that children are so vulnerable that the management of their emotions constitutes one of the principal functions of their school. Although the project of emotional education is well intended, its main outcome is to disempower young people. The therapeutic turn in education also distracts schools from providing a genuine intellectual challenge to young people.

The Dangerous Rise of Therapeutic Education provides a compelling account of the corrosive impact of a pedagogic ethos on the experience of learning in all sectors of education. It shows how the illegitimate importation of therapeutic techniques into schools, colleges, universities and workplaces fails to improve emotional well-being. The infantalisation of learners of all ages is the inexorable consequence of the therapeutic turn. Sadly, the ascendancy of therapeutic education and its regrettable consequences is rarely recognised and even less discussed. That is why this important book is long overdue. It offers an exciting and novel interpretation of a phenomenon through which the current crisis of education is lived and experienced. Every parent who takes their child seriously needs to become familiar with the issues raised by Ecclestone and Hayes. And every educator who wants to educate needs to consider whether they are teachers or managers of emotions.

Frank Furedi,
Professor of Sociology
School of Social Policy and Social Research
University of Kent

Preface

You know something has changed when young people want to know more about themselves than about the world.

(Mark Taylor, History Teacher, South London)

Something has indeed changed. If you ask educators, parents and policy makers what is wrong with the British education system, many will identify too many stressful, demotivating tests, an irrelevant, boring and 'elitist' curriculum, lack of parity between academic and vocational education, rising levels of bullying, disengagement amongst growing numbers of young people and inequality of participation and achievement caused by social exclusion. They will probably also agree with numerous reports that British children are the unhappiest, most stressed and anxious in Europe, fearful about everything from security and consumerism to lack of friends and global warming.

Few educators, parents and policy makers will question the idea that we face a crisis of unprecedented proportions in mental health and emotional problems, alongside claims that the materialism of Western societies, bad parenting and the pressures of schooling and modern life make childhood 'toxic' for the majority of children. Some might agree with neuroscientists that poor parenting damages emotional receptors in the brain permanently, requiring 'repair' through 'nurturing interventions' in nurseries and primary schools. The vast majority will agree that schools generally need to do much more to develop and enhance children and young people's emotional well-being.

We argue in this book that, far from getting to the heart of what is wrong with the British education system and what needs to be done in response, these concerns obscure a profound crisis of meaning which is producing a much more serious change than anything they suggest. We characterise this as the dangerous rise of therapeutic education, with far reaching implications for educational goals and practices and therefore for the ways in which education fosters a particular view of what it means to be human.

Charting the rise of therapeutic education

Sponsored enthusiastically by the British government and supported by numerous academic researchers and a huge professional and commercial industry, a deluge of interventions throughout the education system assess the emotional needs and perceived emotional vulnerability of children, young people and adults and claim to develop their emotional literacy and well-being. From the age of three onwards, day to day activities throughout the education system require children to participate in circle time, Philosophy for Children classes, nurture groups, peer mentoring and buddy schemes. From ten years old, they might do drama workshops to deal with the 'trauma of transition' to secondary school and more circle time in citizenship and personal, social and health education lessons to create empathetic, tolerant and emotionally literate citizens.

Other subjects such as history, English and biology might also be marshalled for emotional literacy. In colleges and universities, students will experience induction programmes that signal all the emotional support on offer, while lectures and assessment processes aim to build self-esteem and make students feel good about themselves. They might take part in group sessions to assess their starting levels of self-esteem and confidence and record their progress and tutorials that elicit and record their emotional responses to their course. In workplaces, activities to deal with stress, harassment, bullying, appraisal and performance review increasingly focus on emotional responses to work while exit interviews help workers cope emotionally with redundancy.

Thousands of teachers, learning assistants, retention officers, disability liaison officers and learning support managers are supported in these activities by growing numbers of children and young people trained to develop their peers' emotional well-being. Buddy schemes in secondary schools train 14 year olds in counselling techniques and psychodrama so that they can act as mentors to 11 year olds moving to secondary school: one scheme in the south-west is called 'Angels' – a nice guy every time life sucks'. The government is currently evaluating a scheme to bring school leavers back into schools as mentors while students in universities can have their peer mentoring activities assessed towards their degree. Teachers, classroom assistants parents and support staff such as canteen workers can attend courses to become 'emotional nurses' and to develop their own emotional literacy and well-being.

As we shall show in the book, there is rapidly growing interest amongst policy makers and many proponents of the activities summarised above in shifting the emphasis from developing emotional literacy and enhancing emotional well-being to teaching children and young people 'the means to be happy'.

Defining therapeutic education

We aim to show how such activities embed populist therapeutic assumptions, claims and processes throughout education, signifying the idea that emotional well-being, emotional literacy and emotional competence are some of the most important outcomes of the education system. We define any activity that focuses on perceived emotional problems and which aims to make educational content and learning processes more 'emotionally engaging' as 'therapeutic education'. We recognize that defining the various activities and underlying assumptions we explore in the book as 'therapeutic' does not accord with specialist definitions of 'therapeutic' from professionals in different branches of psychoanalysis, child and educational psychology and counselling.

Instead, our use of the term relates the activities we explore in the book to the broader emergence over the past 40 years of a 'therapeutic ethos' throughout Anglo-American culture and politics. One feature of this ethos is an exponential extension of counselling, psychoanalysis and psychology into more areas of social and personal life, policy and professional practice. But the significance of a therapeutic ethos as we and others define it is much more than this: it offers a new sensibility, a form of cultural script, a set of explanations and underlying assumptions about appropriate feelings and responses to events, and a set of associated practices and rituals through which people make sense of themselves and others.

We develop our thesis that populist accounts of emotional problems and associated claims are embedded in educational policy and practice through examples of therapeutic activities. We argue that these illustrate the way in which a therapeutic culture has begun to 'influence and arguably dominate the public's system of meaning [and to have] emerged as a serious cultural force' (Furedi 2004: 17). Our analysis shows that only by relating policies and practices emerging in schools, colleges, universities and workplaces to broader themes in culture and politics can we reveal the underlying therapeutic ethos.

Popularising therapeutic orthodoxies

The vocabulary, mindset and assumptions of popular therapy permeate a vast array of lifestyle, confessional and reality television programmes, the huge literary genre of biographies and autobiographies titled in bookshops as 'tragic life stories', women and men's lifestyle magazines, weekend newspaper supplements and the ever-expanding self-help industry. There is a growing array of guide books on mental health.

We begin the book with some random examples of popular manifestations of therapy and everyday preoccupation with emotional vulnerability and we could cite examples *ad infinitum*. As we shall show, not only are educational policy and practice full of therapeutic vocabulary and assumptions, but so too are our personal and working lives. Far from being trivial, random and irrelevant anecdotes, such examples reflect some influential therapeutic orthodoxies. These include claims that past life experiences have long-term negative emotional effects for everyone, and particularly pernicious effects for an increasing minority. The overall message is that, behind our apparently confident facades, we are all, to a greater or lesser extent, emotionally fragile and vulnerable and, as a consequence, we need particular forms of emotional support. A parallel orthodoxy is that if we do not see this, or disagree with it, we are in denial or repressing our true feelings.

Defining the 'diminished self'

Central to our thesis about the dangers of therapeutic education is an argument that populist orthodoxies reflect and reinforce the concept of a 'diminished self'. We argue that the manifestations of a therapeutic culture throughout the education system insert a particular cultural perspective of the self. This 'regards most forms of human experience as the source of emotional distress ... [where people] characteristically suffer from 'an emotional deficit and possess a permanent consciousness of vulnerability' (Furedi 2004: 110/414). A diminished human subject finds exposure to uncertainty and adversity, including disappointment, despair and conflict simultaneously threatening to 'the integrity of the self' and inhibiting of it. A diminished sense of human potential denies the intellectual and privileges the emotional.

Diminished images of students and pupils are rife throughout the education system, reflected in the routine use of labels such as 'vulnerable learners', 'at risk learners', students with 'fragile identities', 'the disaffected and disengaged', 'the hard to reach', people with 'fractured and fragmented lives', learners with 'complex needs' and 'low self-esteemers'. Sometimes, whole groups such as asylum seekers learning English, the children of asylum seekers, working class boys or 14 year olds disaffected with school education, are deemed to 'suffer from low self-esteem' or to be 'emotionally fragile'. 'Low self-esteem' is widely seen as the cause of social and educational difficulties.

Children are internalizing similar ideas: 'feeling stressy', 'being left out' or 'got at', 'having an anxious morning' are routine expressions amongst eight year olds. Older students, including adults on professional development and higher education courses, increasingly describe themselves as 'suffering from low self-esteem', citing feedback and being asked challenging questions in class as 'stressful'.

The British education system has always been prone to labels rooted in discredited psychometric measures of intelligence, such as 'thick', 'stupid', 'bright' or 'low ability'. Labels depicting emotional causes of problems with attitude, behaviour or achievement are much more recent and becoming more prevalent. We argue that they are a predictable outcome of activities that claim to address diminished perceptions and to empower their participants but which end up encouraging people to respond emotionally to day to day challenges. This circularity emerges, as we shall argue, through a changing cultural perspective about the self and its potential.

The emotional state

The British government under New Labour has embraced disparate concerns and psychological explanations about people's emotional states. Policies that require nurseries, playgroups, schools, colleges and universities to address emotional problems and develop emotional well-being embed New Labour's particular view of 'social justice' into educational policy and practice. The goals and institutional arrangements of 'Every Child Matters' require welfare and education agencies to ensure that, as part of being 'healthy', 'safe' and able to 'enjoy' and 'achieve' educationally and socially, children's mental health and well-being are paramount.

Guidance for nurseries and schools, including the Foundation Stage Profile, Social Emotional Aspects of Learning (SEAL) strategy and the National Healthy Schools Standard, and a large number of other initiatives, encourage schools and colleges to address well-being through the curriculum, teaching activities and support systems. SEAL specifies 42 outcomes for 3–11 year olds and 50 for 11–16 year olds and schools are required to assess young children's emotional competence in a Foundation Stage Profile. The National Institute for Clinical Excellence is drawing up guidelines for primary schools to diagnose emotional well-being. Twenty eight instruments are currently used to assess different aspects of 'emotional competence' in different parts of the education, health and welfare system.

Emotional interventions receive large amounts of public funding. SEAL cost £10m in 2007–8, with a further £31.2 million earmarked over the next three years. Anti-bullying schemes cost £1.7 million a year, while peer mentoring currently receives £1.75 million. Another £60 million was added in July 2007 to educational expenditure for schools to improve emotional well-being, phased over the next three years to be £30 million in 2010–11. In October 2007, the Department for Children, Schools and Families (DCSF) announced £60 million for 25 pilot projects to introduce therapeutic interventions in schools for children at risk of mental ill-health.

Psychologists, therapists, counsellors and psychiatrists have never been more influential, creating a thriving commercial industry. The former Department for Education and Skills (DfES) lists over 70 organisations working in therapeutic education, ranging from specialist consultancies for circle time and emotional literacy, mental health and children's organisations to lobbying organisations and pressure groups. Some universities, including Cambridge, have research centres for emotional well-being based on the disciplines of psychiatry and positive psychology. A fast growing consultancy business runs expensive courses in learning to learn, happiness and well-being and emotional literacy, carries out emotional audits of schools and workplaces, assesses the emotional literacy of senior management teams and produces text books and materials for teachers and parents.

Challenging the rise of therapeutic education

Our analysis is a strong challenge to the state's sponsorship of therapeutic education. We relate the rise of therapeutic education to wider cultural and political analysis in order to explore the ways in which politically-sponsored interventions for emotional well-being, and the industry that has grown around them, resonate so strongly with the public and educators alike. Political sponsorship is credible precisely because it uses the language, assumptions and activities of popular therapy, mirrored in the texts and courses promoted by the thriving industry that has grown around therapeutic education.

The book offers an original and provocative critique, based on some key propositions that we consider necessary to state at the outset. First, we do not regard therapeutic education as progressive and benign. Instead, we aim to show that strong images and beliefs about people's vulnerability and fragility lie behind the rhetoric of empowerment and positive psychology. At the heart of our analysis is a challenge to a popular and political obsession with people's emotional fragility and with what we characterise as 'the diminished self'. As we argue, this reflects deeper cultural disillusionment with ideas about human potential, resilience and capacity for autonomy.

Second, we regard therapeutic education as profoundly anti-educational, arguing that whatever good intentions lie behind it, the effect is to abandon the liberating project of education. We aim to show that therapeutic education creates a curriculum of the self that lowers educational and social aspirations in its quest to be more 'personally relevant', 'inclusive' and 'engaging' and to reflect students' 'real needs'. This anti-educational trend has two effects. The first is that, in the name of inclusion, tolerance and empathy, a curriculum of the self introduces activities that encourage people to reveal their vulnerable selves to professionals and a growing array of peer mentors, lifecoaches, counsellors, psychologists and therapists employed as 'therapeutic support workers'. Far from being empowering, this invites people to lower their expectations of themselves and others, and to see others as similarly flawed and vulnerable. The second effect is that, as the book goes to press, these activities and their underlying assumptions are paving the way for more formal attempts to coach 'appropriate emotions as part of developing emotional well-being and 'happiness'.

Our third proposition is that therapeutic education is profoundly dangerous because a diminished image of human potential opens up people's emotions to assessment by the state and encourages dependence on ritualised forms of emotional support offered by state agencies. Therapeutic education replaces education with the social engineering of emotionally literate citizens who are also coached to experience emotional well-being.

Developing our arguments

We explore our propositions through Kant's argument that 'examples are ... the go-cart of judgment' ([1781]1978: 178). In the case of our book, examples are more important than this because they enable us to extract the unarticulated vision of children, young people and adults held by governing elites, those advising policy makers, think tanks, consultants and academics promoting emotional well-being, and professionals at all levels of the system. We use examples of initiatives promoted by government, educationalists and the emotional well-being industry, with occasional anecdotes from practitioners, parents, children and young people experiencing them. We do not claim to offer these examples as systematic empirical evidence. Instead, we use them to explore the fundamental and urgent question that we debate in the book, namely 'What vision of a human being is being presented in the various initiatives and interventions that comprise therapeutic education?' We ask readers to decide if our examples and the conclusions we draw from them resonate with experiences in their own context.

We began separately to analyse the rise of a 'therapeutic ethos' and its effects on different sectors of the education system in 2002. Since then, we have received numerous invitations to speak about our critique, at seminars and conferences and in journalism. Sometimes our views have been received with great interest, occasionally with agreement. More often, though, they have attracted hostility or incomprehension, sometimes strong personal criticism. The arguments we put forward in the book are complex because they draw on ideas and practices across diverse areas of social policy and contemporary culture. But they are especially controversial because they confront an overwhelming tide of support for emotional interventions amongst policy makers and educators from liberal and Left traditions. In particular, our ideas challenge mantras of 'inclusive education', 'personalised learning' and 'learner voice', all embodied in the drive for a more personally relevant, engaging curriculum.

We structure our arguments in the following way. First, we analyse the ways in which populist therapeutic explanations and assumptions permeate widespread support for emotional interventions throughout education. We show how these interventions and their underlying assumptions both arise from, and reinforce, the state's promotion of emotional well-being as part of New Labour's approach to social justice since 1997. Five chapters then provide different types of examples showing the rise of therapeutic education in primary schools, secondary schools, further education colleges and universities. Each chapter evaluates implications for educational goals and practices in each of the four contexts. Chapter 6 shows the incursion of therapeutic activities into workplaces. In Chapter 7, we offer an original chronology of five shifts towards a therapeutic culture, rooted in changing ideas about the nature of the self in Anglo-American societies over the past forty years. In the final chapter, we respond to the main criticisms made of our arguments and offer a proposal for education based on an alternative perspective that we describe as *radical humanist education*. We present this perspective as a basis for starting to resist the trends we present in the book.

Towards a political and educational alternative

Our propositions make it important to clarify our own political and educational position. As a starting point here, we argue that the loose and unthinking application of old labels such as 'left', 'radical' and 'liberal', and the newly coined notions of 'social justice' and inclusion, have all become mantras and no longer mean very much in relation to educational or political ideals. This problem is particularly evident in our attempts to challenge the rise of a therapeutic turn in education which lead routinely to accusations that we are 'right wing' and 'elitist' and therefore 'uncaring', 'old-fashioned' and 'not confronting our own emotional issues'. These emotive, simplistic and inaccurate criticisms make the task of articulating a clear educational position both novel and difficult. Notwithstanding these difficulties, the final chapter offers a strong polemical challenge to the trends that we analyse in the book.

We recognise that, even if we are right in our thesis that the rise of therapeutic education reflects a powerful and unique change that goes beyond most historical forms of social engineering, it is still an unfolding process with implications that are far from clear cut. Nevertheless, we invite parents, teachers, trainee teachers, teacher educators, policy makers, advisers, inspectors, students and the promoters of therapeutic education to engage seriously with our analysis. We invite those who agree that our concerns are legitimate to consider how to resist the trends we identify. We write this with the aim of starting a battle of ideas about what education means in the twenty-first century.

Abbreviations

ABC	*A Basis for Choice* (FEU Publication 1979)
ADHD	Attention Deficit and Hyperactivity Disorder
AFAF	Academics For Academic Freedom
AoC	Association of Colleges
APIR	Assessment Planning Implementation and Review
AQA	Assessment and Qualifications Alliance
ASBO	anti-Social Behaviour Order
ATL	Association of Teachers and Lecturers
AUT	Association of University Teachers
BACP	British Association for Counselling and Psychotherapy
BERA	British Educational Research Association
BIP	Behaviour Improvement Programmes
BTEC	Business and Technology Education Council
CBI	Confederation of British Industry
CEL	Centre for Excellence in Leadership
CPD	continuing professional development
CPVE	Certificate of Pre-Vocational Education (1985)
CUSN	College and Universities Support Network
DCSF	Department for Children, Schools and Families
DFES	Department for Education and Skills
DoH	Department of Health
DIUS	Department for Innovation Universities and Skills
EC	Emotional Correctedness
ECM	Every Child Matters
EI	Emotional Intelligence
ELA	Emotional Literacy Assistant
ELQ	Equivalent or Lower Qualification
EQ	Emotional Quotient
ESOL	English for Speakers of Other Languages
ESREA	European Society for Research on the Education of Adults
EYC	Early Years Curriculum
E2E	Entry to Employment
FE	Further Education

FEC	Further Education College
FEFC	Further Education Funding Council
FENTO	Further Education National Training Organisation
FEU	Further Education Unit
FHE	further and higher education
GCSE	General Certificate of Secondary Education
GNVQ	General National Vocational Qualifications
GTC (E)	General Teaching Council (England)
HE	Higher Education
HEI	Higher Education Institution
HEA	Higher Education Academy (formerly the ILT)
HMI	Her Majesty's Inspectorate
ICT	information and communication technology
IEA	Institute of Employment Studies
IEP	Individual Education Plan
IfL	Institute for Learning
ILT	Institute for Learning and Teaching in higher education
INSET	In-Service Education and Training
ILP	Individual Learning Plan
IQ	Intelligence Quotient
IT	information technology
ITE	Initial Teacher Education
ITT	Initial Teacher Training
LEA	Local Education Authority
LLUK	Lifelong Learning UK
LSC	Learning and Skills Council
LSDA	Learning and Skills Development Agency
NATFHE	National Association of Teachers in Further and Higher Education
NC	National Curriculum
NCVQ	National Council for Vocational Qualifications
NEETS	Not in Employment, Education or Training
NETTS	National Education and Training Targets
NFER	National Foundation for Educational Research
NIACE	National Institute for Adult and Continuing Education
NUS	National Union of Students
NVQ	National Vocational Qualification
ODD	Oppositional Defiance Disorder
OECD	Organisation for Economic Co-operation and Development
OfSTED	Office for Standards in Education/ Office for Standards in Education, Children's Services and Skills
PA	Personal Advisor (Connexions)
PC	Political Correctness
PCE	Post-Compulsory Education
PCET	Post-Compulsory Education and Training

PGCE	Post-Graduate Certificate of Education (or Professional Graduate Certificate of Education)
QCA	Qualifications and Curriculum Authority
QTLS	Qualified Teacher Learning and Skills Sector
QUANGO	Quasi-Autonomous Non-Government (al) Organisation
SEAL	Social and Emotional Aspects of Learning
SEU	Social Exclusion Unit
TEC	Training and Enterprise Council
TES	*Times Educational Supplement*
THES	*Times Higher Education Supplement*
TLRP	Teaching and Learning Research Programme
TUC	Trades Union Congress
UCET	Universities' Council for the Education of Teachers
UCU	University and College Union
UNICEF	United Nations Children's Fund
WEA	Workers' Educational Association

Chapter 1

In an emotional state

Introduction

It is important to understand the interplay between cultural accounts of emotional problems and political responses to them because culture and education offer particular accounts about the nature of human potential, about who we are as human beings and what we are, or are not, capable of. Policy connects cultural perspectives to practice and shapes the ways in which individuals construct themselves as subjects and citizen by attributing various roles, categories and status to people. Yet, people often have little awareness of how this happens, nor little control over the subtle and complex processes it involves (Shore and Wright 2005: 4).

A key strand in contemporary political and cultural accounts of how we regard ourselves and others is an unchallenged assumption that we face an unprecedented epidemic of mental health problems, and that policy makers must respond. The chief executive of the charity NCH argued in the *Daily Mail* on 20 July 2007 that

> the lack of emotional well-being amongst our children and young people is undermining the foundation of any social policy to combat social exclusion, deprivation or lack of social mobility. We urge Gordon Brown and his new Cabinet to commit to tackling this hidden and fast-growing problem.

The goals and institutional arrangements of 'Every Child Matters' (ECM) formalise such concerns by requiring welfare and education agencies to ensure that, as part of being 'safe' and able to achieve educationally and socially, children's well-being is paramount. Communicating with participants after a meeting in October 2007 of an All-Party Parliamentary Group on Well-Being in schools, the Deputy Director of the University of Oxford's Institute for the Future of the Mind said that 'there is overwhelming sympathy for schools to do more to protect and promote the emotional well-being of children and young people', for the APPG to support existing initiatives to do this and to 'make recommendations that carry considerable weight both scientifically and politically' (Sharples 2007; see also Toynbee 2005; Layard 2005).

In this context, renaming of the Department for Education and Skills in 2007 as the Department for Children, Schools and Families (DCSF) is extremely significant because it erases 'education' as a social and political aspiration for the first time. Reflecting popular concerns about unhappiness and emotional problems, schools will promote well-being by eliding welfare and educational goals and activities. ECM therefore enables the state to intensify its responses to popular concerns by incorporating them in educational policy and practice.

In this chapter, we examine how the government has come to sponsor therapeutic education as part of New Labour's approach to 'social justice'. First, we offer examples of popular concern about emotional well-being and the therapeutic orthodoxies that underpin and reinforce this interest. Second, we show a political evolution from ideas about conferring esteem on a vulnerable public to more active promotion of 'the means to be happy'. Third, we summarise how arguments in the chapter lead to a new role for education.

Preoccupied with emotional difficulties

The rise of popular therapy

Coming out of a difficult meeting, a colleague offered an assessment of another colleague's behaviour: 'well, it's obvious she was bullied at school. All the signs are there ...'. Another meeting, a different colleague, another assessment: 'he's got real esteem issues, hasn't he, all that suppressed anger ...'. In a different university, discussions about a grievance procedure over a senior colleague's terrible temper and public humiliation of his secretary led to the union representative's decisions to proceed on the grounds that his behaviour reinforced her 'low self-esteem', shown by the fact that she had received counselling for stress. In 2007, the Trades Union Congress adopted concerns about 'vulnerable' workers as one of its main campaigning themes.

Work is not the only place where everyday explanations for behaviour are offered increasingly in terms of emotional fragility. One section of a bookshop in a small town near Oxford is depicted as 'Tragic life stories': it carries 69 titles. Next to it, the sub-titles of the autobiographies of minor and major celebrities suggest they could easily cross into the other section: tales of 'love and fame' are illuminated through 'battles with addiction', 'low self-esteem', 'childhood abuse' and 'personal demons'. Autobiographies of minor celebrities, ordinary people and of famous and successful people such as ex-American president Bill Clinton, Hollywood actress and political activist, Jane Fonda, British Olympic athlete Kelly Holmes and pop singer Robbie Williams have turned insecurity, emotional 'pain' and vulnerability and 'battles for emotional survival' into a flourishing literary genre of what some call 'cry-ographies', 'path-ographies' and 'diseased victim literature'. Deeper problems of mental illness are also mainstream media fare. British ex-footballer Paul Gascoigne's latest biography, with long transcripts of his therapy sessions and his body map of ailments and their mental causes, was serialised in *The Times* in July 2006.

Celebrities who promote their emotional difficulties are widely praised for doing so, especially if they are men: writing in the British newspaper, *The Guardian*,

Catherine Bennett argued that the rise of public disclosures of depression and self-harm by celebrities were a positive sign because they provide relief to others who suffer so that rather than being a sign of 'a debased deal between victims and voyeurs [it is] the first step towards a mentally healthy society in which everyone feels at liberty to admit mental illness' (Bennett 2005). It is not only celebrities who are commended for their willingness to disclose feelings of vulnerability. At the annual conference of the British National Union of Teachers in 2006, a school teacher who broke down during his account of stress at school was praised for enabling others to come forward and admit difficulties. The popularity of the British film *The Queen* in 2007 was rooted in its portrayal of emotional vulnerability in a figure who epitomises old-fashioned English stoicism and emotional repression.

The popularisation of emotional vulnerability and a therapeutic turn in culture and politics through the 1990s in Britain have been analysed by Frank Furedi and in America by James Nolan (Furedi 2004; Nolan 1998). These trends have intensified since those analyses. Emotional problems and concerns about well-being, with accompanying therapeutic explanations, are a staple ingredient of women's magazines and increasingly feature in men's. In the March 2007 edition of *Psychologies*, for example, readers could carry out self-assessments to learn that they might have low self-esteem, high self-esteem or be in denial about both: in the September edition, they learnt that high self-esteem might mask 'self-love' and be as 'dysfunctional' as low self-esteem. Between March and October, they could add 'approval addiction disorder', 'fear of rejection', 'fear of intimacy' and 'task avoidance disorder', 'responsibility avoidance syndrome' to a long list of everyday aspects of life fraught with unseen or repressed emotional problems but 'explained' psychologicially. Adjacent to sections in bookshops for cry-ographies and tragic life stories, is a vast genre of guides to

'Therapy' is everywhere

'Therapy' was once regarded as a cure or treatment for people who were disturbed or troubled or mentally ill. Now the term has entirely changed its meaning and become a positive value.

Shop signs seduce us with the fashionable appeal of therapy. In one shopping centre alone, we saw 'Food for Therapy'; a hairdresser's called 'Thairapy'; a designer clothes shop called 'Therapy' and 'Nail Therapy'. On the underground and in magazines, there are advertisements for a range of retail therapies: 'Jean Therapy'; 'Shoe Therapy'; Dress Therapy. A night club in central London advertises a 'Therapy Session' on Sunday evenings.

Outside the confines of shopping centres, there is pet therapy, dolphin therapy, dance therapy, art therapy, music therapy, film therapy; there's even a rock group called 'Therapy' - and there are endless so-called 'new age' therapies – magnetic therapy, crystal therapy, inner changes therapy, timeline therapy

> Everyday activities have become 'therapeutic'. Women's magazines and weekend newspaper supplements depict holidays, going out with friends, good sex, the ubiquitous 'me time' for hard pressed women, a glass of wine after work in terms of their instrumental effects on 'self-esteem' and 'emotional well-being': the August 2007 edition of *Psychologies* magazine offered the 'fact' that 'a recent study at the University of Essex found that 90 per cent said that going for a walk boosted their self-esteem'. It is common to describe friends as 'therapeutic' merely for doing what friends do – listening, advising and supporting.

psychological and physical health, comprising self-help guides, diet and childcare books.

Such themes have created a flourishing television genre where a plethora of lifestyle 'experts' from cosmetic and fashion pundits to family therapists focus on emotional vulnerability caused by everyday problems. Professional therapists or presenters acting in the role of therapist use counselling techniques and psychodrama activities to draw out the emotions of their subjects to painful levels and then build them back up again: the more vulnerable and painful the account, the better the cameras like it. Each series of the reality programme 'Big Brother' has a weekly psychological analysis where therapists, psychiatrists and psychologists provide insights about the emotional state and motives of the housemates to an enthralled audience (and its even more enthralled presenter, Davina McCall). In April 2007, psychotherapist Pamela Stephenson Connolly presented a television series of therapeutic sessions with famous people, with the ensuing revealing and emotional accounts widely reviewed in the press.

A twist to depictions of emotional fragility appears in TV programmes such as *The X Factor* and others where experts assess would-be dancers and singers. Here, strongly negative feedback is frequently greeted with howls of derision from the audience and defensiveness or tears from the hapless participants. A programme on bullying criticised such assessments as 'outright bullying condoned by the media' and called for programmes that use them to be banned (Channel 4 2007).

Yet, not far below the surface of such concerns are harsh judgements of people who cannot handle their emotions 'appropriately'. The media spectacle over the alleged 'racist bullying' by Jade Goody of Shilpa Shetty in British 'reality TV' programme *Celebrity Big Brother* in January 2007 revelled in the 'emotional fragility' and inability to deal with confrontation without extreme anger and distress of both sides. Programmes such as 'Wife Swap' routinely depict working class participants as unable to express emotions calmly or reasonably, or 'appropriately and constructively' as advocates of emotional literacy would have it. In everyday life and work conversations, rude or aggressive treatment, especially if from men, is frequently judged as 'emotionally illiterate', 'bullying' or 'harassment'.

What to feel and what not to feel

Lost your middle-aged or your post-marriage confidence? Believe that you can't dress well, lose weight, get rid of old possessions, have good sex in a long-term relationship or deal with your children properly? A heady mix of expert and not-so-expert therapy, tough talk, tearful confession, teaching of technique and joyful redemption are just what you need.

Posh pseudo-therapists/truth-telling 'friends' Trinny and Susannah pioneered an expanding genre of therapeutic make-over television in their 'What not to Wear' series. Over four years, the duo came to parody the role of therapist, eliciting confessions of low self-esteem and other 'emotional issues'. Before being urged to cover up physical faults and receiving fashion advice, hapless participants lay on a therapist's couch while Trinny or Susannah interrogated them about why they had ended up such a sad and drab sight, and offered tearful empathy. The ensuing resurrection of the woman's sexy, sassy, stylish 'inner self' culminated in her grateful tears of thanks.

Programmes such as *How to Survive Sex after Marriage* have taken the make-over genre to new, demeaning depths. Here, three implausibly young and photogenic sex therapists and relationship counsellors require couples to expose their festering resentments, 'anger management issues' and the banal and sometimes difficult tribulations that beset most couples. Painful disclosures to each other are followed by participants' pleas for the experts to 'help' them. Simplistic therapeutic diagnoses and some training in sex techniques are followed by further confessions about the couple's ignorance, sexual redemption (not filmed but discussed to camera) and the obligatory tearful, grateful resurrection.

Formulaic pop therapy, a few useful tips and some stern 'talking to', promise easy 'cures' by blurring the lines between counselling, some elementary psychoanalysis and coaching you what to feel and what not to feel. Having someone to coach you to run better is one thing. Coaching 'appropriate' feelings is quite another.

Toxic childhood

The logical conclusion of being immersed in popular therapy is to see ourselves as all suffering, to a greater or lesser extent, from the negative emotional effects of diverse life experiences and events, where emotional survival of the everyday trials and tribulations of life becomes the ultimate goal. These ideas are reinforced by media and political attention to a plethora of fears about the impact of modern life on how people feel about themselves and their lives, emanating from a wide range of sources (see also Furedi 2004).

Alongside popular interest in emotional vulnerability, attention to these fears has intensified over the past five years. Studies showing a crisis of unprecedented proportions in the mental health and emotional problems of children and young people were widely taken up by academics and the British media in 2007, with widely varying estimates and definitions of problems:

- *The Daily Mail*, 20 July, 2007: a study for the Nuffield Foundation found that more than a million children have mental health problems, doubling the numbers of a generation ago. A survey of over 8,000 children found that a third of those aged 14–16 had 'conduct disorders', such as aggressive, disruptive or anti-social behaviour. Four per cent of children aged 5–16 had emotional disorders such as stress, anxiety and depression, 2 per cent had hyperactive behaviour or attention problems, 6 per cent had conduct disorders, and 2 per cent had more than one type of disorder.
- Spratt *et al.* (2007): 10 per cent of children aged 5–16 have a clinically diagnosed mental disorder, 4 per cent have an emotional disorder and 2 per cent a hyperkinetic disorder, with such problems more prevalent in lone-parent or reconstituted families, jobless families, those on low incomes and those where parents had low qualifications.
- Stephenson Conolly (2007): 40 per cent of the British public will undergo 'psychological difficulties at some time', defining a mental disorder as when someone has 'disabling psychological symptoms, an emotional or behavioural problem or dysfunction in thinking, acting or feeling … all of which can cause distress and may impair how someone functions' (2007: 6).
- *The Guardian*, 5 June, 2007: a UNICEF (2007) survey showed that British young people report the highest levels of unhappiness in Europe, and that today's 16-year-olds are less likely than their counterparts 20 years ago to have a best friend they can trust.
- Alexander and Hargreaves (2007): the first of 32 reports in a major review of primary education, led by Professor Robin Alexander at the University of Cambridge, presented evidence from 'witness sessions' with 757 teachers, parents, teaching assistants and children revealing 'widespread anxiety' about the pressures of testing, fear, insecurity, risk and danger and lack of respect and support between generations.
- Palmer (2006): a book about *Toxic Childhood* was promoted in 2006 through a letter to the *Daily Telegraph* signed by the Archbishop of Canterbury and 110 experts, including academics, psychologists and heads of mental health of children's organisations. It warned that children's lives 'are being poisoned' by materialism, depravity, spiritual breakdown, testing and an arid school curriculum, too much emphasis on rational, cognitive learning, too much freedom, risk adverse parenting (and therefore not enough freedom), technology, advertising and the media.

- *The Guardian* 20 March reported the children's commissioner, Professor Aynsely-Green expressing concerns about children's stress and anxiety caused by the constant pressure of tests, an 'unengaging curriculum', insufficient support for those with emotional or physical needs, lack of participation and 'voice' in school decision-making and widespread bullying that is not being tackled enough (Bawden 2007).

Children's fictional characters are being marshalled in the battle for more emotional support and better understanding. A book in 2007 offered a semi-humorous parody of psychoanalytical accounts of characters such as Tigger, Goldilocks, the Wicked Stepmother in Snow White, Peter Pan and Cinderella, revealing their repressed disorders, syndromes and psychological anxieties. The author hopes to encourage tolerance and understanding of mental illness:

> While it is sad to think of all those characters suffering for so long, it's heartening to know that help is at hand and that they just need to be pointed in the right direction. That's true for everyone, whether they are living in a land far away or just round the corner ... With a little kindness, professional therapy and perhaps some psycho-pharmaceutical intervention, there's every possibility that many of our favourite characters will indeed live happily ever after.
>
> (James 2007: 12–13)

Therapeutic orthodoxies

Talking about behaviours and their causes in terms of emotional states, syndromes, addictions and dysfunctions is assisted by proliferating categories: the latest list from the American Psychiatric Association's *Diagnostic and Statistical Manual of Mental Disorders* identifies over 800 psychological syndromes and disorders that create physical symptoms and behaviours (Nolan 1998). Christopher Lane has shown how this influential list turns once-normal traits such as shyness or feeling nervous about speaking in public into psychological disorders, where shyness has become 'social phobia'. He argues that this is fuelled by drug companies, encouraged by the psychiatry and psychoanalysis professions (Lane 2007). A self-help book for people to diagnose their own mental health by Pamela Stephenson Connolly, well-known for newspaper and magazine articles and television programmes on psychotherapy, translates the specialist jargon of psychiatrists and therapists into everyday understanding (2007).

Depicting everyday responses to life, alongside more serious problems, as treatable pathologies goes hand-in-hand with apocryphal accounts of cycles of emotional dysfunction, deprivation and 'legacies' of trauma, linked to class and economic circumstance. In a book for teachers and parents evangelising about the need for schools to develop emotional literacy, Peter Sharp cites figures from a study based on interviews with 10,000 children aged 5–15, and 4,500 young people aged 11–15, and questionnaires to their teachers, which shows that 14 per cent of children with mental disorders came from social class V compared to 5 per cent from social class I.

Other factors were correlated to the likelihood of childhood mental illness: 20 per cent of children from unemployed parents compared to 8 per cent from employed families; 15 per cent from families with no qualifications compared to 6 per cent where parents had been to university. These accounts lead to sweeping claims. For example,

> ... it is more likely that emotionally literate parents will have emotionally literate children who will go on to be emotionally literate parents themselves ... if a child is given insufficient emotional nuturance, this can lead to poor mental health and ultimately can be lifethreatening: approximately 1 in 4 of us will have a mental health problem at some time in our life, requiring treatment or support from the caring professions ...

(Sharp 2003: 5)

Interchangeable, ill-defined terms such as emotional literacy, emotional intelligence, emotional well-being, self-esteem and mental ill-health, together with proliferating lists of disorders and syndromes, simplistic cycles of deprivation and permanent damage wreaked by 'emotionally illiterate or 'dysfunctional' parents', all reinforce popular therapeutic orthodoxies. These are rife with contradictions: pessimistic determinism of lasting emotional damage and repressed emotional 'issues' go hand in hand with possibilities of emotional resilience, transformation through self-awareness and the promise of fulfilment and finding our 'authentic inner self'. Promises of 'realising our potential' and 'becoming the real me' run up against the low horizons and mundane aspirations of 'accept yourself, or love yourself with all your human flaws' of the therapy industry.

Therapeutic orthodoxies

1 We all suffer from low self-esteem
Oprah Winfrey says that 'lack of self-esteem is the root of all the problems in all the world', a claim reinforced by some psychologists:

> I cannot think of a single psychological problem – from anxiety and depression, to fear of intimacy or of success, to spouse battery or child molestation that is not traceable to problems of poor self-esteem.
>
> (Brandon quoted by Furedi 2004: 153)

2 We all mask our low self-esteem behind confident facades
Self-image acts as a self-fulfilling prophecy because 'self-belief goes hand in hand with the idea that we can never be better on the outside than we believe ourselves to be on the inside'. An article in *Psychologies* (March 2007) warns:

all day long, people are interpreting the congruence between our verbal communication and the non-verbal signals that lie behind what we are saying' he [McKenna] explains ... 'Building a positive self-image makes sure that your automatic reactions come from a sense of confidence and empowerment. That's the only sure fire way to feel good about yourself for ever'.

3 We all suffer lasting legacies from the emotional effects of our childhoods

Those whose carers were distant, cold and remote grow into needy, depressed adults without a sense of emotional well-being

(Stephenson Connolly 2007: 488)

In a television programme purporting to 'research' sex addiction, TV presenter Ulrika Johnsson ended up with her own therapeutic assessment of the 'disorder', and its partner, 'emotional intimacy disorder'. Prolonged personal disclosures and tearful accounts of realisation and salvation led to populist therapeutic explanations: 'wanting to please my father', 'wanting my mother's affection', 'always pleasing other people'. Johnsson's rationale, constructed with a therapist, mirrored magazine articles and self-assessment quizzes that encourage women to see themselves as always at the emotional beck and call of everyone but themselves (Channel Four 2007b).

4 We must accept ourselves and value what we have
Happiness is realising you are a valuable human being and appreciating your own qualities. It is as simple as that. Once you realise your own worth, you know that just being you is more than good enough.

5 It is possible to realise our potential and find our 'real' self
A headline on the front cover of *Psychologies* (August 2007) promised a reader's 'true-life' account of 'how I finally turned into myself'!

6 We can become more self-aware through self-help guides and/or professional therapeutic support

These orthodoxies and their accompanying insights are drawn from an eclectic mix of cognitive behaviour therapy, neuro-science, Freudian or Jungian analysis, transactional analysis or Rogerian counseling. They have become part of the way we explain our own reactions to life, and those of others, at the levels of popular culture and everyday conversation.

In our discussion of the chronology of a therapeutic turn in popular culture and politics in Chapter 7, we make the uncontentious claim that the symbolic date of its rapid rise in Britain was the death of Diana on 31 August 1997. From then until now,

Therapy as humour

Two greetings cards
One has a photograph from the 1920s of a group of adults at a party, laughing hysterically. The caption reads 'we didn't know we were unhappy until we had therapy'.

The second is titled 'door-to-door therapy' and has a hand drawn cartoon of a 1950s salesman greeting a woman answering the door 'Morning madam! Need any help with dream interpretation, dealing with the internal saboteur, harnessing intuition, identifying your energy path or making space for yourself?' She replies 'No, I'm alright this week thanks'.

A full page newspaper advertisement for a car proclaims 'buy this and become the real you'! A speech bubble reads 'I bought this and finally found emotional well-being' (says man in pub).

An article in *The Times Magazine* on Saturday 24 November interviews young people about problems they cause and experience on buses in London.

'They say they don't like seeing kids fighting on the bus – except they clearly do because they all start talking at once about the fights they've seen, with this one getting mashed or bashed, and how it was 'too funny but, like, scary too'. One says with mock solemnity 'Seriously, I am traumatised by the fights I've seen. I have, like, that syndrome'. They all crack up. (*The Times Magazine*, 24 November: 34)

Diana, Princess of Wales remains the model victim and martyr who resonated not only with the media which promoted her in this way but more deeply as the 'people's princess of suffering'. Yet, while Diana gave interest in popular and cultural interest in emotional vulnerability her royal seal of approval, the roots of a therapeutic turn were evident shortly Before Diana's death (BD). In a perceptive column written in 1996 about how the press, campaign groups and legislators were building their activities around victims, Matthew Parris identified these roots:

> Blessed are those who suffer. From the dawn of man, and pace Nietzsche, suffering has conferred status. Suffering invites sympathy and commands respect. Suffering raises the sufferer above everyday reproach and forbids the sneer or gibe. Suffering brooks no contradiction. It confers upon the sufferer a dignity, and a kind of authority, elevating her or him above reproach.
>
> (Parris 1996)

What Parris clearly saw is that critics are chastised and even howled down on occasion as insensitive, uncaring and immoral, if not sacrilegious. The suffering victim and the victim culture that fuels its resonance cannot be challenged, making it a powerful force for politicians. As we show in Chapter 8, our own critique of the trends we identify here attracts similar responses.

However, there was something of a backlash against a preoccupation with emotional concerns and the suffering of victims, and then a backlash against the backlash. Writing in *The Guardian* in 2003, David Aaronovitch argued that

> a disdain for therapy is becoming almost as fashionable now as therapy was in the period after the death of Diana' and he applied a simple test 'Of the people I know who have had therapy, I can't think of any that shouldn't have been there. But I certainly can think of plenty who haven't but bloody well should have ... Too much psychotherapy, you say? There's nothing like enough.
>
> (Aaronovitch 2003)

The therapeutic profession rallied to this challenge, including well-known media psychoanalyst Oliver James, who, in a moment of prescience, predicted what will probably be the first league table to be welcomed when it appears: 'If only they would rethink the purpose of school so that instead of grades, the annual league tables measured how well pupils' psycho-social health had fared ...' (James 2003).

As we show in the next section, policy makers are heeding this call at a rapid rate.

Policy makers need therapy

The emotional effects of social exclusion

It is easy to ridicule the reductionism, contradictions and clichés of popular therapy as pointless and perhaps harmless trivia. It is also tempting to dismiss them as completely irrelevant to political responses to the concerns outlined above. Yet, policy makers have embraced popular therapy with open arms because the incoherent, ubiquitous nature of therapeutic orthodoxies and their symbiotic relationship with cultural accounts of emotional vulnerability and dysfunction, enable the state to show that it is uniquely placed to respond to popular concerns and to develop people's emotional resources.

Responding to emotional vulnerability has been integral to New Labour's belief in what ex-Prime Minister Blair regarded as the 'equal worth of all' and to the ensuing political shift from equality of opportunity to 'equality of esteem' (Blair 1998). A central strand in public policy has been to make those defined as excluded from society and work feel included in social and welfare services, where building self-esteem and responding to expressions of emotional vulnerability enables the state to confer recognition and affirmation (see Furedi 2004; Giddens 1998).

A fundamental principle informing social policy since 1997 is widespread agreement that social exclusion is inextricably linked to destructive influences that damage self-esteem and emotional well-being. This emphasis is evident in reports about children's emotional problems, cited above, reflecting a marked shift from earlier emphasis on the destructive effects of poverty (see, for example, UNICEF 2000, 2007). Amidst vague definitions of 'inclusion' and 'exclusion', education is a key factor in combating diverse material, personal and psychological disadvantages that comprise personal and collective spirals of decline (SEU 1999). In this scenario, social justice is a political response to exclusion depicted as a psychological condition accompanied by: 'feelings of social isolation, lack of contact with other people, a feeling of being trapped, low self-esteem and self-confidence, and feelings of insecurity, hopelessness and depression' (O'Connor and Lewis 1999: 18).

From community arts projects to the regeneration of libraries, this diagnosis focuses on the negative psychological effects of isolation, poverty and unemployment: 'from this perspective, the erosion of civic solidarity and informal networks is recast as essentially a psychological problem' (Furedi 2004: 166). Professor Richard Layard, an economist and adviser to the government on mental health, argues that mental ill-health is the worst form of deprivation while Professor Felicity Huppert, from the Centre for Well-being at the University of Cambridge argues that social and environmental factors account for only 10 per cent of happiness and feelings of well-being (Layard 2007; Huppert 2007).

Concern about emotional well-being is a central theme in the Social Exclusion Unit's account of the effects of low educational achievement and participation on particular groups, such as young people and single mothers. In this scenario, policy makers attribute low self-esteem, feelings of vulnerability and risk to particular groups trapped in a cycle of deprivation. Breaking out depends on educational and welfare initiatives that address the emotional impact of deprivation and the provision of 'holistic' support services that broker welfare, education and work opportunities (SEU 1999). Writing about the need to manage the transition of school leavers to education or training, ex-Prime Minister Blair argued:

> Getting this right offers the prospect of a double dividend. A better life for young people themselves, saving them from the prospects of a lifetime of dead-end jobs, unemployment, poverty, ill-health and other kinds of exclusion. A better deal for society as a whole that has to pay a very high price in terms of welfare bills and crime for failing to help people make the transition to becoming independent adults.
>
> (SEU 1999: 6)

In their depictions of the 'complex needs' caused by cycles of social and psychological deprivation, politicians are careful not to elide structural causes, such as unemployment and communal break-down, with individual psychological 'traits' or attributes of low self-esteem and emotional vulnerability. Instead, claims that emotional dysfunction both arises from and contributes to inequality enable policy makers to focus on its emotional, individual and social outcomes instead of material causes and effects.

Such ideas are taken up enthusiastically by educators. For example, Kathryn James cites a report by the Institute of Employment Studies that found levels of self-confidence and self-esteem were the highest reported outcome of participation in adult and community learning. Invoking the cycle of deprivation, she connects low self-esteem to poor motivation for learning and then connects it to poor health, abusive relationships, unsatisfying employment, poverty, problems in old age and stress. James' definition of self-esteem for adult educators resonates with the therapeutic orthodoxies above:

> Confidence in our ability to think, confidence in our ability to cope with the basic challenges of life, confidence in our right to be successful and happy, the feeling of being worthy and deserving, entitled to assert our needs and wants, achieve our values and enjoy the fruits of our efforts ...
>
> (James 2004: 24)

And echoing *Psychologies* magazine, she adds 'self-esteem is embedded in our perceptions and expressed through our feelings and behaviour' (ibid.).

Although she also relates poor achievement to economic and social deprivation, she argues that educators should address low self-esteem by understanding its effects on adult learners, diagnosing their levels of self-esteem and then adopting strategies to raise it (James 2004; James and Nightingale 2004). Morwena Griffiths defines self-esteem as 'getting and having an attitude, and valuing yourself'. Rejecting individual, psychological explanations of low self-esteem, she links it, instead, to a collective identity rooted in inequality. From this perspective, self-esteem should be a concern of those committed to social justice (Griffiths 2003).

Conferring esteem

New Labour's depiction of the emotional problems of exclusion incorporates therapeutic orthodoxies about lasting legacies passed onto subsequent generations alongside possibilities of cure and redemption. Arguments that genetic factors and social and environmental factors play only a small part in mental ill-health enable the state to offer interventions that develop particular cognitive outlooks and responses. Supporters of this view argue that 'scientific evidence' for such interventions, together with valid and reliable measures of their effects, are emerging rapidly (Huppert 2007).

In early manifestations of New Labour's 'Third Way', the welfare state was seen as crucial for supporting people's psychological well-being and a source of esteem for those needing its services. Influential sociologist Anthony Giddens, one of the architects of the 'Third Way' ideology, argues that 'welfare is not in essence an economic concept, but a psychic one, concerning as it does well-being ... welfare institutions must be concerned with fostering psychological benefits, as well as economic benefits' (Giddens 1998: 117; see also Furedi 2003a, 2004). He argues that governments need to foster 'reflexivity' as a self-defining process that enables individuals to monitor psychological and social information about possible life trajectories, choices and relationships (Giddens 1991). He sees this as a positive trend, arguing that psychoanalysis and therapy flowing from a quest for self-awareness provides a setting and a

> rich fund of theoretical and conceptual resources for a the creation of a reflexively ordered narrative of self. In a therapeutic situation, whether of the classical psychoanalytical type or not, individuals are able (in principle) to bring their past into line with the exigencies of the present, consolidating a story-line with which they feel relatively content.
>
> (Giddens 1995: 31)

The breakdown of collective ties, the rise of individual isolation and the increase in fears of risk and of the future, lead Ulrich Beck to argue that increased individualisation offers opportunities for people to construct more aspects of their 'life explanations' and 'biographies' than ever before (Beck 1992). For both Giddens and Beck, 'reflexive self-awareness' on the part of the public and policy makers alike creates progressive forms of democracy.

Grandiose claims about the 'democratic progressiveness of reflexivity' are a far cry from the British government's attempts to connect with concerns about emotional vulnerability and dysfunction. These extend the state's role in addressing what Furedi calls a 'psychology of exclusion', where '[tackling this] is not simply justified on the grounds that it assists social integration, but also because managing this condition of psychological distress is increasingly interpreted as an integral part of the business of the state' (2004: 167).

In response to these ideas, the publicity, bidding processes and funding criteria for initiatives such as Surestart, community arts and sports projects, playschemes and the use of libraries all claim benefits for self-esteem, confidence and social skills.

Making the most of 'issues'

A social worker friend offered a recent account of bidding for extra funds to support some of his case load of young people leaving care:

> you really have to go to town on their 'low self-esteem' and 'being at risk' and make sure you go on about those above everything else … you talk vaguely about them 'having emotional issues' but you don't define them and this helps too.

Developing emotional literacy

A powerful strand in political responses to pubic concerns is the idea of developing emotional literacy, defined by the influential pressure group Antidote as: 'the practice of interacting with others in ways that build understanding of our own and others' emotions, then using this understanding to inform our actions' by enabling people to:

- Find ways to feel connected to each other and of using their relationships to deal with emotions that might otherwise cause them to lash out in rage or withdraw in despair.
- Deal with the emotions that can render them unable to take in new information, access emotional states such as curiosity, resilience and joy that lead to a rich experience of learning.
- Engage in activities that promote physical and emotional well-being and broaden the range of what they can talk about with each other in ways that make it less likely that they will abuse drugs and alcohol, bully their peers, or engage in other forms of self-destructive activity.

Antidote presents its vision of such a society, where:

> the facility to handle the complexities of emotional life is as widespread as the capacity to read, write and do arithmetic. Antidote's vision is of an emotionally literate society where:
> *families and friends* provide us with emotional security
> *communities* create opportunities for neighbours to connect with each other
> *government* engages us in its deliberations and is responsive to ideas that emerge
> *workplaces* cultivate creativity and draw upon our potential to contribute
> *economic* policy promotes social and emotional well-being alongside prosperity
> *our environment* becomes more sustainable as we embrace change in lifestyles
>   and attitudes
> *schools and colleges* stimulate curiosity, creativity and the desire to learn
> *our criminal justice system* addresses the emotions that drive some of us to crime
> *our health providers* attend to the emotional aspects of physical illness
> (www.antidote.org.uk)

Resonating with popular therapy and the sweeping promises of 'reflexive self-awareness', Antidote asserts that 'emotional literacy involves becoming aware of our inner experience, so as the better to understand other people and through them to experience a sense of connection to the wider community' (2001: 2).

In 2005, the DfES introduced a Social and Emotional Aspects of Learning strategy (SEAL), based on advice from Professor Katherine Weare and colleagues from the University of Southampton who had worked with their local authority's education psychologists and six other LEAs to pilot a number of strategies and interventions for emotional literacy. A report for the DfES, *What Works in Developing Children's Emotional and Social Competence and Well-being*, drew on this work and on a literature reviews of studies in America and Britain that had evaluated evidence for interventions (Weare and Gray 2003).

Primary SEAL was written for the DfES by educational psychologists, a headteacher and subject consultants, supported by the founder of Antidote, researchers in psychology and local authority educational psychologists. It draws on diverse ideas from studies about emotional intelligence, emotional literacy, empathy, social problem-solving, anger management and cognitive development. Its proponents argue that attention to children and teachers' emotional literacy improves standards of achievement, attendance, motivation and behaviour, encourages inclusion, fosters skills relevant to the demands of employers who require high levels of emotional intelligence (including schools which need emotionally literate teachers) and improves mental health. Weare goes further, arguing that attention to emotional literacy will help schools develop 'happier, calmer, more successful children ... improved family relationships and ... significant gains for [parents'] ability to parent successfully' (2004: 15). The usual slippery elision of constructs is evident in such claims but the emphasis is placed on emotional literacy.

A colleague of Weare's and a consultant working with schools to develop emotional literacy adds the following strong claims:

- understanding emotions is directly connected with motivation and cognitive achievement;
- dealing with emotions helps to develop better relationships and a sense of psychological and mental well-being;
- emotionally developed young people are better equipped to live with difference;
- our moral outlook and value systems are deeply shaped by our attitudes and feelings;
- our sense of meaning and purpose is derived as much from our feelings as from our understanding.

(Sharp 2001: 4)

The government's strategy for SEAL claims that:

Research on 'emotional intelligence' has brought a wider view of 'intelligence' to include personal and social issues. Emotional and social competences have been shown to be more influential than cognitive abilities for personal, career and scholastic success, so they need to be central to school and learning to increase school effectiveness. Working in this area can improve educational and life chances.

(DfES 2005a: 8)

Quoting Goleman, the DfES argues that:

Students who are anxious, angry or depressed don't learn; people who are in these states do not take in information or deal with it well ... when emotions overwhelm concentration, what is being swamped is the mental capacity cognitive scientists call 'working memory', the ability to hold in mind all information relevant to the task in hand.

(DfES 2005a: 8)

Such overblown claims derive from work on emotional intelligence, originated by John Mayer and Peter Salovey who defined it as 'the capacity to reason with emotion in four areas: to perceive emotion, to integrate it into thought, to understand it and to manage it' (Craig 2007: 7). Daniel Goleman's best-selling book is credited widely for bringing the idea that emotional intelligence can be measured into Anglo-American popular and political thinking, developing this construct from personal and intra-personal intelligences that comprise 'abilities such as being able to motivate oneself and persist in the face of frustrations; to control impulse and delay gratification; to regulate one's moods and keep distress from swamping the ability to think; to empathise and to hope' (Goleman 1996: 43).

Goleman's ideas were a rallying call about the lack of recognition that emotional skills are given in our 'IQ-conscious world', and his idea that emotional intelligence is more important than traditional measures of intelligence is comforting because it suggests that, whatever people's social and emotional background, they can learn emotional skills (see Stobart 2008). This resonates with the idea that there are 'multiple intelligences', promoted by psychologist Howard Gardener (1999). A bleak view that intelligence is innate and therefore limited to a small pool of people has given way to a more inclusive idea that everyone is a unique combination of separate abilities. This appears to offer a more holistic, humane, liberal view of how children learn and also, what they should learn.

Developing emotional well-being

Practitioners and researchers from the field of mental health also influence arguments that educational institutions need to pay explicit attention to young people's lives. Notions of mental well-being, and the prevention of mental ill-health, expand emotional intelligence and emotional literacy into 'emotional health' and 'well-being'. Authors of a book for schools from a DfES-funded project to develop emotional health and well-being in secondary schools define mental and emotional health problems as a

> disturbance in functioning' in one area of relationships, mood, behaviour or development. When a problem is particularly severe or persistent over time, or when a number of difficulties are experienced at the same time, a child is said to have a mental health disorder.
>
> (Cowie *et al*. 2004: 1)

The emergence of 'emotional well-being' into political and professional thinking moves mental health work from a marginal activity into mainstream education and welfare services. Organisations such as MIND have long campaigned to promote the voice of people with mental health problems who want to feel less marginalised and stigmatised. The world's first mental health publisher has the same mission:

> we want to prove that everything in life is a mental health issue and therefore eliminates the humiliation that people with 'mental illness' feel. This process

is already happening. Do not let your children grow up not understanding people with mental health issues … mental health will become part of the social norm.

(www.chipmunkpublishing.co.uk)

'Supporting mental well-being' is a significant change from a sickness model, where mental health is 'no longer seen simply as the absence of mental illness, but as encompassing emotional health and well-being' (Spratt *et al.* 2007: 415). Schools working with voluntary organisations and health and welfare agencies as part of ECM 'have a crucial role in promoting positive mental health, and in identifying and remediating difficulties' (Antidote 2007).

In parallel to the media's presentation of mental health problems as a progressive development that enables more of us to admit to problems, policy initiatives encourage schools to identify early signs of difficulties in order to prevent problems emerging and to enable all children to admit to problems.

Instrumental outcomes of education

Political interest in people's emotional 'skills' and well-being is, of course, integral to the demands of the labour market. Antidote quotes Lord Putnam of Queensgate, chancellor of the University of Sunderland, to assert that 'Emotional literacy will become as vital to personal and national success in the knowledge of economy as traditional definitions of literacy were to previous eras' (ibid.). Emotional skills and qualities are an essential component of human capital, particularly in the service industry and public sector, and the education system plays a key role in socialising the 'right' forms of emotional labour for different jobs (see, for example, Colley 2006; see also Hughes 2005).

A functional view of emotion is not confined to its role as an economic commodity. Indeed, as a counter to an overly instrumental focus on the needs of employers, organisations such as the National Institute for Adult and Continuing Education argue for public funding for adult education to be maintained because participation produces emotional, personal and social benefits such as raised self-esteem and confidence as part of 'identity capital' (NIACE 2007).

Government-funded research presents 'soft outcomes' as a measurable component of human capital for the economy, but also as having discernible and measurable benefits for reducing depression and mental ill-health and raising self-efficacy, self-worth and social capital (DfES 2006; OECD 2001, 2007). Recent studies on links between educational achievement and social deprivation identify 'personal capital' as a set of positive dispositions such as self-efficacy and an optimistic outlook (Huppert 2007) There are claims that links between a positive learning experience and change in confidence, learner identity and social capital are educational outcomes as important as knowledge and skills (see, for example, Tett and McLaughlan 2007). According to Professor Leon Feinstein, Director of the Wider Benefits for Learning Research Centre, these outcomes and the soft skills associated with them should be defined less by central government and emerge more from what children and young people want from their education (Feinstein 2007).

Creating the means to be happy

Political interest in emotional literacy and the idea that the state must confer esteem and develop the emotional skills of a vulnerable, disaffected public are shifting to a more positive depiction of the state's role and a more optimistic view of the 'problem' that needs to be addressed. A view that the state should pay more attention to happiness and emotional well-being is popularised by journalist Polly Toynbee who argues that:

> we need to put a lot less emphasis on money measures, radically revise definitions of output ... and pay more attention to the state of mind of the public using services, things that cause stress and, more seriously, mental illness and the role of public services in reducing them.
>
> (Toynbee 2005)

In the All-Party Parliamentary Group seminar on well-being in schools, cited above, contributors argued that promoting well-being and happiness was a more positive direction for state education than emphasising emotional vulnerability. Speaking at the seminar for the DCSF, Richard Bartholomew argued that recent reports on the state of children's mental health were over-pessimistic and that government and state agencies need 'good evidence' about ways to develop resilience through interventions in families and schools. Likewise, Carol Craig argues that an over-mechanistic, normative approach to SEAL risks encouraging narcissism and introspection in young children. She favours a less interventionist approach for older children based on positive psychology (Craig 2007).

Some supporters of a more positive approach favour the development of well-being through discrete activities, such as a statutory GCSE in Personal Social and Health Education, to assess well-being as part of such interventions and to have an indicator of well-being in schools' accountability targets (Layard 2007). Others promote the use of teaching methods accompanied by diagnostic and formative assessments in existing subjects to develop broader attributes, dispositions and attitudes associated with positive attitudes to learning (Claxton 2002, 2007; Craig 2007).

A significant feature of current debates around these ideas is a change in language that replaces vulnerability, low self-esteem and suggestions of emotional illiteracy (see box). Yet, despite a positive emphasis, more normative themes are evident. For example, in keeping with themes about 'toxic childhood', Felicity Hubbert argues that interventions for well-being should teach children that 'consumer goods are absolutely dreadful for their well-being' and shift their values to intrinsic motives and altruism (Huppert 2007).

(I-SPY) Spotting the insidious language of therapy

First, familiar language at work and in personal life describes everyday experiences and, even when the words are ordinary, pathologises the concept:

Stress, harassment, bullying, anxiety, being offended, lacking confidence, suffering from low self-esteem, shyness, mental abuse, having inappropriate feelings or showing inappropriate behaviour, being in denial, repressing feelings, needing closure, moving on, having emotional baggage.

In everyday conversations, we talk about ourselves and others as being dysfunctional, traumatised, repressed, having low self-esteem, being emotionally vulnerable or fragile, feeling uncomfortable. Increasingly, we describe those we don't get on with as emotionally illiterate or inauthentic.

Responses such as workplace and trade union help lines, working with counsellors, mentors and advisors, and staff development sessions where childish games and sitting in circles to share experiences and feelings are clearly therapeutic. What is less familiar is that activities such as appraisals, consultation, open door times, debriefing and exit interviews are essentially about how we feel not what we think or do.

Second, there is the educational response to the therapeutic language of vulnerability, suffering and victimhood:

A recent pamphlet produced by an internationally recognised centre for school leadership offered terms about the emotionally competent school: self-esteem, self worth, being ourselves, accepting, respectful, empathetic, responsive, playful, soothing, and feel(ing) secure and confident in [our] own identity.

To this torrent of therapeutic language, we can add that made popular in education and management as a result of Daniel Goleman's book *Emotional Intelligence*, such as schooling the emotions, emotional literacy, emotional competence, and emotional learning, and the extension of this language into bureaucracy and management: emotional audits, the emotional culture of the organisation and emotional or aesthetic labour.

The equivalents of this therapeutic speak in policy documents are terms like empowering, enabling, inclusive, emotional well-being, nurturing, supporting, mentoring and creating tolerant and empathetic citizens.

In teaching, terms like listening, being open and accepting, empathy, creating a relational space, creating a safe and nurturing space, giving learners a voice, enabling children and young people to construct narratives, exploring the true reality of their lived experience, all foster a therapeutic attitude.

Third, the language of positive psychology counters vulnerability and therapeutic responses which have come to be seen as negative:

The new language is much more upbeat, with talk of happiness, well being, optimism, having a positive outlook, the joy of learning, resilience, stoicism, being in the moment, flow, being loved and respected, creating the means to rise to challenges, meaningfulness, altruism and a sense of life going well.

A new role for education

At a seminar on 'Childhood, well-being and a therapeutic ethos', hosted by the Research Centre for Therapeutic Education at Roehampton University in December 2006, 70 representatives from mental health organisations, children's charities, education psychologists, psychiatrists and therapists could not agree how many people needed therapeutic interventions but they all agreed that the scale of emotional problems was 'huge and growing'.

Education was seen as a key site of influence: in his introduction, the director of the research centre argued that

> if we are to stand a chance of our children and ourselves leading good lives, it may be vital for psychotherapists amongst others to examine how we can influence education in general ... Perhaps, therefore, those of us who are psychotherapists need to look at psychotherapy as an educational practice, not only in the consulting room but to see the wisdom for both children and adults to learn from each other and for our society to continue to attempt to ensure that scientific and technical learning, whilst important, is secondary to the resources of the human soul ... thus, education and therapy might be seen not so much abut knowledge but rather about awakening ... by imparting and acquiring through the relational.
>
> (Lowenthal 2006)

In the context outlined in this chapter, his ideas about elevating 'relational and emotional' aspects of life over traditional subjects find a ready audience. Yet, while the idea that Western countries should concentrate 'less on growth and more on the wellbeing of citizens' has captured the zeitgeist, a telling reminiscence from economist Andrew Oswald shows that only 15 years ago, no-one was interested. He recounted how, in 1993, he organised a conference on the economics of happiness and although he put out 100 chairs only 12 people came (Arnot 2006).

Our analysis of the recent turn in political thinking about well-being and happiness suggests that such conferences will become more and more popular and that indicators of schools' accountability for their pupils' well-being will almost certainly appear. Nevertheless, there is still resistance. The onset of interest in therapeutic explanations and responses to problems in schools came quickly into conflict with the educational 'dinosaurs', who, like Gradgrind, want children to know a fact or two: in this early period, some educationalists made explicit that therapeutic education was not just about supporting vulnerable children but was, instead, an attack on reason.

One attempt for more emotionally tuned schools enraged ex-Chief Inspector of schools, Chris Woodhead, who quoted Stephanie Quayle, vice-principal of Cotham School, Bristol as saying: 'We stress the importance of feeling as a counter to the fear that schools have become too rational, full of accountability, efficient rather than effective' (cited in Woodhead 2003). He denounced the notion of 'emotional intelligence' or 'emotional literacy' with its requirement for 'emotional literacy audits' and a belief that children could be 'taught to understand and control their emotions' as 'a fad new sweeping through our schools' and concluding that: 'The preoccupation with emotional intelligence is at best a distraction, at worst a dangerous indulgence' (Woodhead 2003).

We do not regard it as a passing fad. From 2003, although a few academics such as Frank Furedi wrote powerful academic and popular critiques of the sociological effects of cultivating vulnerability, therapeutic education has taken root because it offers a caring ethos and set of practices to support vulnerable children and young people. Yet, as the summary of evolutions in political thinking shows in this chapter, seizing on education as a way of responding to concerns about emotional vulnerability and emotional literacy transforms easily to a concern to teach people what happiness is and how to be happy.

Conclusions

Reports about the emotional state of the nation have generated a largely unchallenged view that education is a key site for a political response. Uncritical support obscures interchangeable, invalid and unreliable psychological constructs and overlooks evidence from the United States that attention to assumed problems of low self-esteem has led to narcissism, depression and lower educational standards (see Stobart 2008; Craig 2007; Matthews *et al.* 2002; Emler 2001). Developments such as SEAL have incorporated self-esteem into emotional literacy and emotional intelligence within the broader, more positive notion of emotional well-being.

Far from being hindrances, an eclectic array of concerns, slippery underlying concepts and theories, together with sweeping claims for the effectiveness of interventions that flow from them, enable government to relate to a therapeutic turn in popular culture. This is being encouraged by a very diverse range of interested parties and stakeholders in the education system. As well as conferring affirmation and esteem, promoting emotional forms of inclusion, and preparing people for the assumed trials of emotional life and for emotional labour at work, we predict that therapeutic education will rapidly come to promote more overt approaches to coaching people's happiness.

Chapter 2

The therapeutic primary school

Introduction

If a primary school is serious about 'supporting' and 'nurturing' children's emotional needs, it has a counselling service available for pupils and their parents to refer themselves, special drama workshops to prepare them and their parents for the transition to secondary school, perhaps supported by older pupils trained as 'angels', a 'chill-out' room for disruptive pupils, massage and relaxation classes for staff and pupils, a health week where all school work, special events and visiting speakers focus on physical and mental health, and a nurture group where children diagnosed with Attention Deficit and Hyperactivity Disorder (ADHD) or Oppositional Defiance Disorder (ODD) can be withdrawn for therapeutic activities.

A school that has truly taken emotional well-being to its heart has inserted emotional and behavioural goals through the teaching of all subjects, cross-curricular activities and the management styles of senior staff. Classroom and entrance hall walls are covered in bright displays that list emotional, social and behavioural skills, 'what makes a good friend', 'our feelings', 'value of the week', children's ideas about 'golden rules' of the school's moral values, and 'rules for breaking friends kindly'. Circle time requires children to discuss their feelings in order to build self-esteem and emotional literacy while philosophy or thinking skills lessons teach them to express ideas 'constructively', 'respectfully' and 'empathetically' as the 'skills' of an emotionally literate, tolerant citizen. The playground may have a 'lonely bench' where children can sit if they want others to befriend them.

The emotionally literate school follows the government's strategy for SEAL and has an assembly programme that covers spiritual, moral, social and cultural awareness (defined, respectively, as a 'sense of identity and self-worth', 'principles to guide behaviour', 'social skills of living and working cooperatively in small and large groups' and 'exploring one's own and others' cultural values and assumptions'). Advisers, consultants and educational psychologists run courses for senior managers to develop their own emotional literacy and to design strategies for the school. Teachers, learning assistants, parents and canteen workers can attend courses run by the local authority on emotional well-being. In some areas, teachers can attend after-school workshops to explore their own emotional problems arising from past and current events, run by educational psychologists.

Political sponsorship of emotional well-being is currently presented as recommendations and guidance, embracing numerous activities that are not officially part of SEAL but which fit it well and which are supported enthusiastically from a range of perspectives. Children will soon come into the primary school already prepared for therapeutic education due to the 'emotional well-being' objectives and guidance in new Early Years Curriculum (see box). In this chapter, we explore how therapeutic education and accompanying claims are taking hold in primary schools. First, we highlight specific examples of the content, process and assumptions in particular interventions. Second, we highlight political and popular concerns about boys as an example of assumptions made about the emotional needs of particular groups. Third, we summarise some concerns about assessment of emotional literacy and well-being. Finally, we evaluate the implications of our examples for educational goals and practices.

An emotional education

Government guidance

State-funded education is aligned with welfare, health and social work activities as part of the statutory goals and requirements of Every Child Matters (ECM) and is the main site for the state's responses to public fears and concerns about mental health, the emotional effects of social exclusion and broader goals for developing emotional well-being and emotional literacy, discussed in Chapter 1.

Combining diverse ideas and sources of support enables the DCSF to promote an inclusive approach to SEAL that aim to encompass 'bright and motivated children' as well as those with emotional or mental health problems (Weare 2004). This approach is supported by OfSTED inspectors who report that children's behaviour is significantly better in schools with a strong sense of community, where its ethos enables children to feel secure, to feel valued as individuals and are safe from emotional and physical harm, and where they are able to discuss their interests and fears in a supportive environment (OfSTED 2005a).

Another report by OfSTED endorses the need to combine various activities and subjects to identify and deal with mental health problems as part of developing all children's emotional well-being (OfSTED 2005a, 2005b).

Therapy for babies (0–3)

- Babies and children have emotional well-being when their needs are met and their feelings are accepted. They enjoy relationships that are close, warm and supportive.
- Making friends and getting on with others helps children to feel positive about themselves and others.

- Children gain a sense of well-being when they are encouraged to take responsibility and to join in by helping with manageable tasks that interest them.
- Children feel a sense of belonging in the setting when their parents are also involved in it.

Understanding feelings

- At times we all experience strong emotions as we deal with difficult or stressful events.
- Adults and children experience a wide range of feelings.
- Children gradually learn to understand and manage their feelings with support from the adults around them.
- Recognising their own feelings helps everyone to understand other people's feelings and to become more caring towards others.
- When each person is valued for who they are and differences are appreciated, everyone feels included and understood, whatever their personality, abilities, ethnic background or culture.

Respecting each other's feelings

- The emotional environment is created by all the people in the setting, but adults have to ensure that it is warm and accepting of everyone.
- Adults need to empathise with children and support their emotions.
- When children feel confident in the environment they are willing to try things out, knowing that effort is valued.
- When children know that their feelings are accepted they learn to express them, confident that adults will help them with how they are feeling.

The learning environment

- Dispositions and attitudes
- Self-confidence and self-esteem
- Making relationships
- Behaviour and self-control
- Self-care
- Sense of community.

(Early Years Foundation Stage Cards – DfES 2007)

According to the DfES, certain emotions promote learning (well-being, feeling valued, feeling safe) while others do not (frustration, anger). Its SEAL strategy for primary schools identifies a large number of skills that can be developed 'within an environment supportive to emotional health and well-being' that equip children to:

Know themselves
- knowing when and how they learn most effectively;
- taking responsibility for their actions and learning;
- feeling good about the things they do well and accepting themselves for who and what they are;
- recognising when they find something hard to achieve.

Understanding their feelings
- identifying, recognising and expressing a range of feelings;
- knowing that feelings, thoughts and behaviour are linked;
- recognising when they are being overwhelmed by their feelings;
- knowing that it is OK to have any feeling but not OK to behave in any way they like.

Managing how they express feelings
- being able to stop and think before acting;
- expressing a range of feelings in ways that do not hurt themselves or others;
- understanding that how they express feelings can change the way others feel;
- adapting the way they express feelings to suit particular situations or people.

Managing the way they are feeling
- calming themselves down when they choose to;
- having a range of strategies for managing anger;
- having a range of strategies for managing worries and other uncomfortable feelings;
- understanding that changing how they think about people and events changes how they feel about them;
- being able to change the way they feel by reflecting on my experiences and reviewing the way they think about them;
- knowing that they can seek support from others when they feel worried, angry or sad;
- knowing what makes them feel good and knowing how to enhance those comfortable feelings.

Setting goals and planning to meet them
- being able to set a challenge or goal, thinking ahead and considering the consequences for themselves and others;
- breaking a long-term plan into smaller achievable steps, planning to overcome obstacles, set success criteria and celebrating achievement. (ibid.: 41)

SEAL offers what its authors call a 'skills-based approach' grounded in children's understandings, values and beliefs. The alignment of skills, values and beliefs mean that the so-called 'skills' in this daunting and prescriptive list are not skills at all but, instead, attributes, attitudes and dispositions that mirror those in articles by life coaches, therapists and psychologists on how to sort out one's emotional life, cited as popular examples of therapy in Chapter 1.

In addition to focusing on the emotional needs of all children, the DfES also approved specialist interventions for widespread use: in 1997, it encouraged primary schools to use 'nurture groups' as a 'resource' that would enable children with emotional problems who did not require individual psychotherapy to make personal relationships. As we show below, these are widely used to withdraw children diagnosed with a range of behavioural and emotional 'disorders' from mainstream classes in order to provide therapeutic support.

Circle time

The underlying principles and processes of liberal humanist counselling are now a staple part of children's primary school experience through activities such as circle time and Philosophy for Children, discussed below. The most well-known and influential proponent of circle time is Jenny Mosley whose work has influenced the DfES and is widely used in primary and secondary schools. Based on her work as an educational psychologist, and with its origins in specialist interventions for children with behavioural and emotional problems, circle time has moved from story telling and 'show and tell' activities to an overtly therapeutic approach to building self-esteem and developing emotional literacy for all children. To Rogerian principles of empathy, active listening and 'reflecting back' and positive regard, Mosley adds emotional warmth, fun, a lively pace and enthusiasm as essential attributes for those running circle time.

Circle time uses group and pair games to help children socialise, build oral confidence and enjoy themselves. Games such as 'pass a smile to the person next to you' and 'cross the circle if you have a pet/have an older brother/like sports' are precursors to what a training film presents as ways to 'move closer and closer to home' (Bliss *et al.* 1995). Games move into personal disclosures, such as 'cross the circle if you feel hurt when someone makes fun of you', 'know that there is bullying in this school', 'know there is bullying in this class', 'would help a classmate who was unhappy'. Rounds of children disclosing in turn might ask them 'what makes you happy', 'what makes you sad', 'think of a change that has made you miserable', 'one things that makes you different from others in the class'. Or children might make an individual display of their personal history, talk about key life events, act in role plays of emotions and reactions about change (perhaps taking on the role of others in the family), make group displays of how to make others in the class happy, such as sharing something, talking to someone who feels lonely, including everyone in games at playtime, and take part in listening exercises and relaxation. Teachers are also encouraged to present their own difficulties, express feelings about particular events and ask children to offer help to them.

Ritual and routine are essential, where discussion and disclosures in rounds allows only the person holding a 'speaking object' to contribute. Children can 'pass' during a round to 'give them time to think' and while, in theory, there is no compulsion to speak, the ritual and warm-up games encourage them to. Teachers remind children of the social, emotional and behavioural skills they will be using and draw attention to these during the session through non-verbal praise, verbal praise, stickers and certificates.

Many children begin circle time at three years of age. Five themes of PSHE, used interchangeably with notions of 'citizenship', are the basis for 40 hours of activity (one session a week) for very young children. The same mix of 'warm-up' games and activities to share and disclose feelings mirror those advocated by Mosley (see Collins 2001).

Mosley regards the wholesale adoption of circle time as a 'cause' that improves teachers' and children's self-esteem, promotes self-understanding and raises standards of behaviour and discipline. Her work promotes circle time as part of a whole school approach, where SEAL is encouraged systematically for staff and pupils: an essential feature is that staff must be able to 'model' the personal qualities and behaviours they expect from children (circletime@jennymosley.co.uk). Supporters claim that circle time enables the excluded or disaffected child to feel included and that it normalises emotional problems by showing that all the children in the group and the teacher experience them to a greater or lesser extent.

Supporters also claim that children enjoy circle time and that it enables teachers to pick up individual children's difficulties and to take action, perhaps by talking to parents, colleagues and other professionals. A colleague in a pre-school centre has been trained by the local authority to regard it as the beginning of an increasingly formal 'trail' of alerting different people to a child's difficulties, beginning with parents and moving onto social workers and other workers.

Circle time to calm us down

When asked what circle time was used for in his school and whether it was a routine activity, Joe, the nine-year-old child of a friend said: 'we do circle time when we all need calming down ... when some people aren't getting on, or when there's bullying. Mostly it's when we're feeling stressed about the SATs'. Asked if he liked it, he replied 'yes, it's nice to be listened to and it calms everybody down'.

Circle time to understand our emotions

Joseph, at the same school, gives another positive account:

First they tell us the L.O. (K: what's the L.O.?) That's the learning objective. They want us to understand our emotions, like how not to get angry when you're only annoyed. It helps us, it gives us courage to speak and it's done in a fun way. Sometimes the teacher asks us to say more about why we feel a certain way but you don't have to say if you don't want to.

Now we're in Year 6, it's not called circle time, it's PSHE, that's personal, social and health education. It's the same but you talk about how to say no to drugs and cigarettes. I don't know what it will be like if we keep on doing at top school next year; it might get a bit boring.

Moving closer and closer to home

Luke, the 6-year-old son of a colleague, says 'we do circle time on Mondays. Sometimes we do show and tell or hear a story. Other times she [teacher] asks us what we did at the weekend. I told them today how Ann and David came round and we went to play football. Then she might ask 'what problems have you had at playtime today'?' When asked if they were made to speak, he said 'when it's something nice, we all have to speak when we are holding the teddy. If it's a problem thing, we don't have to speak if we don't want to'.

Who wants to be a friendship struggler?

Another friend's 10-year-old daughter said that 'going on about feelings is often boring'' and she cited the example of 'friendship strugglers' as making those who had no problems with friendship 'just feel sorry' for them or to see them as a 'bit pathetic. I mean, who'd want to be a friendship struggler?' A boy in her class refers to the school's 'lonely bench' as the 'losers' bench'.

Certifying circle time values

Children can be certified for doing circle time. One product for schools to buy says 'congratulations ... [name of child] you kept circle time values'

- We listen carefully to others.
- We take time to speak calmly.
- We try to think of ideas to help others.
- We are positive and friendly.
- We use our thinking, looking, speaking, listening and concentration skills.
- We can have fun if we act responsibly.
- We take some special issues to the teacher for a quiet chat.

(www.Tts-group.co.uk)

These examples show children using some of the official phrases of their teachers: 'calming down', 'understanding emotions', 'learning objectives', PSHE and 'friendship struggler', and the certificate teaches them the ubiquitous word 'issues'! They also show how difficult it would be for children *not* to speak. Compulsory rounds and games for 'nice' things lead to more probing, intrusive questions that, in the telling phrase of the training video, enable the teacher to 'move closer and closer to home'. After a few years of circle time, it is very unlikely that children would continue to resist speaking about their problems.

Emotions and feelings trees and the worry box

In nurture groups, discussed below, the daily 'feelings tree' requires children to start their day of nurturing routines by selecting a feeling displayed on a tree as representative of how they feel that day and to speak in a circle about why they feel the way they do. In various forms, this ritual is adapted to mainstream primary school activity, sometimes as the beginning of a circle time about how we all experience many different feelings: this aims to develop a 'vocabulary of feelings'.

Many schools require children to make displays of emotions and feelings, with photographs and drawings of different facial expressions and the emotions they might indicate.

Worrying about the 'worry box'

A friend's eight year old child came home in a state of anxiety because she had been asked to write something down on a piece of paper, anonymously, to go into the class 'worry box', from which the teacher would select some examples for discussion in circle time later in the week. When she couldn't think of anything, the teacher said she could go home and come back the next day with something to go in the worry box.

Building 'learning power' for lifelong learning

There is growing concern about the negative effects of testing and targets on pupils' motivation and the ways in which they encourage children and teachers to prioritise the demands of the test and to overlook the development of skills and attributes needed for lifelong learning (see, for example, Pollard *et al.* 2003; Harlen and Deakin-Crick 2002; Claxton 2002). One response is the promotion of 'learning to learn', namely generic capacities that are supposed to help people develop the attributes and dispositions necessary for lifelong learning, what Claxton and colleagues depict as 'helping learners get better at learning' or 'learning power', defined as a 'complex mix of dispositions, lived experiences, social relations, values, attitudes and beliefs that coalesce to shape the nature of an individual's engagement with any particular learning opportunity' (ellionline.co.uk; see also Deakin-Crick 2007; Claxton 2002).

Studies to identify the elements that define a good learner have led to an instrument to diagnose seven dimensions of 'learning power': changing and learning, meaning making, curiosity, creativity, learning relationships, strategic awareness and resilience. Designers argue that 'diagnostic assessment' based on valid and reliable constructs shows that learners achieve well in terms of official targets but are also 'fragile' and 'dependent' learners. The research claims that such interventions make students more resilient, more 'strategically aware of their own learning' and 'less dependent and fragile' whilst also achieving more in terms of standard learning outcomes. A control group became weaker on the learning dimensions, in keeping with the evidence from the whole cohort (www.ellionline.co.uk).

Nurturing learning power

Activities include:

- self-assessment 'using the language of learning';
- pupils and teachers 'share and explore learning power highs and lows' through group exercises and a class diary that records the 'ups and downs' of learning;
- turning highs and lows into a coaching manual for the 10 year old 'learning buddies' who help the new reception class develop their learning power;
- displays of pupils' work show drafts, mistakes, and new directions coming from original ideas rather than the 'mis-leading' and 'off-putting' final polished product;
- teachers share their own doubts and uncertainties about learning, modelling the need to ask questions, and expressing difficulties and fears rather than presenting themselves as the 'unrealistic' paragon of expertise that is the image of most good teachers;
- a 'learning wall' where pupils place Post-Its of notes when they feel themselves 'working at the leading edge of their learning power', or photographs of a special achievement.

(Claxton 2002)

Philosophy for Children (P4C)

According to the Society for Advancing Philosophical Enquiry and Reflection in Education (SAPERE), it is important to differentiate between the study of philosophy as an academic subject and philosophising as a practice of enquiry, as a way of engaging with questions through 'thinking, analysing, creating solutions and new points of view' (Lacewing 2007:5). The question of whether or not all activities presented as 'philosophy for children' are philosophical is contentious (see SAPERE 2007).

We do not engage here in discussion about whether children are capable of philosophical thinking or of 'doing' philosophy. Instead, we argue that the enthusiastic and uncritical promotion of emotional well-being enables the notion to be easily hijacked, especially when it is surrounded by other vague ideas such as 'communities of enquiry' and the ubiquitous and equally vague 'reflection' and 'reflective practice'. While some activities depicted by SAPERE focus on better ways to discuss specific philosophical topics, other interventions presented as P4C are imbued with social and emotional purposes and outcomes, including feeling good about yourself and others, being respectful, empathetic and disagreeing in 'appropriate' ways, how to deal with having 'hurt' feelings or how to help others better (see DfES 2005a).

Scripting 'appropriate' responses

A project run by Antidote introduced two P4C classes in a London inner-city school during a four-year project that tried out a range of interventions for emotional literacy. A DVD shows two separate classes of 20 eight year olds from diverse ethnic backgrounds. Sitting on the floor in a circle, the teacher asks individual children to remind everyone about the 'ground rules'. They recite them enthusiastically: respect for others' points of view even when you don't agree with them; listening until the child has finished what she or he is saying; trying to understand their feelings; saying what it is you don't agree with before stating your own views; not interrupting.

The teacher has a topic: it might be a painting, or photograph with a theme, such as 'poverty in Africa' or be more open-ended, like 'what does this picture tell us about nature'? The teacher 'models' the right behaviours for conducting a discussion, with positive reinforcement of each child's contributions, praise for good behaviour and enthusiastic thanks at the end for how much she has 'enjoyed our philosophy class today'. The children are thoughtful, respectful of each other and say, as children do, sweet and engaging things about the topic. If they disagree, they must use a particular form of words, such as 'I don't agree with you, Hannah, because', before putting their own point of view.

In this example, it is hard to see at first what might be questionable, not least because the engaging ways that children talk in the film, both in the lesson and when interviewed about it afterwards, and the enthusiasm of everyone featured, all combine to obscure critical analysis. But listening to the dialogue and the justification for doing it makes it quickly apparent that this has little or nothing to do with 'philosophy' or even a 'philosophical way of thinking and talking'. In this example, the teacher never challenges the children about the content of what they say, whether it is 'logical' or 'reasonable': all views are accepted unconditionally. It is therefore far from clear what, if anything, the children learnt about poverty in Africa, or about the nature of nature!

The DfES seized eagerly on claims that P4C brings emotional and cognitive learning together. After a lengthy discussion of a 'typical' activity, a story called 'Lion, Mouse and Human' from the SEAL 'Good to be me' theme, the document lists approvingly certain comments from children about what they had learnt:

- The monster didn't share to start with because she didn't understand how to share.
- I learnt that if someone is horrible to you, don't be horrible back, just say how it feels and try to be nice to them.
- You must share.
- Quite a lot of stories go from bad to good.
- I learnt not to get in fights.

(DfES 2005a: 57)

According to the DfES and Antidote, teachers involved in projects to introduce P4C are overwhelmingly enthusiastic. For example,

For me, P4C has been an amazing way of unlocking children's thought processes, emotions and imaginations, and giving me a far greater insight into the way they feel about themselves and their relationships with other people in their lives.

(DfES 2005a: 58)

Similarly, children, teachers, parents and the head teacher in the Antidote film (cited above) like the informality of the process and talk enthusiastically about the far-reaching effects of doing these sessions on confidence, self-esteem, behaviour inside and outside the classroom and on the children's motivation to learn other subjects.

Smoothing transitions

Researchers, teachers and policy makers regard the transition from primary to secondary school as so 'unsettling, daunting, stressful' that it can de-motivate up to 40 per cent of 11-year-olds badly enough for them to 'never' recover, thereby causing a marked dip in formal achievement (Frankel 2007). A host of other changes are seen to need special treatment in order to help children 'embrace change' and 'build resilience', such as moving between classes each day, experiencing different teaching styles, moving between different locations and from one set of expectations to another (Tew and Park 2007).

According to Tew and Park, 'primary-secondary transition is sometimes written about as an experience of loss for young people, to be understood in terms of the processes associated with mourning or grief' (2007: 23). They list a series of emotions associated with grief: denial, anger, bargaining, depression and acceptance and argue that, although many children see opportunities provided by secondary school as exciting, the 'confused' and 'ambivalent' feelings of loss and gain need to be 'managed and eased'. The article encourages schools to do this by eliciting and sharing feelings, encouraging 'closure' of relationships that will be ending through activities such as exploring scenario cards, drawing storyboards, doing role plays and asking children to write responses from agony aunts or problem pages. In some schools, children can take part in 'drama workshops' about transitions, alongside their parents.

Psychodrama for the 'trauma of transition'

A DVD *Ready or Not* aims to show teachers and parents how they might help children cope with transition to secondary school. A series of drama workshops led by theatre educators encourage children to 'express their hopes and fears' about transition. Activities include 'the memory chair', where each child comes to sit and recalls something they will miss about primary school, and 'stop the script' where children do short role plays of something they fear at secondary school and the other children offer suggestions for changing the outcome.

Older children are brought in to 'dispel' fears, rumours and myths and to offer positive examples of life at secondary school. The head teacher talks about the challenge of change, the need to 'cope' with it, to manage a process that, while a 'natural part of growing up', needs support and clear 'strategies' that children can use. In contrast to adults' pessimistic tone, some of the younger children are excited, happy and optimistic, looking forward to 'proper science lessons with experiments', 'new friends and experiences' and 'real teachers who know about different subjects'.

But these examples are fleeting and sporadic compared to time spent on anxieties, the 'challenge of change', what is like to 'feel small in a big place' and to 'leave your friends behind'. In the same vein, identical activities are presented in ideas for circle time to deal with transitions to primary school for four-year-olds (Collins 2001).

The older children advocate safety and conformity : one child asks what to do if he is lost in his first few days. The peer mentors tell him to 'make sure you ask someone wearing a badge that shows he is a bully counsellor because you can't trust other children not to play a trick on you by sending you the wrong way'. Another says that secondary school is great but sometimes you can be targeted as a 'swot' or 'nerd' by children who are 'less able than you'. He tells the children that if they conform and work hard, they will get on and do well (Hughes *et al.* 2007).

One of the most striking things about the sessions is the absence of dramatic interest or creativity and, instead, their similarity to training in psychodrama techniques for practitioners in mental health and counselling. Pessimism permeates the DVD: despite claims to focus on 'hopes' as well as 'fears', the role plays, 'fictional' situations presented to children and the narrator's voice-over all emphasise fears, concerns and worries.

Nurture groups

Nurture groups have a long history as a specialist approach for children with emotional and behavioural difficulties who are not seen as needing individual therapy or counselling. The 35-year-old 'Nurture Group' movement was originally designed for children who lacked the personal resources needed for school. Offering an optimistic vision of looking forward rather than pathologising children on the basis of their past experience, nurture groups provide routines and developmental strategies to improve poor personal organisation, self-control and awareness, and understanding of their surroundings (Boxhall 2003).

Supported by the DCSF and its predecessor the DfES as a good behavioural strategy, their use in UK primary schools has been steadily increasing since 1997 as one of the main ways to deal with rising levels of emotional and behavioural difficulties (EBDs) (Bailey 2007). Rooted in developmental psychology, they offer an early intervention based on withdrawal from mainstream classes, mainly for children diagnosed with Attention Deficit and Hyperactivity Disorder but also for those diagnosed with Oppositional Defiance Disorder. There is a widespread view that 'oppositional' and 'defiant' behaviour at five years of age leads to a worsening of social and emotional problems as children progress to secondary school, so early therapeutic intervention is vital (see Cornwall and Walter 2006).

The groups, with their strict routines, continuity of staff and tightly scripted 'nurturing norms' of appropriate ways to 'say sorry', 'calm down' and 'monitor your noise levels', are considered an appropriate intervention for a broad range of troublesome behaviour. In a study of how nurture groups were implemented in two primary schools, Simon Bailey observes that actual diagnoses and being 'at risk' of a diagnosis were both criteria for children's referrals to the groups (Bailey 2007). His study also illuminates how therapeutic orthodoxies permeate judgements of individual cases, where difference comes to be synonymous with emotional and behavioural deficit, where overt behaviours either conceal private 'trauma' or reveal it overtly, and where constructs such as 'attachment' or 'esteem' shift arbitrarily. He argues that 'two fuzzy, ill-defined concepts feed off each other and onwards into further reaches of psychiatric description' (Bailey 2007: 16).

As well as showing how constructs extend into new areas of psychiatric description, the study highlights how easily the language and assumptions of therapy become unthinking and routine, turning quickly into simplistic labels and negative judgements. Staff describe how activities such as the 'feelings tree', described above, enable them to 'dig into the home lives' of the children. Such digging leads invariably to what Bailey calls 'recurring' themes in nurturing orthodoxy including what the founder of nurture groups calls the 'developmental impoverishment' of the child's home situation (Boxhall, quoted by Bailey 2007: 12).

In Bailey's study, there are examples of children adopting some of the same self-fulfilling statements and labels used by staff to describe their own behaviour and its causes. He concludes that 'far from effecting the compassion and healing which its instantiaters no doubt desire, such internalising shifts attention from systems and structures, which limit and define, to the emotional deficit of the individual which is deemed fit for further manipulation' (ibid.: 17).

Using the existing curriculum and everyday life

The government and its schools' inspectorate and other bodies such as the Qualifications and Curriculum Authority (QCA) advocate that all subject areas can be used imaginatively to develop SEAL, with citizenship and personal, social and health education (PSHE) as especially important. The QCA offers numerous ways that schools can adapt the existing curriculum, such as the national literacy strategy, in order to help children deal with their experience and adapt to school. For example, this provides children of asylum seekers with 'opportunities for personal, reflective talk and [life story] writing'; 'activities such as music, drama, art and storytelling assist [newly arrived children] in understanding their experiences and managing difficult memories and feelings' (QCA 2005).

Everyday emotional literacy and well-being

A friend's daughter was excited that her school was going to use a visit by a travelling circus as an opportunity for children to practise circus skills. Far from encouraging this as a great opportunity to learn juggling or trapeze artistry, the leaflet for parents said that this would 'boost children's self-esteem, make them more confident and teach them social skills'.

But schools don't have to lay on such extravagant activities. There are many opportunities for teachers to 'model' emotional literacy and, in the language of nurture groups, to 'dig into' children's emotional lives. Chatting to a child while supervising bus duty is one such possibility, while playground fights, squabbles and bad classroom atmospheres enable children and teachers to 'share' how they each feel when such situations arise and to find ways 'together' to avoid them.

In a similar vein, the QCA advocates helping children of newly arrived immigrants or asylum seekers to regard play and sports as opportunities to 'cope better' and show resilience and manage experiences of loss and change. The social and emotional aspects of physical exercise and games are therefore as important outcomes as health, fitness and skill. As Susannah Wright shows, these examples of social and emotional outcomes are identical to claims amongst nineteenth-century proponents of moral education that teachers should model the right 'moral' behaviour from the same activities (Wright 2006, 2007).

New Labour's new boys

The idea that schools must develop the emotional well-being of all children runs alongside concerns about specific groups, particularly boys and, more specifically, working class boys who are being excluded from schools in ever higher numbers. In the minds of policy makers, many parents and teachers, boys are a special case: highlighting it here reveals the influence of popular orthodoxies on current policy in this area.

In their analysis of shifting cultural and political ideas about the 'problem with boys', Becky Francis and Christine Skelton explore various perceptions about the problems that face boys which have emerged over the past 20 years. These range from girls who are disempowering them, schools who are failing them and the effect of 'natural differences' where they are naturally clever but lazy, difficult to motivate, competitive, independent and intolerant of inadequate teaching. Yet, many of these perspectives overlook class and cultural differences and economic contexts (Francis and Skelton 2006).

Under New Labour, a view that boys have a responsibility to 'achieve' is overlaid with concerns about laddish behaviour. For example, in a consultation document, *Boys Will be Boys*, produced in 1996, the government argued that 'the very future of our society depends on reconnecting young men and boys – particularly in the most economically and socially deprived areas – with a sense of belonging and identity which will provide both hope and self reliance' (Francis and Skelton 2006: 66). The government's emphasis on the emotional effects and causes of social exclusion, discussed in Chapter 1, means that boys who are not achieving as they should or could, are not merely disruptive and excluded but also emotionally vulnerable and 'at risk'.

In this vein, books for teachers and parents, and the government's own texts about the problem with boys, emphasise the emotional effects of social exclusion: the experience or perception of alienation; isolation; lack of identity; low self-confidence; low self-esteem; passivity; dependence; bewilderment; fear; anger; apathy; low aspirations; helplessness. As Francis and Skelton show, a significant feature of the claims and government response to them is that they are both drawn from popular texts rather than academic studies.

As Furedi shows, such assumptions are culturally and historically specific: at different times and in different contexts, characteristics now seen as 'repression' signal, instead, stoicism, resilience and independence (2004). By the time working class young men go to university, they face negative orthodoxies about their class and masculinity from government agencies and universities that focus on the likelihood that they will 'drop out' of higher education (see Quinn *et al.* 2006). According to

Therapeutic orthodoxies about boys

Underneath male bravada, boys are fragile learners

Boys' self-esteem as learners is far more fragile than that of most girls, not least because boys resort to bravado to cover over the shame they would experience if they 'actually showed their fears about not messing up' (Pollack quoted in Francis and Skelton 2006: 71).

Men are emotionally more illiterate than women

Men and women display 'typically' different 'emotional styles' that make women more emotionally literate (see, for example, Weare 2004; Sharp 2001).

Repressing feelings causes lasting emotional damage

> When they [boys] are upset or afraid, they feel ashamed: sometimes the shame is buried deep and the boy gives the impression of being unaffected; sometimes the shame kindles anger which is self-directed and turns inwards, possibly leading to depression; at other times, the anger is outwardly expressed through kicking, fighting, shouting, destroying something or being rude.
>
> (Neall quoted in Francis and Skelton 2006:71)

Traditional attributes of masculinity damage boys' educational and social success

> The idea that boys' 'negative feelings' about themselves produce 'self-harm' and exclusion fits well with ideas that many men cling to outdated images of masculinity, where failure to disclose vulnerability ensures that they become incapable of handling emotions maturely and are seen as little more than 'autistic control freaks'.
>
> (Furedi 2004: 35)

Francis and Skelton, the overriding image from popular and political texts about boys is that 'trying to be a boy' in today's society places them under psychological pressure: the DfES paper 'Nationally Healthy School Standard to Raise Boys' Achievement', produced in 2003, observes that the tension between an inner, caring and vulnerable person and outward expectations of 'laddishness' will not create a 'caring masculinity'.

The psychological, emotionally-tuned emphasis in popular and policy responses to the 'problem' with boys accords with the government's ideas about social justice and exclusion. In response, the DfES encourages schools to use assemblies and tutorials to address 'issues' related to developing a 'caring masculinity' (exemplified by sensitivity and consideration), which provide boys with 'time to talk' about the need to reject violence, 'talk out' aggression and openly express feelings without fear of embarrassment. In this way, a culture is being developed that enables a boy 'to be himself', rather than having to live up to a tough male stereotype (DfES, quoted in Francis and Skelton 2006: 73).

We can therefore add the therapeutic orthodoxy of 'finding your authentic self' to the list above, providing that boys are seeking the authentic self of caring masculinity.

Assessing emotional literacy and well-being

Presenting emotional intelligence and emotional literacy as domains of learning has led to numerous formal and informal assessment instruments. A report for the DfES identifies over 40 instruments for assessing different aspects of emotional competence, used in a variety of ways in educational contexts and in multi-agency work as part of Every Child Matters, and judges 28 of these as suitable for use in practice (Stewart-Brown and Edmunds 2003). Uses include: helping teachers, practitioners and others to identify children with poor emotional competence (screening); identifying children's emotional strengths and weaknesses in different settings (profiling); identifying ways to support children's emotional development (improving practice) and monitoring emotional development (monitoring progress) (2003: 10–11).

The transition from research instrument to public assessment has a long history in education. According to Gordon Stobart, just as measures of IQ became reified creations that labelled and shaped their recipients, proponents of emotional intelligence proponents of emotional intelligence fall into the same trap as those who promoted old forms of IQ, where their attempts to offer alternative forms of 'intelligence' end up as reified constructs that are reinforced by schemes of assessment that have limited validity (Stobart 2008). As we showed in Chapter 1, these problems are compounded by disagreement about the extent to which emotional 'skills' are biologically based, or specific and situational. Once beliefs are turned into pseudo-scientific constructs, a common-sense agreement that these can be measured and developed then emerges. This leads to disparate skills being reduced to single judgements.

Problems with reliability and validity are not merely the arcane concerns of psychometricians. Education has a time-honoured tradition of taking strongly held beliefs, developing assessment methods to support them, reifying the ideas through supposedly scientific measures and then, in some cases, speculating on their biological underpinnings: a related example is certain models of learning styles (see Coffield *et al.* 2004).

Lucy, Emma and Roy learn the ropes

Lucy

The QCA's Foundation Stage profile requires teachers to assess children's personal and social development in relation to 'dispositions and attitudes' and 'social development'. The 8-year-old daughter of a friend was assessed in the following cheery but stern tones:

Statements 6, 7 and 8: s/he contines to be interested, motivated and excited to learn; she is confident to try new activities, initiate ideas and speak in a group; she maintains attention and concentrates.

> 7 Lucy is keen and enthusiastic! She loves to join in with activities and discussions. Sometimes she is a bit too enthusiastic! She needs to allow others time to talk/have a turn, and needs to listen carefully to instructions! 6 and 8 – Lucy's ability to spend time and care on activities is developing all the time …

Statements 4 and 5: s/he works as part of a group or class, taking turns and sharing fairly; she forms good relationships with adults and peers.

> 4 At the start of the year, Lucy needed some adult support to take turns and share. She likes to lead but this can lead to her appearing a bit 'bossy'. She has a really good sense of humour and likes to have fun! 5. Occasionally, she may unintentionally appear a bit cheeky. We are helping her to reflect on these times and this has improved enormously during the year.

Emma

In hushed tones at a parents' evening, a friend was asked if there was anything that might be worrying her 8-year-old daughter, Emma, because she didn't like to talk in circle time when the topic was personal. If nothing was wrong, then 'perhaps', said the teacher, 'she has low self-esteem'. When the parents asked Emma if there was anything wrong, she said 'the things the teacher asks us to talk about are private, they're home things, things just for us to talk about'.

Roy

An outer London primary school employs 'emotional literacy assistants' (ELAs), to deal with problems of low self-esteem and poor motivation. Roy is a cheery, freckled-faced five-year old who skips in to his class – a little late – and he is welcomed by a warm and positive ELA:

> ELA: How do you feel today, Roy?
>
> ROY: t's my birthday and I'm going to McDonald's and it's nice and sunny, Miss ... It makes you feel nice, Miss ... and happy!
>
> After a while the ELA probes ... :
>
> But are you sure there's nothing worrying you ...?
>
> *Non-academic children*
>
> A colleague working in a primary school observes: 'at least we can talk to parents about a child's emotional and personal development when we can't find anything good to say about their child's academic progress'.

Lucy is being trained to 'reflect on her behaviour' with a supportive 'other'; Emma is learning that she has repressed 'issues' and her parents learn to be anxious about their daughter's repressed issues. Roy is learning that uncertainty and anxiety are normal and that he should talk about such feelings; while 'non-academic' children and their parents learn that at least their emotional development is important.

Of course, teachers have always judged and labelled pupils' social and behavioural characteristics. Yet, defining emotional constructs as banks of statements that are recorded in detail, together with the simplistic assumptions often underpinning everyday informal judgements, takes assessment into new areas of dubious validity and reliability. Despite these problems, focusing on social and emotional characteristics is a useful diversion for children who do not do well in conventional assessments.

Implications for educational goals and practices

Imposing the orthodoxy of 'appropriate' feelings

Taken together, examples in this chapter show a restricted set of ritualised 'strategies' that promote 'appropriate' responses and feelings and reinforce, both explicitly and implicitly, two therapeutic orthodoxies. One is that expressions of hope, happiness and excitement or difficult behaviour merely hide 'repressed' fears and anxieties, and the other is that enabling children to articulate their repressed fears in a 'supportive' and 'safe' environment enables them to be 'dealt with'.

Activities that comprise therapeutic education require children to conform to tightly prescribed techniques, a vocabulary and underlying therapeutic principles. The Antidote film showed that ritualised exchanges, with their conformity to demonstrating appropriate behaviours and speaking the language of 'respecting' and 'understanding' each other's 'views' and 'feelings' turns P4C into scripted behaviour management modelled by the teachers. Similarly, the examples of children talking about circle time show how they internalise the language and rationale. Whether or not children like these activities, they are learning to express their emotions through formulaic, compulsory rituals and associated assumptions about what comprises a good relationship between teachers and pupils and between pupils.

Coaching attitudes and dispositions

As we argued in Chapter 1, optimistic support for policy in this area obscures underlying pessimism about social problems and hopes that developing emotional literacy and emotional intelligence might mitigate them. The belief that developing emotional intelligence can stem a rising tide of social problems, particularly violence, leads to Goleman's view that we need to 'school the emotions'. His claims that emotional intelligence will reduce violence, depression and stress, improve health, family life, remove prejudice and improve organisations have, as we showed in Chapter 1, been taken up by supporters of emotional literacy and emotional well-being. As Craig argues, Goleman presents emotional intelligence as a panacea that schools can foster in exactly the same way that the self-esteem movement did in America a decade or so earlier (Craig 2007).

The language of emotional skills, competence and literacy also disguises strongly normative views about desirable attributes, attitudes and dispositions and reduces subject knowledge to eliciting knowledge about feelings and the coaching of 'appropriate emotional responses'. The disingenuous citing by the DfES of 'the ancient Greek ideal 'know thyself' as a working goal of P4C in its SEAL strategy sounds like an endorsement of philosophical enquiry. As Guignon shows, this injunction has been widely misinterpreted throughout history (2004). Instead, the rituals associated with a populist version of 'knowing yourself' amount to no more than scripted forms of social training. Children are learning a behavioural script and learning that they need professional support to elicit and manage their feelings and those of their peers. Circular language and practices are mirrored in SEAL guidance, textbooks on emotional literacy and well-being, training courses and the activities discussed in this chapter.

Despite claims that children can opt out of having to respond in circle time, psychodrama workshops and P4C, the popular orthodoxy that repressed feelings conceal inner trauma makes it hard to see how children can do this without being labelled with 'having issues'.

The idea that we can coach appropriate attitudes and dispositions is evident in Sharp's advice to parents about 'emotional coaching':

> if coaching is taken as a process involving 'giving hints' and 'training' and perhaps even 'modelling', then the distinction between this and telling is that the aim is to allow the coached child to make their own choices and mistakes in the context of a safe and secure environment.
>
> (Sharp 2003: 64)

He adds that learning from experience is 'self-coaching', advocating that parents keep logs of emotional incidents, write reflective diaries, analyse them and set targets for different ways to deal with their own and children's emotions. However, some parents have told us that children bring home written suggestions that the family should 'de-brief' everyone's day using circle time rituals.

We do not know how many schools are encouraging parents to reflect, self-coach and set themselves emotional targets, although similar approaches are promoted in some parenting classes.

Infantilising and normalising emotional difficulties

We argue that such interventions and their associated assumptions infantilise children, making them suggestible to fears, problems or 'uncomfortable feelings' that they may or may not face and they normalise the bad experiences of a minority of children as universal difficulties that 'we all have'. The overall effect is to insert expectations of structured support and 'nurturing'. Principles of 'inclusion' and de-stigmatising emotional difficulties inserts a continual self-awareness that is likely to mean that all children must empathise with the emotional problems of some of their peers by finding and admitting some of their own and by taking part in the same interventions. This is reinforced by requiring teachers to disclose their own fears and vulnerabilities.

Despite claims to promote emotional well-being, resilience and optimism by eliciting children's positive feelings about particular events as well as their fears, the language of 'vulnerability', 'fragility', 'nurturing' learning power and dealing with difficult emotions overwhelms positive feelings and responses. In the DVD about transitions cited above, there is a strong sense that it is the teachers' and parents' fears that fuel the children's, and that encouraging the children to express their fears does more to put them in their minds than to bring out what is assumed to be there. A concern to promote safety, and to avoid stress, tension, conflict, difficulty and feelings of exclusion and embarrassment, extends to the banning in some schools of certain sports activities and playground games.

Labelling children and their families

Therapeutic education presents roots of difficulty and dysfunction as, simultaneously, individual, social and biological, fixed and changeable. The feelings and behaviours that teachers attribute to their pupils through formal and informal assessments create simplistic labelling and judgemental stereotypes rather than genuine understanding of children's feelings, motives and behaviours.

Invalid and unreliable assessments lead to labels and judgements about the ability of families, particularly working class families, to deal with children's emotions. We have noticed this anecdotally in conversations with teachers and parents, and Bailey observed it in his study of nurture groups, discussed above. The *Community Soundings* report about primary education revealed many negative judgements about parents held by teachers and teaching assistants about inadequate parenting, the need for classes in remedial parenting, low parental aspirations, passing the socialisation buck to schools, parents' emotional illiteracy (Alexander and Hargreaves 2007).

Such views are hardly surprising. Not only does therapeutic education lead schools to take on an extended and intrusive role in children's socialisation, but the emotional well-being industry peddles a strong, negative message of emotional determinism. Quoting American psychologists, Stobart raises the spectre of more insidious labels: 'Most frighteningly, in distilling this complex entity [of emotional intelligence] into a single quality, might we not some day soon be reading a book touting the advantages of an emotional elite and the deterioration brought to our society by the emotional underclass' (Matthews *et al.* quoted by Stobart 2008: 69).

Conclusions

Few, if any, proponents of the activities discussed in this chapter regard their goals and methods as 'therapeutic': indeed, Guy Claxton rejects this attribution strenuously (2005, 2007). In contrast, we argue that all the activities in this chapter insert a powerful therapeutic ethos into educational contexts, through a prescribed vocabulary of feelings, simplistic explanations and assumptions about feelings and responses to events, and a repetitive set of rituals. Their underlying orthodoxies encourage children, parents and teachers to make sense of themselves and others in particular ways that are almost impossible to challenge. Whatever the rhetoric of empowerment, such interventions suggest that all children, to a greater or lesser extent, are emotionally vulnerable and that they need scripted forms of nurturing and support. Activities discussed in this chapter move the therapeutic demand for routine and predictability, once reserved for specialist behaviour management strategies, into mainstream social training.

Policy makers hope that SEAL will permeate schools:

> Without their concrete realisation in behaviour, competences remain potential rather than actual ... Programmes which attempt to build emotional and social competences must include extensive, *routinised, regular and* predictable work to develop specific skills across the curriculum and reinforce these skills by pupils' real life experiences across the whole school ...
>
> (DfES 2005a: 37, our emphasis)

The government offers suggestions about how schools can find their own way towards developing emotional and social skills. Yet, the breadth of interventions embraced by SEAL, the sweeping claims that accompany them and their growing routinisation make therapeutic education far more significant than requiring sensitivity to children's emotional needs and ways of dealing with the problems of a small minority: good schools and teachers have always done those things. Instead, therapeutic education is transmogrifying the liberal goal of educating the 'whole child' into an emotional interpretation where children as both a subject and a curriculum can be coached 'subject' and 'curriculum' that can be coached and assessed. As we aim to show in the next chapter, secondary schools turn pupils' worlds further inwards.

Chapter 3

The therapeutic secondary school

Introduction

Before a political shift in 2007 towards the idea that schools should actively promote happiness and well-being, the government presented the scale of emotional deprivation as so great that schools and other agencies can no longer leave emotional skills and well-being to parents. In this context, psychotherapists and the emotional literacy pressure group Antidote advised the government on how to introduce emotional literacy in secondary schools. Speaking on *Woman's Hour* on BBC Radio Four in December 2006, Brett Kahr, a psychotherapist, articulated why this is necessary:

> time to talk, time to feel good about yourself, to create citizens of the future; the ability to talk is the most important skill we can give these children. The skills spread into the playground, onto the street and into the estate. Not bottling up emotions, lay it all out at school and go back home and make it up, say sorry. People don't talk about it at home – mum is rushing around worrying about everything, whereas at school there's a specific time to feel comfortable and say what we want. If we put angry, depressed and sad feelings into words, we won't act them out. It is a joint responsibility between teachers and parents; the painful reality is that many parents are not in the best state of mind – mentally ill, abusers, in marriage break-ups, whereas teachers can nurture.
>
> (Brett Kahr on Woman's Hour, Monday 14 December 2006)

Concerns about the need for schools to pay attention to the emotional needs of children intensify in the case of teenagers:

> It is not too fanciful to see, behind the youth culture of raves and drugs, sport and celebrity, the rise of teenage pregnancy and fundamentalism, the shadow of insecurity: the feeling of not being able to get a grip on the miasma of choices and opportunities ... No wonder so many young people clutch at the first kind of boy or girl, the first shallow ideology that comes along. It's not so much that young people live in poverty ... as they do not know where to turn for direction and value. In such a state, algebra and parts of speech can seem a little beside the point.
>
> (Claxton 2002: 48)

Despite the continuing resonance of these images, political interest in finding ways to promote and assess 'happiness' and well-being is leading to a different, more positive approach to therapeutic education from the one developed through SEAL and discussed in the previous chapter. In this chapter, we explore how therapeutic education resonates with ideas that schools should develop 'soft skills' in order to make education more 'relevant'. First, we show how interest in personalised learning and learner voice, learning to learn and assessing soft skills erodes belief that young people need subject knowledge. Second, we explore how advocates of interventions for young people with behavioural, social and mental ill-health problems want therapeutic principles to be integrated with broader educational goals. Third, we show how the emotional work being undertaken by young people in peer mentoring schemes is integral to therapeutic education. Fourth, we show how subject disciplines are increasingly being hollowed out and marshalled for emotional outcomes amidst a plethora of other instrumental outcomes. Finally, we highlight implications of therapeutic education for definitions of a 'broad and holistic' education and for views about 'subjects' worth teaching in schools.

Listening to learners

Personalisation and learner voice

It is becoming commonplace to castigate adults for failing young people by not 'listening enough' to what they are telling them. Citing a survey of 3,500 11–25 year olds by the Industrial Society which reports young people as fearful of challenge and future opportunities and trends, Claxton argues:

> Schools are seen as failing to equip young people with the ability to learn for life rather than for exams ... That last sentence is key. Remember this is the voice of today's youth (not some sociological theory). They are telling us they are floundering, and that we are not teaching them how to swim. That's why they turn off from school ... they are not intrinsically lazy or bolshy or lacking ability: they are disappointed in our reactions to their predicament and flailing about.
>
> (ibid.: 48)

One response is 'personalised learning' which aims to help children to develop 'individual interpretations of the goals and values of education. At the end, the child should be able to tell their own story of what they have learnt, how and why, as well as being able to reel off their qualifications' (Leadbetter 2004: 16). As vague and slippery as 'well-being', this notion has not come from academic research or practice developed on the ground in schools: instead, it is essentially a political creation (Johnson 2004). A crucial impetus for making personalisation as influential a political idea as privatisation was during the 1980s is to find a narrative for public service reform that cuts across ideas about social inclusion and social justice in education and other areas of public policy (see Leadbetter 2004).

Finding ways to 'enable' young people and their parents to engage more deeply with education and other public services is not merely about personalising educational outcomes and processes through individual support, mentoring and more choice about pathways and options. In the context of the emotional state discussed in Chapter 1, personalising education also requires the state and its agencies to respond to feelings about educational processes and outcomes. For example, the think tank DEMOS points out that

> understanding users [is] ever more important ... not only asking users to help us find the solutions, but also to define the problem in the first place ... Improvements in education and health come from complex interactions between people.
>
> (DEMOS 2005)

As a political response, therapeutic ideas about 'the co-production of the learning experience', 'self-enhancement' and 'self-realisation' encourage schools to elicit more authentic expressions of 'needs' and to respond to young people's feelings about their experiences by offering more individualised approaches to educational choices and emotional engagement.

Educators have responded positively to the idea of personalisation, arguing that, while there are problems with definition, numerous activities in schools exist to promote it, including strategies for assessment for learning and learning how to learn and promoting opportunities for 'learner voice' (see Pollard and James 2004 for discussion).

Learning to learn for lifelong learning

Personalisation and listening closely to what learners feel about their learning is central to Guy Claxton's enthusiastic advocacy of how to build learning power in secondary schools from strategies children learnt in primary school. For Claxton, 'being a good learner is not just a matter of learning a few techniques like mind mapping or brain gym. It is the whole person: their attitudes, values, self-image and relationships as well as their skills and strategies' (2002: 15). From this perspective, schools need to develop people who 'know what to do when they don't know what to do', whether that is how to 'figure out where they've gone wrong in a sum' or 'fallen out with someone and want to be friends again' (ibid.).

'Skills' associated with building and sustaining 'learning to learn' are seen as crucial to successful transitions between primary and secondary school. In some areas, secondary schools have created a new foundation stage, organised to provide a 'well-known, safe and secure' environment that is like a primary school. Children spend a substantial amount of time on developing 'learning to learn' skills and attributes, taught by one class tutor with specialists brought in for other lessons or take part in whole days devoted to learning and thinking skills for students and staff (see Kurlbaum 2007: 43). One headteacher describes the role of this class tutor for the first four years of secondary school as 'shepherding' (Frankel 2007).

Subjects can be marshalled to develop a positive self-concept, social skills and emotional sensitivity through teachers setting up discussion of how the teacher and learners feel when learning, encouraging students to see how they learn 'emotional control' (through waiting their turn and being persistent through difficulties) and resilience by 'bouncing back' when learning goes badly (Weare 2004). These claims extend the already huge list of skills and attributes Weare defines as emotional literacy into broader characteristics of learning to learn.

Learning to learn and learning power seem to be endlessly adaptable. In the latest political turn towards more positive images of emotional interventions, a more upbeat vocabulary is used: 'giving young people the means to be their own happiness creators and maintainers', where strategies for learning power encourage pleasure, joy, flow, optimism, curiosity, self-efficacy, engagement, resilience and stoicism, mindfulness, holistic approaches, developing the means to flourish (Claxton 2007). As we showed in Chapter 1, this language embraces that of positive psychology (Huppert 2007).

Learning to learn

The ideal 'learning power' student

A young boy is preparing for his first day in secondary school. Worried and also excited, this child gets out his 'learning diary' to remind himself of how his learning had gone in the previous week, what new learning methods they had discovered, and what his 'thoughtful' teacher had written on his diary in response to his thoughts and disclosures.

> As he's thinking about the challenge of the new school, he can hear Mrs S's voice in his head, suggesting he writes down a list of hopes, fears and expectations so he can compare these with what he actually found … [he] picks up the journal that he keeps by the bed and writes for a few minutes. Having prepared himself as much as he can, he closes the book, turns out the light and falls asleep.
>
> (Claxton 2002: 9)

Activities

- Create a learning to learn poster with the crucial five Rs: resilience, resourcefulness, responsibility, reasoning and reflection.
- Buy learning to learn products: 'Building Bridges' by Alite, a series of 36 fully resourced lessons to help with transfer to secondary school. L2 by Alite – 60 hours of teaching materials, including lesson plans and student profiling software (Kurlbaum 2007).
- Ensure that every teacher includes at least one aspect of learning to learn in every lesson.

- Hold six 'super learning days' when pupils first arrive at secondary school, with older children as 'lead learners' to mentor them (Kurlbaum 2007.
- Encourage regular reflective writing about 'What I enjoyed most this week', 'What did I do that was difficult?', 'What did I do to get round my difficulties?', 'What have I noticed about my learning?', 'How can I help others with their difficulties? Take the diaries in and write personal comments on key points, disclosing your own ways of dealing with difficulty and ideas about future learning (Claxton 2002).

Assessing soft outcomes

In Chapter 1, we showed that interest in personal, social and emotional outcomes of participating in education aims to counter an over-emphasis on instrumental economic and employer-led outcomes, and to combat perceptions by students and growing numbers of their parents and teachers that education is boring, irrelevant and demotivating. Soft outcomes are presented as 'wider benefits of learning', thereby appearing to offer more benign instrumental goals than merely developing 'human capital' for the labour market.

A group of trainee teachers was asked recently what outcomes they wanted their pupils to learn from schooling and they identified the now familiar long list:

Empathy; self-awareness; social competence; resilience; creativity; reflectivity; the ability to self-evaluate/self-assess; enthusiasm for learning; being a good citizen; happiness; being caring; being respectful, tolerant good team players; applying knowledge; learning to learn; problem-solving; communication; self-management; making a positive social contribution.

(Hargreaves 2007: 81)

Supporters of these goals claim that collaborative learning and assessment methods will develop them whilst also developing subject knowledge. For example, the task of sharing meanings from a text students have read '[builds up] a rich picture of collaborative learning ... students take responsibility for knowing what needs to be known and for insuring (sic) that others know what needs to be known' (Hargreaves 2007: 189). Designing formative and summative assessments to capture these outcomes improves students' ability to retain subject-knowledge and to make more flexible use in its application, and, therefore, leads to better success than traditional learning (ibid.). Integral to these processes and outcomes are notions such as 'allowing a learning voice', 'learning about their own learning and being socially active and responsible' (2007: 191).

Many proponents of learning to learn appear to regard the emotional outlook, attributes and skills associated with them as more important than subject content. Hargreaves sums up this position in her challenge to 'old' ideas about teaching and assessing subject knowledge:

> I am questioning whether a version of learning as acquisition and using information and skills still has the social currency it had before the information revolution in which information is readily available but wise application of it still depends on choices made by social beings.
>
> (2007: 191)

These ideas re-define education as 'learning' and learning, in turn, as participation and as a social contribution that develops generic attributes and capabilities for the increasingly complex situations people must deal with. Although subject knowledge is reiterated as important, this becomes a mere token gesture.

Some researchers define many soft outcomes as components of 'personal capital'. Citing research by Bynner and Feinstein, Tim Oates, Director of Cambridge Assessment, identifies attitudes, values and 'affective aspects of personal identity' which determine whether children learn early on that they can achieve, or whether they 'write off their own chances' in a self-perpetuating cycle of failure (Oates 2007). From this perspective, personal and emotional cycles are at the heart of social cycles of deprivation, where barriers to developing personal capital link inextricably to future deprivation and poor life chances. Oates argues that personal capital can be assessed formatively and summatively, both through specific indicators and measures and through broader approaches such as learning to learn.

The constructs that are claimed to underpin 'soft outcomes' and the processes that lead to them are constantly elided in accounts cited here, along with behaviours and skills, values and attributes. Attempts to define this vast array of soft outcomes and processes lead to interest in new forms of formative and summative assessment. According to Hargreaves, 'for an assessment for learning [method] to be valid, its learning outcomes must be socially appropriate for learners of the 21st century' (2007: 185) Not only are these outcomes much more broadly defined than those encompassed by conventional assessments of attainment, but the methods they lead to were designed originally for diagnostic and formative purposes based on self-report by learners (see, for example, Daugherty *et al.* 2007). Despite the significant difficulties this raises for validity and reliability, soft outcomes are increasingly a target for developing summative measures and accountability indicators.

Specialist interventions

De-stigmatising mental illness

We showed in Chapter 1 that a powerful impetus for addressing the emotional problems and 'needs' of children young people in schools is the idea that if all children express and evaluate their own and others emotions, those with serious problems will feel less excluded and stigmatised. Some schemes aim to do this by developing emotional well-being and emotional literacy for everyone. For example, PATHS is an intervention of 60 lessons with discrete units on self-control, emotions and problem-solving and activities including didactic instruction, role play, class discussion, modelling by teachers and peers, social and self-reinforcement (Cowie *et al.* 2004). The 'alternative thinking' curriculum comprises:

Self-awareness

Self-monitoring and recognition of feelings
Building a vocabulary of feelings
Making links between thoughts, feelings and behaviour

Personal decision-making

Self-monitoring of actions and recognition of their consequences
Distinguishing between thought-led and feeling-led decisions

Managing feelings

Self-monitoring of 'self talk'
Challenging negative self-messages
Recognising triggers for strong feelings
Finding ways to handle fears, anxieties, anger and sadness

Handling stress

Self-monitoring for signs of stress
Recognition of sources of stress
Learning to use relaxation methods

Empathy

Understanding others' feelings and concerns
Recognising that different people have different perspectives

Personal responsibility

Taking responsibility for self-management
Recognising consequences of actions and decisions
Accepting feelings and moods
Persisting to achieve goals and commitments

Conflict resolution

Understanding the difference between need and want
Using a 'win–win' model for negotiating solutions

Winning hearts and minds

'My Life in School' survey

The 'My Life in School checklist' requires young people to act as 'peer researchers' to carry out a 'survey' or 'audit' of problems experienced by vulnerable, disaffected and withdrawn children who might be 'at risk' of developing mental health problems, and then to suggest actions and work with staff on possible strategies. Young people from the school's council (if it has one) help to set the aims and objectives, design the research tools, administer questionnaires and interviews, help analyse data and draw conclusions and disseminate findings in writing and presentations to governors, teachers and other young people. One example of a questionnaire requires children to say how often in a typical week they experience a range of positive and negative behaviours from peers (Cowie et al. 2004). In some schools, this activity can be assessed towards a GCSE in Citizenship.

Circle of friends

A colleague working as an educational psychologist for a local authority describes a well-known technique used to integrate young people with social and emotional problems into mainstream schooling.

> Christopher is looked after. He's had the most awful life you can possibly imagine and he's painfully shy. But he's really keen to get qualifications and turn his life round. My approach was to find the most able, confident, popular kids in his class and go in before we placed him in the school to talk to them at length about his problems and get them to agree ways of bringing him into social and class activities. It transformed him. But what really brought tears to the eyes, was when Christopher's circle of friends did a presentation to the governors. They had researched all about his problems, all the social and psychological explanations for them. It changed everyone. The alternative to doing this sort of awareness raising is to put kids like Christopher in a special school.

Working with 'troubled' and 'troublesome' young people

The idea that specialist therapeutic interventions once reserved for a minority of children, such as 'circle of friends' and nurture groups, have a much wider potential for all children is advocated by Cornwall and Walter (2006). In their account of a school which introduced therapeutic education for young people with serious behavioural and emotional problems, Cornwall and Walter argue that interventions for all children are 'rich with therapeutic potential'.

> therapeutic education values the social and emotional transactions involved in learning, and this includes the psychology of learning, the process of teaching and learning, personal growth, life skills and the transfer of a humanitarian culture.
>
> (Cornwall and Walter 2006: 12)

Calling for therapeutic educational principles to permeate schools, Cornwall and Walter offer characterisations of education and ask readers to select which they prefer:

- competition for success in life – linked to passing exams and gaining recognition/accreditation;
- social engineering to produce 'worthy' citizens;
- training to make sure that enough people have sufficient 'basic skills' for work;
- education to give young people skills to succeed in life and cope with society's demands;
- self-actualisation – to achieve personal potential and liberty;
- personal growth and fulfilment that encourage lifelong learning.

(2006: 39–40)

In case readers of their book are in any doubt which to chose, the last three bullet points comprise a worthwhile, 'humanitarian' education. Advocating therapeutic education to benefit all pupils as well as helping 'troubled, troublesome and vulnerable' young people succeed, the authors list approaches that all teachers should use to counter the current failure of education to engage and motivate significant numbers of young people:

- recognise and contextualise the learner's characteristics and work effectively with them;
- be more sensitive to learners' individuality (and humanity) and listen better;
- develop strategies that will better inform daily lesson delivery and planning;
- use positive relationships to counter the insecurity of current educational 'challenges';
- be more creative and flexible in planning and delivery, challenging constraints to teaching that emanate from a narrowly defined and subject-based curriculum;
- move beyond simple behavioural technologies and into more holistic, nurturing and therapeutic approaches.

(Cornwall and Walter 2006: 40)

Being an angel

Peer mentoring and mediation schemes

In 2003, one-third of all secondary schools had mentoring schemes where adult volunteers agree to be role models and tutors to help young people defined as 'at risk' of failing General Certificate of Secondary Education (GCSE) examinations to acquire study skills and motivation (see Colley 2003b). In some local authorities, people trained as 'life coaches' visit schools to help school leavers decide what to do next and learn how to plan to realise their goals.

A more recent feature of mentoring initiatives is buddy and peer mediation schemes. Some train 14 year olds as 'Angels' – A Nice Guy Every Time Life Sucks. After completing training in counselling and taking part in psychodrama workshops, Angels wear badges in school showing their status as mentors. Their training requires them to remember and act out some of their own childhood difficulties and to learn some basic psychology about the causes of children's low self-esteem, family and education problems. They can then volunteer to mentor children through the traumas of going to a new school, dealing with bullying or friendship problems or the everyday problems of school life. As the two accounts show below, many mentors find the experience extremely positive.

Being an angel

Bella is now 16 and doing A-levels at an FE college. She has always wanted to do a degree in Performing Arts and Drama. After her experience as an Angel, she is now thinking of following this with an MA in Psychodrama.

> As an angel, I had to go on duty in the playground and other full areas at break time and sort out any disputes that happened there. I also went to our school 'angel base' where kids could come and talk to an angel if they had any problems, so that we could help them sort it out. We also helped out at open evenings and put on plays in assembly to show a good example to younger kids, get people involved and just generally promote kindness rather than arguments! We went round to different schools to perform plays, do drama workshops, read poems and entertain the younger kids whilst joining in with their anti bullying projects and helping them out. If the children joined [the school], then we would be there for them [and to] look out for them and show them round.
>
> Our goals ... were to make the school safer and friendlier, to promote equality, to have fun and be creative in our ideas on how

to help people, and to give everyone a kind of safety net so that arguments could be settled rather than develop into fights. We also wanted to encourage people to be aware of everyone around them and to respect everyone else. We went on 2 residentials, one weekend and one a few days a week for 2 weeks. The weekend one was to work with younger children and see what kind of things worried them so that we could make our school better for them to come up to. Our school paired up with a group of kids from a school for teenagers with behavioural problems and mental disabilities and we took them out for a few days a week and hung out with them at our school so they could take part in our angel scheme and we could learn a few things from their peer mentoring scheme too.

When asked how she responded to our argument that her role was therapeutic and encouraged vulnerability rather than combating it, she said:

I definitely wouldn't describe the angels as a therapy lesson for kids– it was just a campaign for people to be more tolerant and to sort out any problems amicably. It was fun as well– we weren't made to go, we just wanted to meet new people and learn a bit more about our school and the people in it.

In article on Teachernet, Sam Baldwin, a Year 12 pupil at Seaford College in West Sussex, describes how his scheme immediately attracted 15 volunteers: as he points out, from a 'cohort of 55 that's a fair proportion!'. The teenagers went on a two-and-a-half-day intensive course run by the Samaritans. Sam observes that

this proved to be very interesting and rewarding and will be a skill that we will be able to continue to use for the rest of our lives. It is also a skill that is very important in this day and age, allowing flexibility in many demanding situations in modern-day life'. The course trained them to be 'listeners and not counsellors' using small private meetings to 'allow us to aid each other in ways to help the [person's] situation, or if the matter was one that would affect the school and its policies then it would be passed on to be dealt with externally, if need be, with all discretion.

Mentors wear badges to distinguish them 'from the general "crowd" ...', working to

[make themselves] available to listen ... allowing as much time as necessary to listen to the whole problem. We try to make the environment suited as much as possible to the [person's] request, such as a classroom or study. However, sometimes they like just to talk around other people just out of earshot so not as to look as though they are describing a problem they have encountered.

His scheme is advertised through posters around the school, presentations to every year group and an assembly where two members of the group arranged and performed a short piece to illustrate some of the situations that mentors are trained to help pupils deal with. Samaritan trainers visit mentors to 'de-brief' their experiences and to offer help with particular situations. Mentors can also attend conferences such as those run by Childline on bullying so that they can offer new ideas to the school for improving the scheme.

He quotes typical problems pupils bring:

> I have been lonely since the start of the year and needed someone to talk to. Thanks to the peer listeners I got some good support from someone I knew and trusted. (Year 12)

> I wanted to tell someone about my parents splitting up but it's not unusual anymore, I didn't think anyone would care. The peer listeners did, and it feels better not to have it on my chest any more. (Year 9)

> What do you do when someone isn't hitting you, but they're making your life hell? I don't want to tell a teacher 'cause I'm not a grass. I went to a peer listener and they helped sort things out for me. Now I don't get any bother from the bully. (Year 9)

Changing the subject

Personal, social and health education (PSHE)

According to Weare, PSHE can be 'emotional literacy by another name', covering positive self-concept, self-protection, making relationships, resisting pressure, stress management and negotiation (2004: 90). In addition to developing P4C classes in primary schools, Antidote has been developing activities for PSHE that encompass personal development and self-awareness, problem solving and team building, tolerance and diversity.

A typical example is an activity where teachers encourage 'metaphor and problem solving' through drama about being on a desert island that engineers conflict and encourages young people to develop roles to deal with it, reflect on feelings, explore differences, develop understanding of themselves and others. At key moments in the 'game', the teacher stops the activity and asks students to plot themselves on emotional thermometer and, at the end, to use a coloured chart to record how 'engaged they were in the session'. This provides the teacher with 'instant feedback about those who need individual attention'. Antidote's activities are being piloted as a PSHE module for all schools to use.

There is a move away from PSHE as a vehicle for encouraging young people to avoid harmful behaviour and hedonism towards considering more worthy, important attributes seen to comprise personal well-being, such as fighting for justice and altruism. These ideas come from the increasingly influential subject of positive psychology, where modes of cognition are 'positive ways of thinking', 'looking on the bright side', 'savouring the moment', 'believing in change'. According to its advocates, teaching children, young people and their teachers how the brain works shifts their mindset and is a powerful influence on their belief systems (Huppert 2007).

The most widely quoted success story of implementing these ideas is a series of PSHE lessons in the independent school, Wellington, which has just appointed the country's first teacher of well-being. The head teacher of Wellington argues that

> teachers, like parents, want children in their care to be mentally and physically healthy and intelligent in the roundest possible sense, and that's what teaching the skills of well-being is all about … There is no more important objective for a school than to help teachers help its pupils find out who they are and how to lead happy and decent lives. The more deprived the area the more vital this version of schooling is.
>
> (Seldon, quoted by Beadle 2007: 6)

Writing in *The Guardian*, award-winning school teacher Philip Beadle looks enthusiastically to Wellington as a source of 'real radicalism' in its introduction of a well-being curriculum with lessons written by Nick Baylis, Professor of Positive Psychology at the University of Cambridge. Beadle advocates the wholesale introduction of emotional intelligence and well-being in place of the 'failed citizenship experiment', adding that 'the ability to recognise happiness when it occurs and to have it defined as something, perhaps the only thing, worth aspiring to, is not, as one critic put it, Orwellian or Stalinist, but a fundamental of decent schooling' (ibid.).

Supporting this approach, Layard regards PSHE as a 'cause' that demands a new style of 'missionary' to develop this ethos with students and, more broadly, across all activities in schools. He argues that a key question for policy makers should be 'Are children happy, not are they tested?' and that once an evidence-based curriculum is developed, it should become statutory (Layard 2007).

Citizenship

The original remit of Citizenship, introduced as a statutory subject at Key Stages 3 and 4 in 2002, encompassed social and moral responsibility, community involvement and political literacy and aimed to revitalise political interest and activity amongst young people seen as apathetic and remote from Britain's parties and institutions (see Crick 1998). A teacher of politics in a London comprehensive school argues that many advocates of Citizenship hoped to instil a new set of moral values in today's young people. Yet, even the group charged with contributing a set of common values into the Crick Report failed to agree on what they are (Rooney 2004).

One effect is that Citizenship has become a leaky, porous subject prone to an endless series of political fads and preoccupations. From special lessons on political parties and institutions, to cross-curricular themes, 'citizenship' encompasses everything from countering homophobia to global warming and conservation. Cross-curricular themes allow a diverse range of relevant topics to be covered: for example, a crisis of farming in 2007 encouraged lessons on farming, nutrition, world poverty, animal cruelty and the effects of farming on greenhouse gas emissions (Kneen 2007). In 2007, a series of gun shootings led the awarding body EdExcel to propose a qualification on community leadership for safer cities and to propose this as part of the Citizenship curriculum. As we showed with the example of the My Life in School survey, Citizenship also encompasses the personal behaviours and attributes of emotional well-being and emotional literacy.

Extreme eclecticism means that, as Rooney also argues, the subject redefines personal behaviours and viewpoints about contemporary issues into moral values and redefines political participation as any activity that instils the habit of participation (ibid.). From this perspective, students undertaking surveys of emotional well-being in schools, taking part in school councils and being a peer mentor are evidence of participation.

Redefining behaviours as values is reinforced by regarding the subject as a way of expanding concern about the self into considerations of others. For example, Weare highlights how Citizenship teaches social responsibility and social skills, conflict resolution, anti-bullying, anti-racism, respect and tolerance of difference, assertion and negotiation. The government's advisory group on Education for Citizenship and the Teaching of Democracy in Schools presented self-esteem as a 'core skill' while guidance to schools on the teaching of sex and relationships makes self-esteem integral to valuing yourself and fits the popular orthodoxy that promiscuity arises from low self-esteem and peer pressure (Crick 1998).

Traditional subjects

Traditional subjects also offer opportunities to develop emotional literacy and well-being:

- the arts (dance, painting, music, literature) through seeing, listening and taking part; expressing emotions through movement, sound and picture, rehearsing personal problem-solving, developing empathy by reading and hearing about others with the same experiences and understanding the causes of emotions;
- English Language by developing 'an emotional vocabulary', developing a positive self-concept through talking and writing about the self, creating a sense of coherence through family history; increasing empathy by writing stories;
- biology through understanding the physiology of emotion including own body reaction, understanding how the brain works and the centrality of

emotion to how we think, learn and experience the world, emotion in animals and our 'common ancestry';

- history through understanding the cause of emotion through biography and the relative impact of individual versus social forces in shaping events, developing personal coherence through family and local history, understanding emotion in major events such as war, terrorism and atrocities and the role of positive emotion in humanitarianism such human rights and the abolition of slavery.

(Weare 2004: 92)

Leaving aside some of the dubious assumptions about the dominant place of emotion in biography and action, particularly in social movements and events, and the idea that animals have emotions, this list indicates the extent to which traditional subjects are being marshalled for therapeutic education.

Capturing 'social, emotional and moral performance'

The hollowing out of subjects to accommodate all the interests discussed so far is leading to more radical calls to change the purposes and content of traditional subjects. A view that developing generic capacities and outcomes is the key purpose of schools is now widespread amongst many teachers, researchers, parents and policy makers (see, for example, Hegarty 2006; White 2007). We can take as typical in its content, but unusual in it bluntness, a recent book from the Association of Teachers and Lecturers (ATL), appropriately titled *Subject to Change: New Thinking on the Curriculum*. This sets out the proposition that 'Education is assumed to be primarily about the development of the mind', but ... this is a 'misunderstanding' (Johnson *et al.* 2007: 69–70). A new skills curriculum is needed for all children, which will be relevant and different:

> The major difference from previous curriculum models is that it should consider the needs of the whole person without assuming that the academic or intellectual aspects should have a higher status than the others. The first truly comprehensive curriculum should rebalance the academic, situated in the mind, against those parts of humanity situated in the body, the heart and the soul. Curricula may well be designed by people for whom the mind predominates, but those designers should see that the twenty-first century requires a population with higher levels of social, emotional and moral performance, and a regenerated capacity for doing and making.
>
> (2007: 71)

The shift here from the intellectual to the emotional, from the mind to the body, typifies what we have called the therapeutic turn. The authors of this proposal to dismantle subjects in favour of 'skills' state: 'We need a bit of honesty in this analysis. Most people are not intellectuals. Most people do not lead their lives predominantly in the abstract. It is not clear that it is preferable to do otherwise: the world cannot survive only through thought' (Johnson *et al.* 2007: 72). John White adopts a similarly hostile tone to criticise the 'Victorian elitism' and irrelevance of old school subjects (2007).

In a more conciliatory vein, the Universities' Council for the Education of Teachers (UCET) responds to ECM by arguing that secondary school teachers will need to 'adjust' the way in which allegiance to their subject asserts their specialist expertise. Rejecting popular caricatures of teachers only interested in examinations and 'crowding heads with facts', they reassure teachers that subject study remains integral to education, and that 'subjects are educational resources of remarkable power, offering unlimited scope for realising an enormous range of educational purposes ...' (Kirk and Broadhead 2007: 13).

Yet, after loading this 'enormous range' of purposes (which encompasses all the soft outcomes discussed above) into subjects, they continue:

> ... under ECM, the educational purpose of learners will depend on how resourcefully teachers will be able to draw on their subject knowledge base, and how readily they will jettison the monocular professional vision that is associated with blinkered use of the subject ...

in order to develop an extended professionalism that removes 'old dichotomies' between ...

> teaching a subject and enabling pupils to learn how to learn, or even being a learning coordinator or consultant; between the cultivation of learners' achievements and fostering their well-being; and between personalisation and the promotion of high standards.
>
> (2007: 14–15)

Implications

Changing the meaning of humanist education

Therapeutic education in secondary schools continues a trend from primary schools where the principles, goals and practices of specialist interventions for a minority of children extend increasingly to all children. A significant effect is to give educational psychologists, counsellors and psychiatrists an extremely powerful voice by redefining 'humanist' education as 'humanitarian'. This finds a ready audience of educators disenchanted with testing, an emphasis on skills for the labour market and a target led system that ignores the needs of the 'whole child'. Many professionals, parents and academics therefore welcome attention to the overlooked affective aspects of students' experience.

There are three broad strands to this interest. One is that, in order to foster an appetite to learn, schools need to redress what Claxton regards as the 'toxic' balance of tests, the pursuit of instrumental credentialism and a situation where too many demands overwhelm students' capacities to cope, thereby creating stress (Claxton 2002). Instead, teachers need to create activities that model the claimed assumptions about the language, priorities and attitudes of the lifelong learner. These ideas have been taken up by the Qualifications and Curriculum Authority which now promotes 'personal, learning and thinking skills' as the heart of the secondary school curriculum and the basis for cross-subject themes and activities.

The second strand is interest in creating humane and humanitarian schools that reject the 'increasingly hegemonic influence' of a high performance perspective of targets, effectiveness and their associated 'technologies' of learning styles, differentiation, emotional intelligence and personal targets. These turn the 'personal' into the 'functional' so that schools neglect the fundamental educational goal of

> learning to be human ... learning to live in personal relation to other people ... because our ability to enter fully into human relations with others is the measure of our humanity, for inhumanity is precisely the perversion of human relations.
>
> (Fielding 2007: 406)

Finally, a very wide range of notions about 'the whole person' is implicated in a view that schools are failing to listen to children and to prepare them for a changing world. Citing Alvin Toffler's argument that we have to understand the future if we are not to do 'tragic damage' to those we teach, Claxton identifies the usual list of apocryphal features of technological, environmental and social change, arguing that the idea that

> schools could and should be systematically preparing young people to thrive under the stressful conditions they will increasingly meet is only now catching on ... Most people agree that the only thing we can say with any confidence about the year 2025 is that there is not much we can say about it with any confidence.
>
> (Claxton 2002: 46–7)

The pursuit of humanitarian education redefines fundamentally what it means to educate the 'whole person'. In the transmogrification of humanist education as 'humanitarian' education, learning a body of worthwhile and inspiring knowledge, or learning to love particular subjects, or aspiring to excel in them, have become invisible as educational goals. Indeed, in therapeutic language, such ideas signify 'dysfunctional' teachers who care more about their subjects than students and who use this to maintain 'inappropriate' power relations. In a recent seminar where Kathryn argued this point, a colleague said that such teachers have 'serious emotional baggage'.

Dismantling demands for subject knowledge

Concerns about difficulties with schooling fuel calls to dismantle 'irrelevant' and 'boring' subjects in favour of learning for life. The hollowing out of subject disciplines has gone a long way through their reincarnation as vehicles for 'relevant', 'real life' learning in which emotional literacy and well-being play a key role. This is reinforced by activities that encourage teachers to surrender their inappropriate, outdated authority by playing down subject expertise and, instead, admitting their own vulnerability about learning.

Disenchantment with subjects also distorts initiatives developed to improve the quality of subject teaching and students' cognitive progression within subject domains, such as formative assessment (see, for example, Black *et al.* 2003; Black and Wiliam 1998). In a recent conference about well-being in schools, formative assessment presented in its more populist incarnation as 'assessment for learning' was offered as a means of fostering a positive attitude as part of well-being (Harrison 2007). In the political and cultural context we have presented so far, a variety of pedagogic and assessment approaches can end up as therapeutic, whatever the intentions of their originators.

Turning young people's worlds inwards

Educational activities have always produced affective and social outcomes alongside cognitive or practical ones. Yet, dressed up as developing emotional skills and well-being, the training of appropriate attributes, dispositions and values encourages children to see themselves, their feelings and opportunities to participate as the most important topics they can learn about. Notions such as learning to learn, personalisation and learner voice are vehicles for engaging young people emotionally with schooling, turning cognitive and intellectual dimensions of learning and thinking into preoccupation with the emotions and feelings of 'doing' subjects. The notion of 'engagement' is therefore much more significant than mere 'participation' or 'motivation'.

Guilt about 'not listening' enough to young people's anxieties and their feelings of not being listened to, of being worried and scared, lead to beliefs that stressed-out and anxious young people cannot cope with, and do not want, a traditional subject-based curriculum. Instead, there is a growing orthodoxy that they want a more personally relevant and 'engaging' education where adults and their peers listen to them. This view erodes subject disciplines and encourages a curriculum which assumes that topics and processes can only be engaging if they relate to the self.

Conclusions

Although therapeutic education in secondary schools continues, trends in primary schools, its particular manifestation at this stage of the education system reflects a much deeper change in ideas about the purpose and content of education. Fuelled by intense disillusionment with a traditional subject based curriculum and traditional assessment, a desperation to show that adults are listening to young people's interests and anxieties is turning humanist and holistic education into humanitarian education.

Lack of a confident, inspiring vision for education creates a vacuum into which a plethora of instrumental attributes, skills, values and dispositions can be inserted, alongside every latest political fad or whim. It is very likely that therapeutic education will quickly accommodate the idea that the search for 'true sources of satisfaction' should be the core value of schooling, where the overarching question is 'Are the children happy?' (Layard 2007).

The porosity of schools and traditional subjects, the sheer weight and speed of initiatives, and all the concerns they are supposed to address, make debate about therapeutic education extremely difficult. As a contribution to this much-needed debate, we have aimed to illuminate how therapeutic education in secondary schools jettisons and disdains the intellectual in favour of emotions.

Therapeutic orthodoxies that any opposition is dysfunctional emotional baggage add a further twist. We argue that this has dangerous implications for education. Whatever well-meaning aims accompany them, the activities discussed in this chapter are reactionary because they do not lift young people out of everyday problems, whether these problems are banal or serious. Instead, therapeutic education immerses young people in an introspective, instrumental curriculum of the self, and turns schools into vehicles for the latest political and popular fad to engineer the right sort of citizen.

Chapter 4

The therapeutic further education college

A further education (FE) college in the Midlands has recently instructed teaching staff on Entry to Employment and adult literacy and numeracy programmes not to ask challenging questions in class or write critical comments on students' work in case these damage their self-esteem. In a recent presentation to new staff at a pre-1992 university, the vice chancellor described students from 'non-traditional' routes such as Access and vocational education courses in FE colleges as having 'emotional baggage' that presented a challenge for universities used to 'traditional' students. As part of inspection requirements, tutorials in colleges ask students to discuss emotional difficulties and record the outcomes, whether students initiate this or not, while some classes for adults ask them to diagnose their levels of confidence and self-esteem and record their progress with smiley and sad face stickers.

Over the past 30 years, the 'typical' FE learner has undergone a significant identity change in the minds of policy makers, academics and growing numbers of professionals. From positive goals to offer an alternative to school, a second chance for education or opportunities for high quality vocational training, whole groups, such as 14–16-year-olds doing vocational options, young people wanting to experience a different environment from school, asylum seekers, adults learning English and Maths and adults seeking a route into higher education, are now routinely depicted as having 'low self-esteem', 'emotional issues', 'dispositional barriers to learning' or, as the Social Exclusion has it, 'complex needs'. A well-meaning but diminished language increasingly portrays FE students as disaffected, disengaged, hard to reach, marginalised, excluded, disaffected, vulnerable, at risk, having fractured lives and fragile learning identities.

Over the past 15 years, the FE sector has experienced more restructurings and resulting turmoil than any other sector, with profound effects on clarity of purpose, resourcing and conditions of service (see *Journal of Vocational Education and Training* 2007, Coffield *et al.* 2008). It has also been subject to a long series of radical changes to curriculum and assessment systems. Government regards FE colleges as crucial for 'delivering' goals of social justice, through a combination of raising levels of skills for the labour market, fostering habits for lifelong learning and addressing the social and emotional damage of exclusion. A series of major policy reviews have required colleges to increase rates of participation and achievement and they now provide for almost 4 million students, a rise of 1 million from 1993. It is widely accepted that 'dispositional' barriers to these goals, such as problems of attitude, negative perceptions of learning and expectations, are attributable to emotional damage created by previous learning experiences and outcomes. One effect is to channel large amounts of resources into an array of support services.

In this chapter, we explore the shift in FE colleges towards a strong caring and nurturing ethos that has become a goal in its own right. First, we explore how the management of transitions for school leavers inserts images of risk and emotional vulnerability into post-16 education and leads to particular forms of assessment. Second, we explore how diminished images of students affect ideas about suitable college experiences, and show their roots in a therapeutic pedagogy which began in the 1980s. Third, we offer examples of courses that prepare students, including FE teachers, for emotional work in various contexts. Finally, we evaluate implications for educational goals and practices in FE.

The therapeutic transition

Defining 'complex needs'

Many young people come into FE from mentoring and support systems that manage the transition from compulsory schooling. It is therefore important to examine the assumptions and activities of these transitions and their effect on images of the 'typical' FE student. Intractable cycles of social, economic and emotional deprivation are integral to New Labour's depiction of the problems facing many families, children and young people. As we argued in Chapter 1, these ideas combine strong images of determinism and fate with possibilities of escape and transformation through a variety of types of support and assessment. Educational achievement is seen as fundamental to individuals' social and economic progress.

Political attention focuses particularly on the transitions of children, young people and adults between education and welfare systems, and through educational sectors (see DfES 2003). In research, policy and practice, the concept of transition has expanded far beyond navigating social, material and practical aspects of life to encapsulate many aspects of relationships in work, education and personal life, alongside major turning points and milestones. A key change is that policy makers and many education and welfare professionals regard transitions as posing fundamental risks to a sense of self and identity (see Ecclestone *et al.* 2009 for discussion).

Although the transition from school into training, work, education or unemployment has always been a focus for intervention, it is seen as especially problematic in the context of an emotional state, discussed in Chapter 1. School leavers with poor or no qualifications are seen as acutely 'at risk' and to have what the SEU defines as 'complex needs' that make them vulnerable to a host of risks including crime, drug abuse, marital problems, early pregnancy, unemployment and ill health (see SEU 1999). The vision of society offered by the Social Exclusion Unit in its account of youth transitions, *Bridging the Gap*, is of an 'irredeemably individualistic, competitive and fragmented' one (Turner 2007: 155). Under New Labour, questions about the effects of structural conditions on people's capacity to exercise agency are relegated in favour of finding ways to help people adapt positively to social conditions (see also Colley and Hodkinson 2001).

We showed in Chapter 1 the influence on social policy of reforming structures in favour of emotional forms of support. This is especially apparent in the formation of the Connexions service in 2001 which provided a youth support service combining vocational and training advice, the welfare case management of social work and the informal support and access to re-creation of traditional youth work. Youth services have been reformed to be more proactive and less liberal in their approach (DfES 2002b, 2005a). A personal adviser brokers these services and support systems, supported by volunteer mentors and we discuss their role in the next section.

An ex-youth worker who trains personal advisers observes that policy makers portray life experiences and events, such as being the child of single parents, permissiveness, poverty and exposure to some extremely risky situations, as if they are automatically a 'one-way ticket to a life of deprivation, ill-health and mental misery' (Turner 2007: 153). Not only does this contrast with ideas in earlier eras that many young people's rites of passage were marked by risk and even danger, but it is also important to note that this fate is by no means a typical outcome (ibid.; see also Newman and Blackburn 2002).

Engaging and assessing young people

Portrayals of risky transitions lead to extra support for those deemed to be 'at risk' of dropping out of the education and training system. The role of mentoring is crucial and, as Helen Colley shows, it redefines old notions of providing 'advice, training and/or counselling by an experienced person to a junior or novice, through a relatively informal, dyadic relationship' into an intensive form of 'engagement mentoring' (Colley 2003b: 86). Mentoring has become a huge education and welfare intervention around the world and in 2003, one-third of British schools were using mentors, usually older people acting as 'role models' and coaches to help students targeted as borderline cases to gain their GCSEs (Colley 2003b). We showed in Chapter 3 that thousands of children and young people are becoming peer mentors, expanding the remit of mentoring schemes into peer support for a wide range of everyday emotional problems.

'Engagement mentoring' targets young people seen as disaffected, alienated and difficult, and therefore 'unattractive' to mentors in other types of mentoring scheme (see Colley 2003a for detailed discussion). This combines the searching out of young people's own interests and perception of needs with targets that 're-engage' them with institutionalised norms, structures and pathways. It involves high levels of emotional labour from mentors in order to:

> [bring about] a significant shift in the values and motivation of the young people, their skills and abilities, and their interaction with the wider environment. The overall objective is to move the young person from a position of alienation and

distance from social and economic reality, to a position of social integration and productive activity.

(European Commission 1998, quoted by Colley 2003b: 92)

Engagement mentoring runs alongside other approaches as part of a remit for the Connexions service to continue the Common Assessment Framework of ECM. This requires practitioners to share information about children and young people and their families with other professionals and to target services at individuals identified as being at risk, including interventions such as cognitive behavioural therapy, motivational interviewing, brief solution-focused therapy and neuro-linguistic programming.

Such approaches go hand-in-hand with constant informal and formal assessments, with formal diagnoses of starting levels of skills and attributes, regular self-assessments and reviews to record progress and achievement. In school leavers' transitions, Turner describes how interventions such as solution-focused therapy and counselling are intended to complement the main approach to fostering behavioural change, namely the Assessment Planning Implementation and Review tool (APIR). This combines prescriptive setting and reviewing of detailed, personalised targets with therapeutic explorations of the young person's attitudes, plans for the future, perceptions of barriers and the resources they can draw on.

In this scenario, 'resources' comprise the human and personal capitals of the personal adviser, the young person and other people he or she can draw on for help. In addition to the APIR, therapeutic techniques are designed to 'work for client change' deriving from what Turner terms the 'problem as opportunity orientation' of solution-focused therapy. In this approach, 'the therapist facilitates the discovery of hitherto unknown resources for framing questions in such a way as to only elicit responses that provide tangible evidence of client self-efficacy' (Turner 2007: 152). As we showed in Chapter 1, the idea that 'self-efficacy' is a resource that enables someone to identify other 'resources' is integral to the idea of 'personal capital' where psychological and emotional attributes are redefined as 'skills' that enhance opportunities and survival in life and the labour market.

Assessing and monitoring personal capital

Mentoring roles and practices, together with constant assessments, are a cornerstone of programmes that provide a bridge between transition from unemployment into support, and from there into education or training at work, such as Entry to Employment (E2E). The combination of engagement, support and personal discipline is especially marked in E2E programmes. As the latest in a long line of initiatives over the past 30 years that have aimed to offer something useful and motivating to a variety of young people, E2E targets those who hated school, or have serious personal and social problems or who were excluded from school. The scheme requires them to plan an individual programme made up from life and social skills activities, job seeking tasks, recreation, basic literacy and numeracy qualifications and accreditation for social and community activities.

An assessment regime of very prescriptive and detailed target setting, regular group and individual reviews of progress in relation to personal behaviour, attitudes and dispositions, is accompanied with an empowering rhetoric of 'students taking ownership of their own learning', of 'becoming independent learners'. It requires very high levels of commitment, patience and emotional labour on the part of teachers who must respond day by day to the trials, tribulations and triumphs that individuals present.

Every activity, from making breakfast in the kitchens that E2E centres invariably have, induction programmes to going ice skating, is rich with potential for the tutors to assess individuals' behaviours and for evidence of meeting targets. Yet, the prescriptiveness, short timescale, intensive assessment and huge expectations of getting young people into work or education within 26 weeks, some of whom have extreme social and emotional problems, make E2E exhausting for teachers both emotionally and practically (see Ecclestone 2009).

Assessing yourself

Mapping your life

In an E2E programme, George is engrossed in drawing a detailed, creative map of his life and hoped-for future to help him to identify where he needs to go and how he will get there. He is engrossed in his work and while he is given encouragement by the tutor, the map is clearly his own and he is very proud of it:

> We've been making roundabouts with roads coming off it, what we want to do in our lives, what we've got planned ahead of us for our future, what's important to us ... It's nice to sort of look at yourself in a different way and see what you actually do like and sort of think about it. Just, I don't know, sort of think about your future a lot more, just sort of get a lot more out of yourself in that situation.
>
> (Andrews in Ecclestone 2008)

Assessing your 'learning'

A typical weekly self-assessment checklist for E2E encompasses:

- What have you done this week?
- What do you want to do?
- What new things have you learnt this week – and that could be about yourself!
- What have you enjoyed, hated or found boring?

A typical lesson self-assessment on many vocational education courses encompasses:

- What did you learn in this lesson about the topic?
- What did you like?
- What did you find difficult?
- What did you find boring?
- What did you learn about yourself?
- What did you learn about your learning?

Although E2E is a stark example of assessment that, simultaneously, supports and disciplines its subjects, it is a mistake to see such approaches as confined to students with serious social and other problems, and therefore not relevant to other FE students. E2E's combination of counselling, mentoring and strong target setting is integral to support services in colleges, such as retention officers, personal learning managers and tutorial systems. The same combination also underpins the Individual Learning Plan for adults doing literacy and numeracy programmes and the competence-based approach of National Vocational Qualifications (see Torrance *et al.* 2005; Ecclestone 2009).

Disciplinary assessment is a logical outcome of 30 years of competence-based and portfolio-based assessment that require individuals to collect and record

Learning to disclose

How do others see you?

A method widely used in life and social skills courses in the 1980s encouraged teachers to experience it before using it with students. 'Johari window' required participants to reflect on themselves in relation to four 'windows', to discuss what they had written about each with a partner and then for the group to offer insights about other participants in relation to the four 'windows':

- what is known by the person about him/herself and is also known by others – open area, open self, free area, free self, or 'the arena';
- what is unknown by the person about him/herself but which others know – blind area, blind self, or 'blindspot';
- what the person knows about him/herself that others do not know – hidden area, hidden self, avoided area, avoided self or 'façade';
- what is unknown by the person about him/herself and is also unknown by others – unknown area or unknown self.

Assessment, planning, implementation and review

Young people and their advisors construct a personal version of a template that offers a graphical model in the form of a wheel with the client at the hub and each spoke representing a different feature of their life world such as friends, family, education and work. The adviser helps the young person sub-divide these sections further, through a series of concentric circles radiating out from the centre and encourages him or her to 'map' for themselves where they are positioned in the major aspects of their lives. A sequence of assessment, planning, implementation and review and aims to 'facilitate reflection' on where changes might be made and what 'resources' these changes might necessitate (Turner 2007).

Catching confidence

A 'record of achievement' for adults on courses for literacy and numeracy, family and parenting classes, leisure and craft activities records learners' perceived levels of confidence and asks for evidence against statements such as 'I feel confident when I meet new people', 'I feel confident to speak to one person I do not know'. Group and individual activities involve putting smiley or sad face stickers against different statements and discussing how people feel about them, and then recording individuals' responses (Eldred et al. 2005). A tutor using this approach argues that 'evidence of confidence is often lost in discussion and activities ... I am keen to use it to "officially" record personal growth' (ibid.: 11).

personal, work-related and educational 'evidence' of achievement against prescriptive criteria. Not only do these forms of assessment offer opportunities for 'digging' and 'moving closer and closer to home' in a similar way to activities in nurture groups and other therapeutic interventions described in earlier chapters, but they also lead to extreme forms of coaching the students through the criteria (see Torrance et al. 2005; Ecclestone 2007a). A liberal humanist ethos masks confession alongside self and external surveillance: as Usher and Edwards argue, this is a pastoral form of governance which 'enables individuals to actively participate in disciplinary regimes through investing their own identities, subjectivities and desires with those ascribed to them by certain knowledgeable discourses' (1998: 215).

In a context where the concept of transitions has expanded far beyond a limited phase within the domain of careers services into numerous threats to an individual's security, such approaches seem benign. Yet, underlying images of identities at risk and vulnerability are deeply inscribed in them. And, as Turner argues, old ideas of youth as a rite of passage in which individuals exercised agency, made mistakes, took risks and forged a character out of direct experience, are a stark contrast to prescriptive regulation through intensive personal support and assessments that employ a therapeutic rhetoric of empowerment whilst requiring high levels of disclosure and self-assessment (Turner 2007).

Students progressing to college from schools will become more and more familiar with such approaches, having been well-trained in circle time disclosures, supported to 'reflect' on their less palatable behaviours (as Lucy was in Chapter 2), made to write reflective diaries and to answer a stream of questions about their feelings of enjoyment, frustration and difficulty and what they have 'noticed about their learning'. Examples in previous chapters showed that subject content and insights take second place in these processes or, increasingly, have no place at all. In examples discussed here, subject learning is invisible and self-surveillance is the priority.

The therapeutic FE experience

Dealing with vulnerable students

A principal of a large, successful college told an FE research conference in 2002 that colleges need to prepare students for a life of uncertainty. Quoting a pop song from that year by M People which was used to advertise the freedom of the open road in a certain French car, she said that FE has to help its students and teachers 'look for the hero inside yourself'. Yet, far from an inspiring vision, her heroes were vulnerable and uncertain in the face of a scary, threatening future, not sure of truth or knowledge but sure of themselves and aware of the attributes, dispositions and attitudes they would need for a life of uncertainty, retraining, and lifelong learning (Limb 2002).

In a study of the wider benefits of further education, involving 2,729 FE practitioners, 92.5 per cent of respondents agreed or strongly agreed that 'experience of improved self-esteem' was the most important wider benefit of FE (Preston and Hammond 2002: 8). Yet, the concept of self-esteem as a goal only gained purchase over the previous decade. According to Furedi, a Factiva search carried out on all UK papers failed to find any citation of the term between the years 1980 and 1985. In 1986, there were three citations. A year later, it grew to 15 and by 1990 there are 103 citations. In 1995 there are 456 citations, which more than doubled a year later. During the next six years, citations increased every year and stood at 3,349 in 2001 (Furedi 2004a).

Although these meanings of vulnerability have a specialist, social work origin, they are no longer confined to those adults and young people with significant social and health problems. Instead, 'vulnerability' has taken on a much more generic meaning. A recent report for NIACE drew on projects from the Adult and Community Learning Fund to argue that growth in confidence and self-esteem are 'highly significant to learners returning to study after a long time and/or who felt that their experiences in initial education had been unfulfilling' (Eldred et al. 2005: 2). The authors acknowledge political and funding pressures to identify 'learning gains and achievements' in low level or non-accredited programmes. In response, they propose that diagnosing and assessing levels of confidence and self-esteem are integral both to policy targets and good teaching, learning and assessment methods. Their definition

From social work case work to education

All E2E learners are vulnerable

An E2E coordinator in a college defined vulnerability as follows:

> This is a tricky one and only yesterday I had this conversation with the college's child protection team as we have to pass on information to them about this type of student. I asked what the criteria would be for this and it would mainly be students who are from the care system. However, I have students who live independently in supported housing that I would also put in this category and those who I know would also be considered vulnerable, those with parents who for example are ex drug or alcohol abuse, those with violent families – basically it would be most E2E students – even those who have violence issues have at sometime been bullied themselves, so could also be considered vulnerable. I think each learner has to be assessed individually and they can also become vulnerable whilst on E2E – they have a row and leave home, tell you they have been raped or are going out with a 47 year old! It's a minefield and by nature of who E2E learners are and the issues they come with, I would consider them all to be vulnerable.
>
> (Ecclestone 2009)

Catching all learners?

A creative arts lecturer working with young people with serious behavioural disorders, such as ADHD, said:

> I use the 'v' word all the time, every day, five days a week. Our learners *are* vulnerable, vulnerable to inappropriate relationships with adults, harmful and self-harming behaviour, all sorts of things. But I admit it's also a catch-all phrase and it can be a stereotype.

of confidence includes values associated with emotional literacy: *Confidence is a belief in one's own abilities to do something in a specific situation. This belief includes* feeling accepted and on equal terms with others in that situation (ibid.: 3, our emphasis).

One piece of advice to tutors using the materials and activities with their students is

> be non-judgemental and actively develop equal opportunities practices. Learners revealed that their low levels of confidence were because they felt failures, isolated, different or excluded. Not being judged seemed to help them build confidence in their identity as learners.
>
> (Eldred *et al.* 2005b: 19)

Another publication of materials to develop the self-esteem of hard to reach, marginalised and excluded adults presents building confidence and a sense of well-being as enabling them to make the most of their potential so that they can participate fully in society (James and Nightingale 2004).

A vocabulary of vulnerability is also routinely applied to students on mainstream courses. At a seminar with awarding body officials, researchers and practitioners about reforming 14–19 assessment at the Nuffield Foundation on 11 October 2007, the vice principal of a college described how assessment systems need to 'support' students rather than test them. Citing the example of young men following a construction course, he said: 'assessment needs to develop students' sense of self, their identity, by building confidence and esteem. These kids are terrified of failing again and we need to re-engage them with learning'. The ensuing discussion prioritised emotional and social needs over assessment to develop craft skills: when questioned whether the language of esteem and identity reflected a new 'type' of student or a change in professional images of them, the group agreed overwhelmingly, that young people and adults coming to FE are much more emotionally fragile than in previous years (Nuffield Review 14–19 Education 2007).

As Elizabeth Atkins shows in her detailed study of teachers and students on a level 1 general vocational course, images of students at risk, vulnerable, and in need of 'emotional attachment and nurturing' lead them to regard students' emotional needs as integral to a progressive educational ethos. Despite their reservations about the quality and usefulness of the qualification students were taking, their concern for confidence and esteem led them to prioritise positive attitudes and dispositions to engagement rather than pushing students to learn content or to do difficult tasks. Although students enjoyed the course and its activities, and believed they worked hard, Atkins argues that their positive views were predicated on lack of demand placed on them and on feeling valued. She concludes that their experience cannot be called education in any meaningful sense (Atkins 2007).

Inducting students into emotional support

At a staff conference in one of the England's largest college providers of higher education, the disability liaison officer from the local university urged staff to begin identifying students' emotional difficulties from day one of their FE course. He told FE tutors that of 2,800 students at the university who required support in 2006 for physical and mental barriers to learning, 300 had a physical disability, 100 had clinically diagnosed, serious mental health problems and the rest had either dyslexia or low level anxiety and stress disorders. Acknowledging that numbers of the biggest group were rising each year, he described the provision of support under the requirements of the Disability Rights Act as creating 'an epidemic of learnt helplessness'. Nevertheless, he told FE tutors that 'being troubled and asking for help are difficult for people', placing a positive duty on colleges and universities to initiate a dialogue. Induction courses should therefore de-stigmatise support and 'open their doors' to students needing help (Broxtowe-Smith 2007). Numerous college tutors

Inducting students into college life

What about the 2 per cent?

A tutor from a sixth form college sought advice from a university about what to include in the induction programme. After a staff development day it was decided to invite distinguished academics and public figures who could offer inspiring and challenging examples of how education can change your life. 'That's all very well for most of our students', said the principal, 'but what about the 2 per cent who won't find it inspiring?'

Big Mother watching you

In the foyer of a college in Kent, a huge poster of a kind, motherly looking woman, advertises 'Dora the college counsellor'. The poster announced that she was there to give students help and advice of any sort. Next to the poster is a folder full of lecturers' and students' comments about what a lovely, helpful woman Dora is. One lecturer said: 'she is the most important asset this college has'.

Dropping in to stop dropping out

A college in the south-east employs four full-time retention officers. They work in a friendly, informal room where students can drop in without appointments. If a student is assessed as being 'at risk' of dropping out of college, he or she drop in to see the retention officer to talk over the problems that are making them late or absent and to collect a lateness or absence note to take to course lecturers. As a colleague pointed out, students often arrive late with an official note, saying 'I was just having coffee with my retention officer'.

report that their induction programmes emphasise barriers to learning and all the support available whilst playing down educational content and assessment unless too much of this puts people off.

Offering therapeutic pedagogy

Many liberal educators believe that

> Much of what passes for education is dull and of little relevance for learners ... It is time to build a high-trust, democratic education system that respects learners and their experiences, listens closely to their expressions of interest and need, builds partnerships between teachers, learners, parents, the community

and employers so that young adults learn what they wish to learn, and how they wish to learn.

(Harkin *et al.* 2000: 140)

The language of learner voice, personal engagement, letting learners decide what they want to learn, and claims about the lack of democracy between adults and younger students, tune into the concerns we have discussed in previous chapters. In FE, such notions are another logical outcome of the steady incursion of a non-specialist therapeutic approach from the late 1970s. An influx of young people and adults displaced by mass unemployment into employment schemes and new forms of vocational education began 30 years of a series of short-lived assessment and curriculum initiatives. Building on initiatives that began after the raising of the school leaving age in 1972, such as new approaches to the Certificate in Secondary Education, these included Records of Achievement, the Certificate of Pre-Vocational Education, the Technical and Vocational Education Initiative, social and life skills, personal, social and health education, the Unified Vocational Programme for young workers and General National Vocational Qualifications.

Always presented in grandiose terms as the latest solution to an intractable problem, these programmes placed learners' responses to life, work and educational events and experiences at the heart of teaching, subject content and assessment whilst aiming to instil appropriate attitudes and dispositions for social and working life (see Ecclestone 2002 for detailed discussion).

They also brought a new type of teacher into FE. Trained (as Kathryn was) in the principles and practices of Rogerian group counselling and transactional analysis, a youth work ethos and activities associated with careers education, a social and life skills curriculum was promoted as a progressive alternative to didactic methods and old-fashioned, boring subjects. The social and life skills of early schemes offered a distinctive pedagogy where young people and adults invariably sat in comfortable chairs in circles (however large the group), took part in games to mix the group, build confidence, get people talking and to disclose personal aspects of their lives, accompanied by endless group discussions with flip charts and multi-coloured pens. Assessed through various evolutions of competence-based checklists, records of achievement and portfolios that emphasised self-assessment and one to one tutorials, this curriculum came to permeate staff development activities and gradually replaced liberal and general studies with communication studies and personal social and health education through the 1980s and 1990s.

FE colleges were therefore doing therapeutic circle time as a mainstream activity long before primary schools! The rationale for this alternative was predicated on the same apocryphal tales of social and technological change, uncertainty and fear of the future evident in current justifications for therapeutic education. For example, Alvin Toffler's *Future Shock* was widely cited in textbooks on social and life skills and typical SLS activities were to create group flip-chart posters and individual life maps of fears and hopes about the future (see Hopson and Scally 1980). Yet, older proponents of these ideas appear ridiculously optimistic compared to the fearful tales

A Basis for Choice: 30 years of progressive education?

Published in 1979, A Basis for Choice (ABC) was written by the Further Education Unit. As a response to the rapid emergence of employment schemes developed by the then Department for Employment through the Manpower Services Commission, ABC castigated the 'elitism' of craft and technician courses, the 'inaccesibility' of teaching and assessment methods and the image of FE as being a second chance for academic qualifications at Ordinary level (now GCSE) and Advanced level.

In their place, ABC advocated a more 'progressive' curriculum of core and basic skills such as team working, problem solving, communication, personal development and a much broader, more elementary approach to vocational education. For its advocates, ABC was a 'radical alternative' for goals of equality of opportunity, widening access and 'social justice' (see Avis 2007).

The therapeutic approaches of circle time, portfolio-based tutorials and assessment activities encouraged by ABC began the process of dismantling traditional FE.

of risk in contemporary education that we discussed in Chapters 1 and 3, where Toffler's updated predictions are still influential (see Claxton 2002). The thesis of the 'risk society' is widely cited in educational writing and it contrasts starkly with older goals, as Beck argues:

> Whereas the utopia of equality contains a wealth of substantial and positive goals of social change, the utopia of the risk society remains peculiarly negative and *defensive*. Basically, one is no longer concerned with attaining something 'good' but with preventing the worst: *self-limitation* is the goal which emerges. The dream of class society is that everyone wants and ought to have a share of the pie. The utopia of the risk society is that everyone should be *spared* from poisoning.
>
> (Beck 1992: 49, original emphasis)

Preparing people for an emotional life

FE's changing curriculum?

Therapy courses

There are 517 colleges and universities offering 2,262 therapy courses, amongst them many 'Beauty Therapy' courses but with a good smattering of 'Crystal Healing' 'Stone Therapy' and other new age interests. And 337 colleges, universities and private companies offer 456 'Emotional Intelligence Courses'. (Source Hotcourse.org.uk 24.10.07)

The window of an FE college shop in Kent contains adverts for courses in craniosacral therapy, massage therapy, group therapy for men with sexually transmitted diseases and highlights 'behaviour therapy' as something to learn in the mothers' and toddlers' group. There are courses in advocacy training, peer mentoring, counselling, becoming a befriender and learning to listen.

And not a philosophy, history or real craft course in sight.

Emotional needs and eating for ever?

In a 14–16 option in health and social care at one college, young women did a quiz on diet and health problems from a teenage magazine, prepared a display of eating disorders and their causes and designed a survey of classmates' diets.

One of two young women on an advanced health and social care course researched her sister's mental health problems while the other steered all her assignments to understanding her own abusive childhood (Ecclestone 2002).

Exploring your own and others' eating habits can carry on at university. Advertisements on toilet doors at a local university ask students to volunteer to be interviewed for a dissertation project on nutrition and the 'emotional issues' affecting eating habits whilst at university.

NIACE's 'Big Conversation'

Adult education has come a long way from leisure and craft activities, liberal studies and community political action. What is most valued in adult education in 2007? 'Essential skills' for 'staying healthy', 'self-esteem', for 'looking after yourself', for stopping 'socially isolated people' from 'being lonely, helping people 'relax' when stressed, giving them 'a sense of well-being', ensuring people's 'employability' and making employees 'feel valued'

From history classes to reminiscence therapy

In a reminiscence therapy class, the tutor says that Ray's 'a brilliant laugh' in discussions about the Second World War. When it's his turn to speak, he puts a chamber pot on his head as if was a German helmet: 'Ray helps everyone else to talk and everyone has fun. It really helps their memory.'

Learning to 'emotionally labour'

As Jason Hughes shows, workers' emotional intelligence is now seen as a necessary part of human capital in workplaces and, therefore, popular in staff and management training (Hughes 2005). In her study of young women learning to become nursery nurses, Helen Colley shows how the curriculum, teachers' and students' expectations and the day-to-day practices of working in nurseries socialise the young women into emotional labour. She locates the changing nature of identity, dispositions and practices for these young women in a socio-political context, exploring the effects of class and gender on emotional labour (see also Bates 1991).

Her detailed analysis offers a compelling account of the processes and effects of developing an overtly emotional approach to doing a job and Colley uses it to raise questions about what sort of curriculum content and pedagogy these young women should experience as part of their nursery-nurse training. Drawing on a strong tradition of critical pedagogy in FE and adult education that aims to raise awareness of personal responses and then develop a political understanding of broader structural conditions, Colley argues that designers and teachers of vocational courses need to enable young women to explore their emotional labour as a basis for 'resisting' its oppressive characteristics, or at least for understanding them better (Colley 2006).

Raising customers' self-esteem

A friend's recent trip to the clothes and accessories shop 'Monsoon' was enhanced by staff highly trained to engage emotionally during the choosing of earrings. Prolonged eye contact, a touch on the arm, a compliment, a question about how she was, a little disclosure about the assistant's own taste in jewellery, a warm and sincere smile all sealed the deal!

An undergraduate doing a Saturday job at Debenhams' department store described the image of customers they are trained to have: 'they tell us that many women might not be confident enough to ask for advice and that we must make a special effort to raise their self-esteem for the short time they are in the shop'.

In a DfES seminar on personalised learning in post-16 education in January 2006, staff training officers from British Gas and Selfridges Department Store showed how modern companies now regard customers' emotional needs as being as important as their practical and material ones. Photographs of uncertain customers wondering what to choose in Selfridges culminated in one of an escalator full of despondent, naked customers of all ages going up, and happy, stylishly clothed customers going down. Staff in both companies are trained in elementary psychology about self-esteem and 'well-being'.

Love your charges!

A flyer for Helen Colley's local nursery advertises: 'Fledglings: offering care, love and education' (Colley 2006: 15).

In addition to preparing students for jobs with high levels of emotional labour, teachers have to develop their own. More intensive work practices, the casualisation of the FE workforce and large numbers of students who face varying degrees of compulsion to attend college, demand new forms and levels of emotional support. This is often at a high emotional cost to lecturers themselves, both in terms of demands made by students and in adjusting to roles they might not have expected to play (see, for example, James and Diment 2003; Gleeson *et al.* 2005; Avis and Bathmaker 2006; Atkins 2007).

Perceptions that students in FE require more emotional support than they did in the past, students' own presentation of themselves as needing it and pressures on a heavily part-time teaching profession, have not only created a more emotionally tuned role for lecturers. These factors have also created a huge rise in counsellors, retention support officers, anger management mentors, personal tutors and learning support managers. A widely told wry joke amongst college staff is that there are more support workers than there are students to support!

Whether teachers are designing more sensitive approaches to teaching and assessment, asking students to fill in lesson evaluations about what methods and activities they like and do not like, reading and commenting on students' reflective logs, or adopting an emotional focus for critical pedagogy, they are increasingly expected to identify and respond to students' emotional needs. And, as examples of circle time, P4C and learning power showed in Chapters 2 and 3, teachers are also required to surrender their subject authority and to reveal their own uncertainties: indeed, too much commitment to subjects is now seen as 'dysfunctional'.

Training emotional teachers

One response to demands for more emotional labour is help trainee and in-service teachers explore their own emotional well-being and to address lack of self-esteem and confidence. For example, a study of trainees' ideas about confidence and barriers to developing it defined 'cognitive components' as encompassing 'knowing your strengths and weaknesses and knowledge'. Emotional components included feelings of being relaxed, an absence of fear or anxiety in class teaching, while confidence based on performance comprised a range of skills and competences in planning, performing and coping with the environment (Norman and Hyland 2003).

A study of FE trainee teachers' 'identities' after progressing to university from their course at a college explored their emotional responses to being students in higher education. The study showed a divided group, with some students adopting an identity as 'down-to-earth, practical and non-academic' students who 'hated jargon and long words', and those who saw overcoming barriers to learning a new academic language as opening up a new world (Evans and Martin 2003). Arguing that students experience 'disjuncture', where feelings of alienation, anger, frustration and confusion, are both visible and invisible, the authors assert that widening participation for students who do not regard themselves as having identities associated with particular courses, such as teacher education, requires more research to 'identify the tangible and non-tangible barriers that prevent students being 'at ease' in their educational surroundings ...' (Evans and Martin 2003: 163).

A number of self-evident truths emerge from such studies: teachers need to be confident and to develop a range of skills, attitudes and knowledge; we all develop confidence through social relationships and meaningful learning activities; some environments are more likely to do this than others, whether at work or in formal education. These obvious insights are then aligned with calls for more studies to explore confidence in specific situations in order to develop ways of overcoming the barriers that learners' lack of confidence creates and to ease their experience.

Using yourself as a focus for teaching

A lecturer is planning a session for a leisure studies class. He has collected information on the neurological basis of learning, and particularly on how learning is affected by nutrition. He sees it 'as a good way of tying the course content into their own lives and habits as learners'. He also has material about how people with different kinds of mental illness might learn differently and how leisure centres might support their learning better:

> His own brother suffers from severe depressions and Rob feels strongly that students should learn to understand more about mental health issues. Again, he is going to try to link this with their own learning, maybe through a visualisation exercise, getting them to look at how their mental functioning is affected by their moods (how anxiety prevents you from concentrating for example, or how depression makes you focus your attention inwards rather than outwards). He starts thinking about how this applies to himself, and wonders if he could set up a public action research project on his own moods for students to observe.
>
> (Claxton 2002: 63)

Exploring and assessing narratives and biographies

Growing disillusionment with subject-based crafts and knowledge in FE, concern about social exclusion and an aversion to functional, employer-led outcomes lead some educators to advocate an overtly therapeutic pedagogy. For example, Linden West argues that adapting people to the imperatives of the market and treating them as no more than commodities means that lifelong learning should become something

> central to the struggle we all share, to create a life on more of our own terms ... Learning, in this holistic, psychological perspective, moves centre stage in a postmodern world where we are forced to make choices, and compose a life, without confident reference to inherited templates, established knowledge or undisputed authority ... It is about learning to be more of an author of our own lives, with the help and support others and their stories, rather than feeling overwhelmed, stuck and powerless.
>
> (West 2004: 141)

A four-year research project as part of the Teaching and Learning Research Programme explores how formal and informal learning through people's lives intersects with structural and personal changes to create changes in identity and agency, researchers argue that eliciting in-depth narratives and biographies of individual lives enables participants to understand and then change their responses to problematic situations. Biesta and Tedder argue that enabling people to understand their own agency 'requires learning about the composition about one's agentic orientations and how they 'play out' in one's life. On the other hand, it requires learning about how one might change the composition of one's responsiveness (Biesta and Tedder 2007: 135; see www.tlrp.org/projects/learninglives).

Identities, usually wounded, damaged, fragmented and uncertain, have become strong themes in research in post-compulsory education (see, for example, Ecclestone 2007). Emotional aspects of identities are of growing interest. For example, a forthcoming conference at Canterbury Christ Church University of the ESREA Life History and Biographical Research Network calls for papers on 'Researching and Theorising the Emotional Dimensions of Learning and Researching Lives: a neglected species'? (www.canterbury.ac.uk).

Interest in 'celebrating learner voice' as a way of encouraging more adults to take part in further and adult education is leading to projects funded by the Learning and Skills Council that draw on 'biographical approaches' with individuals and small groups and offer accreditation of life experience towards credits on award-bearing courses. This version of accrediting prior learning has a long history in further and adult education, although earlier versions aimed to assess prior experience against pre-defined work and educational criteria.

Implications

Repairing learners' fragile identities

Beset by assumptions that FE is no longer a second chance, but a *last* chance in fighting cycles of deprivation, saving the economy and repairing the emotional damage wreaked by schools, and subjected to repeated restructuring, colleges are more prey to images of students 'at risk' than any other sector of the system. In a policy context that emphasises cultural and psychological deprivation over material and structural factors, it is hardly surprising that practitioners and managers see themselves on the front line of a fight to repair the emotional damage of earlier failed interventions.

The logic of this portrayal means that, by the time young people get to college, all the safeguards of 'early interventions' in families, primary and secondary schools, and the inoculation promised by a good education, have been squandered. The pathologising, psycho-medical language of 'interventions' is integral to these depressing images, reinforcing the idea that FE is part of welfare rather than education.

Although colleges have always catered for young people and adults with social and psychological problems, the stereotypes they now engender exercise a powerful influence over how all FE students are seen. It is therefore important to balance such images with the overall profile of learners in FE colleges:

- 56 per cent of 17-year-olds in full time education in FE colleges come from the bottom three socio-economic groups;
- 29 per cent of learners are from relatively disadvantaged postcode areas;
- 14 per cent of learners are from non-white ethnic groups;
- 8.2 per cent have a declared disability or learning difficulty.

(Avis 2007: 69)

Stereotypes and preoccupation with barriers to learning create a self-fulfilling prophecy where high levels of emotional labour from teachers and support services reinforce the images they respond to. A circular logic of widespread expectations that needy students have to be nurtured, concerns about students' feelings and a focus on fostering attributes, dispositions and attitudes for work, all create images of diminished learners.

We have aimed to show that a spectrum of patronising, banal and disciplinary assessments are not merely offered to students deemed to be vulnerable and at risk but, instead, are used with many students in FE. Examples of assessment discussed in this chapter show that disciplining personal behaviour is integral to reviewing and recording achievement. We argue that, whatever empowering rhetoric is used, emotional support and intrusive monitoring do not make an educational experience for young people whose life chances depend on something much better than this. Such experiences are profoundly anti-educational.

Creating cautious teachers

Teachers in FE are trapped between relentless targets, auditing, repeated restructuring and growing numbers of students who do not want to be in education but have little alternative. They face pressure to intensify emotional labour in order to maintain a professional integrity based on an ethos of care which signals the distinctiveness of FE from other parts of the education system. We have argued that teachers in FE have to expend more emotional labour, because students increasingly come to expect this, because images of their vulnerability make it hard not to offer it and perhaps because paying attention to feelings is easier than teaching and learning difficult subjects and crafts. Therapeutic education does not require subject specialists.

In response to these pressures, researchers suggest that we need to know more about teachers' and learners' emotional responses and 'identities' and that we need more research to tell us common-sense, even banal, things about confidence, self-esteem and barriers to learning. In turn, there is an assumption that such insights help teachers find more effective ways to elicit students' accounts of their emotional barriers and then to build teaching and assessment activities around them. A linked assumption is that doing this well requires teachers to understand their own lack of confidence and fragile identities so that they can empathise with students. These assumptions and the resulting practices turn confidence as a *by-product* of learning something substantive like a craft or academic subject into an explicit focus for attention as a *pre-cursor* to learning or a subject in its own right.

Of course, as all teachers know, there is a fine line between a caring approach and having the confidence to know when to challenge students to go further than they might like or want. The danger in exercises that 'facilitate' and assess self-esteem and confidence is that they elevate these commonplace by-products of good teaching into central goals of learning, creating a desire to 'ease' and 'smooth' discomfort and to avoid challenge and risk.

We argue that however well-meaning its intentions, diminished introspection produces strongly normative assumptions about what denotes a good FE teacher. In contrast to encouraging expectations of emotional closeness in response to diminished images of students, professional distance and expertise and strong positive images of students are necessary to build skills and knowledge, challenge students' ideas, criticise their work so that they can improve, and to take risks. Pushing and cajoling students who might not want to work hard, be too unconfident to speak or to take on difficult tasks cannot emerge from cautious over-sensitivity to how students feel. Instead, caution and over-sensitivity prioritises attention to feelings because this is easier than teaching and learning difficult subjects or crafts.

Such problems are reinforced by teacher education where research and reflective practices that 'expose' disjunctures and fragmented identities encourage negative introspection and reinforce comfortable or safe identities. Instead, we argue that empirical study might more usefully explore how the demands for attention to students' emotional well-being affect the teaching and assessment practices of teachers and teacher educators (Ecclestone and Hayes 2008).

Conclusions

Powerful images of people at risk permeate the FE sector where students are between the 'security' of school, higher education or work. Its purposes and activities increasingly focus on pessimistic images of risk and vulnerability and the need to elicit and manage people's personal and psychological capital in the name of enhancing their 'personal resources'.

In contrast to schools and universities, 30 years of therapeutic pedagogy and support systems have created an 'ethos of care' that is integral to the values and purposes of all FE colleges. A crucial shift in educators' thinking from earlier manifestations of therapeutic education is that self-esteem and confidence are now precursors to meaningful learning or, in the latest demeaned use of the term 'learning', as precursors to mere *engagement*.

In the past, educators saw these aspects of education as by-products of good teaching where students achieved something tangible and important. Our examples in this chapter suggest that learning has become almost anything but learning in any meaningful educational sense. Instead, teaching and assessment emphasise responses to the processes involved and responses to yourself as a responsible target-keeper, an 'engaged' participant or a 'reflective' learner.

We do not agree that a better alternative is to help teachers and students understand how 'discursive practices' of teaching, assessment and mentoring 'construct' their identities in negative ways, or to understand their emotional and material oppression. We argue that the political and cultural context we have outlined makes these responses therapeutic and therefore unable to resist the images and practices explored in this chapter. A more pressing problem is that goals for colleges to offer valuable second chances for high quality education and craft training are little more than a distant, romantic memory.

Chapter 5

The therapeutic university

Introduction

What was once an almost monastic environment of secluded calm disparaged by philistines as 'the ivory tower' now seems to be a place where it is widely assumed that staff and students may need counselling to cope with all aspects of university life. Increasing numbers of students and staff accept this assumption and see the services and support systems on offer as unexceptional. Unhesitatingly, they openly present themselves as having emotional and social problems. The greatest minds and brightest young people now find that the opportunity to pursue truth and wisdom in the 'groves of academe' is an emotional treadmill. This change leads us to ask what has happened to the life of the mind to make it an emotional rather than a critical business.

We could simply extend our argument and say that there are many discernible activities in the university that are just like those in schools and colleges that we have discussed so far and which we could characterise as part of a therapeutic education. We will give some attention to these activities but they are not central to our argument. Instead, the evolution of the therapeutic university comes from much more subtle changes to what key thinkers see as the fundamental purpose of higher education and from the preparation of teachers to 'deliver' that purpose. We argue therefore, that the rise of the therapeutic university has even more serious implications than a therapeutic school or college because belief in knowledge and reason, and optimism about their progressive and social consequences, are at stake: once these are at risk, the ideal of the university begins to disappear.

In this chapter, we explore four trends that simultaneously reflect and create therapeutic higher education. First, we discuss the rise of concern with emotionally vulnerable students and emotionally vulnerable academics. We identify vulnerability as not merely a general vulnerability; rather it is a specific emotional risk that students and academics are presumed to face because of their intellectual orientation. Second, we discuss the rise of professional and inter-professional therapeutic and counselling courses and how they are legitimising therapeutic education and therapeutic approaches throughout society. Third, we discuss the new philosophy of the therapeutic university as professors of higher education are defining it. Finally, we look at the rise of therapeutic teacher training and how it is changing the nature of learning at university.

- *Exam and study stress:* Out of control, panic attacks, *feelings of inadequacy.*
- Bereavement: Loss, anger, loneliness, sadness and depression.
    (Source HUCS 'Student Counselling in Universities' website)

The issues we have italicised refer to things that were once part of being a student and motivators for learning and knowing. The rest are, for the most part, the everyday ups and downs of young people's emotional lives. Printing such lists in every university encourages students to see these as problems that need more attention than they would naturally give them, and the website warns against the 'have a stiff drink' form of advice. Student services have, of course, a vested interest in exaggerating these problems but they could not do so if they did not resonate with students' self-perception of their own vulnerability.

Students may come to university already predisposed to think of themselves as needing help with any changes and do not find it problematic to ask for 'help'. This change is significant since, only a few years ago, students who had problems tended to get on with things because they did not want to be seem as weak or incapable of coping. Of course, that was sometimes a problem if they had real difficulties. Now everyone looks for a difficulty to declare, like the hundreds of students who register themselves as 'dyslexic' when the problem, if it exists, is exceptionally rare. The normalising of a range of difficulties and learning difficulties has led to some students using this as a way of getting extra help and avoiding criticism from fellow students and lecturers. It also represents an emotional shift in which having a problem that affects learning is seen unproblematic or even as a positive personal attribute.

Expanding self-harm

A research project at Roehampton University exploring incidents of self-harming behaviour at university is creating a typology of self-harm that ranges from not getting enough sleep and eating unhealthy food, to binge drinking, illegal drug-taking and self-wounding. The aim is to de-stigmatise 'traditional' images of self harming by running workshops to show that most, if not all of us, self-harm to a greater or lesser extent (Best 2007).

Even if students leave their parents and their new professional parents behind and are ready for an intellectual challenge, they will learn that academic life is fraught with dangers that could affect their emotional health and well being. Their first week will be spent on 'Induction' courses designed by administrators, student services and academics that will be about advice and support and little else. The assumption of such courses is that young people are increasingly unable to cope with the changes involved in leaving home and going to university. There is rarely much about the challenge of ideas, about thinking the unthinkable and saying the unsayable, features of learning that are the essence of university life.

It's learning Jim, but not as we know it!

Academics have problematised the 'student experience' and made the simple act of getting away from home a traumatic moment of identity crisis. Examples from a 2007 conference and the publicity from a book summarise how academics now see their students ...

Conference theme: student experience?

Students' lives today – it's learning but not as we knew it!

Home or away? Issues of identity, engagement and what it means to be a student.

How students' experience of family change and disruption may inform their learning.

The fragile will to learn ...

'There is an extraordinary but largely unnoticed phenomenon in higher education: by and large, students persevere and complete their studies. How should we interpret this tendency? Students are living in uncertain times and often experience anxiety, and yet they continue to press forward with their studies. The argument here is that we should understand this propensity on the part of students to persist through *a will to learn*.

This book examines the structure of what it is to have a will to learn. *Here, a language of being, becoming, authenticity, dispositions, voice, air, spirit, inspiration and care is drawn on.* As such, this book offers an idea of student development that challenges the dominant views of our age, of curricula understood largely in terms of skill or even of knowledge, and pedagogy understood as bringing off pre-specified 'outcomes'.

The will to learn, though, can be fragile. This is of crucial importance, for if the will to learn dissolves, the student's commitment may falter. Accordingly, more than encouraging an interest in the student's subject or in the acquiring of skills, the *primary* responsibility of teachers in higher education is to sustain and develop the student's will to learn ...' (our emphasis).

(Barnett 2007: *A Will to Learn: Being a Student in an Age of Uncertainty*)

Despite the assumption of vulnerability, we believe young people do not want to be students seen as needing therapeutic interventions, even when disguised as supporting their fragile 'will to learn'. Higher education still exists in disciplinary form and students still 'read' subjects. It is true that degree programmes are increasingly inter-disciplinary and professional, or skill-oriented, but they do not explicitly offer any sort of 'therapeutic higher education'. However, this bold statement needs a caveat since Barnett's claim to offer something new to the 'philosophy' of HE belies the way in which the 'fragile' learner is now a reality for whom academic study itself is problematic.

Academic study puts fragile learners at risk ...

We are also aware of the different sorts of demands which different programmes of study make upon students, such as in the field of Health Care. For some people, a caring role at work can mean that they are always seen in this role, even outside work and so it can become hard to attend to their own needs and feelings, which may go unmet. In addition, Health Care students are faced, sometimes on a daily basis, with loss in their work and this can make it doubly hard if they are dealing with their own losses such as a relationship ending or bereavement. Similarly, the pressures of life in schools dealing with the issues of young people can make considerable emotional and physical demands on students in teacher education.

Students studying in the disciplines of Psychology, Sociology or the Expressive Arts may find themselves re-examining areas of their lives which have previously seemed unproblematic to them. On the other hand, students working in competitive sports have other types of emotional issues to confront and resolve. For other people it is not a particular event that is bothering them but more a general feeling of anxiety, stress or feeling low.

('A Guide for Students – Counselling and Supervisory Services' – a leaflet issued by a new university)

Students reading the above in their induction week and scanning the publicity for their professors' books may well have 'a general feeling of anxiety' about doing their academic work. What you would normally expect from being at university, namely challenging experiences and changing your mind about your most precious beliefs and prejudices, are now projected as something that must be carefully and 'sensitively' handled. The not-so hidden assumption is that the intellectual challenge or change in general is something that people may find difficult to cope with. On this basis, every philosophy student should have a personal counsellor while belief after belief is challenged and possibly undermined for ever.

Therapeutic activities for staff

Students are not the only ones who are made vulnerable by university life and they may find that their lecturers are in counselling as well. One post-1992 university in the north west of England displays posters offering all staff free counselling at any time, alongside a 24-hour paging service. When we began to research this aspect of university life, we were surprised how ubiquitous counselling was for academics. We do not want to down-play the increased demands of academic work, particularly in post-1992 universities but a sense of proportion might help the drift towards seeing the demands of a lecturer's role as psychologically damaging. We discuss in the next chapter how the assumption of vulnerability is common in every workplace but it is alarming that this assumption is so powerful in academia.

It's lecturing Jim, but not as we know it!

An assessment and four free counselling sessions are available to any member of staff who:

- has relationship difficulties;
- has suffered bereavement/loss;
- feels under the sort of pressure which interferes with their capacity to work efficiently and effectively;
- is so stressed that they are unable to function properly at work;
- feels in a rut with their work or personal life and cannot make any moves further;
- suffers from debilitating depression, panic attacks and other stress related symptoms.

(A service offered by a 'research' university.)

We would be tempted to see this list of academics' problems as extremely dubious except that it is clear that academics do feel that they are vulnerable and victimised. The concern with 'stress' and 'bullying' is common to all unions in the public and private sectors and we discuss this in more detail in the next chapter. What is different in the university sector is that the relationship with young people makes the language of the playground easy to appropriate. When the campaign group Academics For Academic Freedom (AFAF) was launched and reported attacks on academic freedom, it received publicity on the 'bullied academics' website although it was billed as demanding a 'right to be offensive'. It seems it is impossible to escape the 'victim' label even when you are being confident about the academy!

Visit www.bulliedacademics.com ...

The therapeutic professional

Roehampton University has a 'Research Centre for Therapeutic Education' at whose seminar series we have both spoken and engaged in a dialogue with proponents of sophisticated forms of therapeutic education. The centre leads the Economic and Social Research Council's (ESRC's) research seminar series on emotional learning. It is a centre of growing prestige and influence and is 'one of the largest and most comprehensive providers of therapeutic education, training and research in the UK'. The centre has a truly academic orientation and is open to critical approaches such as ours. It was an early starter in what has since became a rush to set up centres and develop programme areas to offer courses in 'emotional intelligence', 'emotional literacy' and 'emotional well-being'. 'Happiness' is not on the programme list yet but it is probably only a matter of time before we see a foundation degree in the 'subject'.

Postmodern therapy ...

The Research Centre for Therapeutic Education at Roehampton University is developing methodologies for investigating:

- The educational implications of postmodernism and other changes in contemporary culture for (phenomenological / existential, humanistic, behavioural and psychoanalytic) therapeutic practice, theory and research.
- Therapeutic education as a form of teaching and learning.
- The most appropriate means of preparing practitioners, lecturers, trainers, supervisors and researchers.
- The inter-relationships between therapy, education, management and health and their implications for individual organisational and community health.
- Ethics as the basis for therapeutic practice.

The following are currently [2007] of particular interest:

- Therapeutic education and well being.
- Relational learning.
- Learning communities.
- The training of psychotherapists, counsellors and counselling psychologists.
- Methodological implications of continental philosophies.
- Emotional learning and involvement processes.

(Source – 2007 publicity leaflet)

We discussed in Chapter 4 the range of counselling and therapy courses as well as courses with a therapeutic orientation in FE. Our estimate was that there are some 517 colleges and universities offering 2,262 therapy courses, amongst them many 'Beauty Therapy' courses but with a good smattering of 'Crystal Healing' 'Stone Therapy' and other new age interests. More tellingly, as we said in Chapter 4, there are 337 colleges, universities and private companies offering 456 'Emotional Intelligence Courses'. Many of these are in FE (source: Hotcourse.org.uk, accessed 24 October 2007).

The field is opening up in HE led by centres like Roehampton's where many courses are well-established and accredited. This is not true of all as a article in the *Guardian* commented some years ago: 'There are a huge number of courses that aim to teach counselling skills, but only a few will prepare you for a new career in the field or gain you accreditation from the British Association for Counselling and Psychotherapy (BACP)' (Curphey 2002). To gain BACP accreditation, you must complete at least 200 hours of practical work and 250 hours of theory. How many of thousands of therapeutic workers that we have shown are working in the education system have this degree of training? What do we say about the courses that do not train people properly or are run by quacks and mystics?

People who are ill certainly need therapeutic help, but within a therapy culture even the best courses become purveyors of a therapeutic ethos. Their approach is easily generalised to people who might be less well or temporarily unwell. From there, as we argued in Chapter 1, the assumption is that most people will be vulnerable at some time. We would argue not only should you not get involved in therapy if you are not trained but that the vast majority of people do not need counselling or therapy. We have noted in discussions that specialists often encourage the generalisation of therapeutic approaches when they argue that calling some people emotionally unwell is an oppressive cultural determination. We might easily conclude that if we don't make such determinations, we are all to a greater or lesser degree mentally ill. One speaker, a trained counsellor, at a conference we spoke at asked the large audience if any of them could put their hands up and say with certainty that they had excellent mental health. Only a few hesitant people put up their hands.

We argue, however, that the spread of therapeutic training, sanctioned and reinforced by universities, is a symptom and not the cause of the rise of therapeutic education. The universities are certainly adding to the therapeutic culture by offering more and more courses of a dubious nature but they can only do so if they have a wider philosophy which justifies this.

The philosophy of the therapeutic university

At the apex of the educational system, the university is not immune to the influences that we have shown to be at work throughout the education system. More than that, it is often the university that is the source both of the specific ideas we have discussed and, more importantly, it provides the intellectual framework for these ideas. That said, there is no book that sets out an explicit philosophy of something called the 'therapeutic university'. Yet most 'innovative' and 'critical' books about the changing nature of the university express an understanding of the university that we would argue is of a therapeutic nature.

Uncertainty

It is in the work of Ronald Barnett, Professor of Higher Education at the Institute of Education, University of London, who, although he does not use the phrase and would disown it, comes closest to articulating the philosophy of the 'therapeutic university'. Barnett is the author of a series of books on the changing university and has been called the most important contemporary thinker on the philosophy of higher education. What we find most valuable, particularly in his later writings, is a clear articulation of a philosophy based on theoretical studies of risk society and what he calls 'supercomplexity' that defines the therapeutic culture in higher education.

No single statement encapsulates the shift that has happened in the university better than Barnett's bold assertion that in the twenty-first century: 'Knowledge and control are not, thankfully, available. (That belief partly led to Auschwitz.) What is both necessary and possible – just – is an enlightened societal self-monitoring' (Barnett 2000: 68). Barnett clearly understands and describes very clearly the academic project of disinterested enquiry. He identifies internal threats to the intellectual heritage of disinterestedness, seeing this as a conflict between the managerialist value of performativity and the academic value of collegiality (Barnett 2000: 25–30).

If this conflict was central we could look at issues such as 'job insecurity' and think of how to tackle the conflict of values from the point of view of academic workers. Yet, even this discussion could only begin if we assumed that a defence of disinterested inquiry should be undertaken. Barnett does not want to do this. Instead, he seeks to reposition the university within wider society devoid of the 'ideological baggage ... of spreading the light of reason' (Barnett 2000: 69). Rather than spreading the light of reason, the university is to re-organise itself around the 'uncertainty principle'. This will transform it into an institution that

> (i) contributes to our uncertainty in the world (through its research and consultancy); (ii) helps us monitor and evaluate that uncertainty (through its work as a centre of critique); and (iii) enables us to live with that uncertainty, through both the operational capacities and the existential capacities it promotes (in its pedagogical activities).
>
> (Barnett 2000: 69)

The publicity on the book adds 'to revel in our uncertainty' to point (iii).

Barnett is not a lone voice. A recent book on the university in the knowledge society, pointedly entitled *Challenging Knowledge*, argues that he is correct, and that the university must, 'allow society to live at greater ease with uncertainty' (Delanty 2001:155). This is because it is one of the 'few locations in society' where the discourse of the 'challenge of technology' and the discourse of 'culture' interconnect (2001: 158). This claim exaggerates the role and importance of the university in helping to overcome the cultural damage done by capitalism and managerialism.

The new role on offer, however, is the only one possible when you give up on the pursuit of knowledge, namely, that the university has a 'communicative role' (2001: 11) in the 'knowledge economy'. This can only mean that it has a 'therapeutic' role. Barnett and his epigones are providing us with an account of what would be better called the 'therapeutic university' The therapeutic university has an ethical purpose, to make people feel safe and secure, and the pursuit of knowledge does not feature in it at all. This vision of the university is an articulate celebration of the loss of confidence in the academy.

There is little opposition to theorists of risk and uncertainty who celebrate the social condition of uncertainty that they argue should be reflected in the university. Their audience is largely administrators and, until the advent of teacher training courses for higher education, they were not read by most academics. This is likely to change and the consequences will be more profound, as we show in our discussion of teacher training below.

Love

Another writer who provides a therapeutic philosophy within a defence of subject knowledge against the compliant, functional, skills-based agenda pursued by government and university management is Stephen Rowland (2000, 2006; Rowland *et al.* 1998). Rowland argues well against a philistine view of higher education and proposes that 'Intellectual love ... provides an excellent basis for intellectual enquiry' (2006: 111). His work is also a partial defence against those, like Barnett, who have effectively abandoned subject-based knowledge in the university. However, he recognises that,

> It is difficult to speak of love. Definitions seem oddly out of place. Sometimes the word seems to mean nothing more than a positive feeling towards its object. At others it appears as merely an expression of sentiment. Yet it also represents the most significant form of human commitment possible.
>
> (2006: 110)

His interesting explanation of what he means is influenced by Spinoza's notion of intellectual love as the desire for 'knowledge of God' in a secularised form:

> The ideal conception of intellectual love is useful in the more secular context of this discussion of enquiry and what it is to love one's subject. The object of intellectual love's desire, the subject matter is never fully known. We may come to know better, but we can never know completely; we can find out what we wanted but this leaves further questions for enquiry, further knowledge desired.
>
> (2006: 111)

Rowland began his exploration of 'love' in teaching in the university (see Rowland 2000). What he now offers as a philosophy of the university builds on the ideas he put forward in relation to teacher training. Yet, developed into a philosophy of enquiry, it misdirects us by pointing to our 'love' of our feelings for knowledge rather than our knowledge. We are encouraged to concern ourselves with what it means to 'love' knowledge rather than to focus on the subject knowledge we actually have or seek to know. Rowland's concern is with our feeling about our subject is an extension of the child's concern with the inner world rather than the outer. We might actually hate the process of enquiry, of going 'the bloody hard way' as Wittgenstein called it, but still be committed to our subject.

Emotions

This exploration of 'love', although a genuine attempt to defend academic disciplines, is one aspect of the therapeutic turn towards the emotions in writings about the university. Another academic, Alan Mortiboys, who runs staff development courses at the University of Central England, has made a case that teachers in the university should focus on the emotions and 'emotional intelligence'.

Mortiboys promotes the idea of teaching with 'emotional intelligence' and developing 'social and emotional' competencies in lecturers because of the central role of the emotions in rational decision making (Mortiboys 2005: 3). There is straightforward error in thinking here, for no matter how we are emotionally involved, or not, in intellectual work we pursue that work in a *disinterested* way. We are not and must not be intellectually or emotionally biased in the pursuit of knowledge. Emphasis on the emotions in higher education is irrelevant, a time wasting activity based on a generalised notion of personal vulnerability.

Become an emotionally literate lecturer

- discover how you relate to your learners;
- shape the emotional environment;
- listen to your learners effectively;
- read and respond to the feelings of individuals and groups;
- develop self awareness as a teacher;
- recognise your prejudices and preferences;
- improve your non-verbal communication;
- acknowledge and handle your feelings.

(Mortiboys 2005)

The assumption of vulnerability already pervades the university. Even when work is supposedly intellectual, it is presented in emotional ways. Not only in 'safe spaces' or through 'poster displays' is work seen as an expression of a person's feelings as much as of their intellect – but at research conferences, poor or boring papers are listened to with respect. There are few questions other than requests for clarification. To be critical is to be hurtful. This situation certainly exists in education and the social sciences, and there are already expressions of it in 'harder' subject areas. Science, for example, is being undermined by environmentalism and precaution just as it is in schools. One discussion even urges those interested in interdisciplinarity to reflect on the Gaia hypothesis because it helps explicate the role of metaphor in science. The message is loud and clear: take seriously the ambiguous and confused notion that the Earth has emotions.

Meanwhile, academics who engage in criticism too enthusiastically with student groups may be subject to complaints, as some now undergoing disciplinary action have discovered while colleagues increasingly ask what people feel about something. Not just in that colloquial way in which 'feel' is synonymous with 'think' but how they respond emotionally to some position, argument or event. We discuss in Chapter 6 how universities offer staff development sessions at which academics are encouraged to express their views. Being empowered to express views is a therapeutic and emotional activity, not a critical one. It is about acceptance and hence compliance, rather than academic freedom. Anyone who ventured criticism in the context of this therapeutic management style would be very unpopular for not playing the game. Indeed, such events often involve just that: infantile game playing justified as a means to allow people to express themselves freely.

We argue that none of these changes has anything positive to contribute to academic life. And they will get a firmer hold on the academy as the new generation of teacher-trained lecturers enters the profession influenced by sessions that emphasise the emotional side of working in higher education. Emotions, after all, cannot be questioned: they just are.

When we reduce the expression of ideas to the expression of emotion, or see them as equally important, academic freedom is further weakened. Individual academics are subjected to more restrictions that are based on the subjective feelings of students, colleagues and managers. And rational debate is debased because emotional freedom is the basis for intellectual and social atavism since the strength of emotion decides matters. The result will be quietude in the face of emotional correctness or, and this is the greater danger, 'emotion wars', a British counterpart to the US 'culture wars'. If this happens, university teaching will need to be increasingly a therapeutic rather than a critical activity in order to restrain emotions.

Work like Mortiboys' on the importance of the emotions will encourage university bureaucracies to promote policies that undermine academic life. Emotional freedom is a safe option for bureaucracies because it gives individuals and groups the right to express themselves in an uncritical climate but all they talk about is their feelings.

The growing emphasis on emotions in the academy says much about the widespread withdrawal from intellectual and public life into relativism, subjectivity and feelings. The emotions are the last bastion of this cultural retreat. Mortiboys suggests that 'I think therefore I am' should be replaced by 'I feel therefore I am' as the slogan of our time (2005: 142). Our response is to emphasise that the university is, the home of reason and that the more it embraces the emotional, the less it is a university.

Therapeutic teacher training

We argue that teacher training for higher education indicates how strongly the turn towards the therapeutic university is beginning to gain a very strong hold. Since the creation of the Institute for Learning and Teaching in higher education (ILT), as a result of the Dearing Report of 1997, and its successor the Higher Education Academy (HEA), patterns observed in teacher training in FE where functional and prescribed content are mixed with a humanistic delivery, are producing an accelerated therapeutic turn.

Our claim that there are many explicit proponents of the therapeutic approach in teacher education is based on our long experience as teacher trainers for lecturers in further, adult and higher education. Even before the advent of teacher training for university lecturers, enthusiasm for the explicitly therapeutic approach of Carl Rogers and an acceptance of a seemingly democratic, egalitarian, non-directive, non-judgemental 'facilitative' teaching ethos have long been cornerstones of teacher training for further and adult education

In addition to university managers, tutors and students on teacher training courses read books expressing the new therapeutic philosophy of education for HE. Straw polls of our academic colleagues show that, for the most part, academics working in the traditional subject disciplines know nothing of their works or their names. This situation will not last, and the *THES/HE* is now giving space to the views of Barnett, Rowland, Macfarlane and other professors of higher education.

Their work is mostly known in teacher training for HE. We now give three examples of academics whose work is significant in promoting therapeutic teacher training and in creating not only the therapeutic university but lecturers steeped in a therapeutic philosophy which they will pass on to future generations of students.

Innovative therapy

Therapy is the explicit focus of John Cowan's *On Becoming an Innovative University Teacher: Reflection in Action*, published in 1998. Cowan reverses the role of technology from something that is used in a conscious way to initiate change to one where its influence will change our consciousness. Cowan's main themes are how the new technologies 'provoke' reflection and how his own personal and collaborative reflection has improved aspects of university teaching. The influence of Carl Rogers' therapeutic 'person to person' approach to learning is both explicit and recommended (Cowan 1998: 142–6).

Cowan identifies three conditions to be met if Rogerian 'growth promotion' is to be successful. First, teachers must 'unearth their immediate thoughts and feelings, and … make these available to their students without editing or censoring' (1998: 143). This resonates with advocacy of a similar approach in strategies for learning to learn and circle time in secondary and primary schools, as we showed in earlier chapters. Second, that teachers 'make themselves transparent to the learner, who can then see right through to what the teacher actually is, within their relationship' and equally that they have 'a positive and accepting attitude to whatever the student is, or thinking or doing, at that moment. It is a prizing of learners as imperfect human beings …' (1998: 144). Third, that the teacher 'accurately senses and assimilates the feelings and personal meanings which the student is communicating …' (1998: 144).

The notion behind such an approach is the reconstruction of the teacher–student relationship as building the self-esteem of both. Rogerian therapy sees the self as something to be 'esteemed, actualised, affirmed, and unfettered' (Nolan 1998:3). It is 'liberating' because, in a quasi-religious way, it sees all human beings and their impulses as essentially inclined towards good (Nolan 1998: 4). We are a long way from the traditional concern with subjects and critical thinking and the dismissal of any concept of innovation in the methodology of teaching as 'spoon feeding'. The concern is now with making advances in building up student self-esteem.

Reflective therapy

The language is not always overtly therapeutic but the therapeutic approach lies behind the current vogue for talking about 'reflective practice'. This is true even if we talk of 'critical reflection' that recognises the existence of particular power relations in reflective practice (Brookfield 1995a: 130). The relocation of the discussion of 'power' to person to person relationships within a classroom is part of the 'liberating' (transformative, empowering, emancipatory) language of therapy, whether or not that debt is recognised:

> … critical reflection is inherently ideological. It is also morally grounded. It springs from a concern to create the conditions under which people can learn to love one another, and it alerts them to the forces that prevent this. Being anchored in values of justice, fairness and compassion, critical reflection finds its political representation in the democratic process. Since it is difficult to show love to others when we are divided, suspicious, and scrambling for advantage, critical reflection urges us to create conditions under which each person is respected, valued, and heard. In pedagogic terms, this means the creation of democratic classrooms. In terms of professional development, it means an engagement in critical conversation.
>
> (Brookfield 1995a: 26–7)

Positive feelings only allowed ... no gripes about workloads

Jane, a lecturer at a new university gave this irate account of her education department meeting ...

> At the beginning of our department meeting, we were all asked to go off in groups of four so that each could identify one thing they valued or had achieved that they could come back and share with others. This would, we were told, develop a positive attitude towards our work at the end of term. We may be primary education lecturers but we don't need our self-esteem working on by the Head of Department. What we do need is more time to do research. Instead of being able to raise real issue of workload, we get 'circle-time'.

Two important features of this critical reflection are that it avoids self-laceration and 'grounds us' emotionally (1995a: 23, 24). It also fosters trust by treating students as adults and acknowledging peer learning. Brookfield's discussion of critical reflection culminates in a purely therapeutic model of practice: 'A teacher who encourages students to point out to her anything about her actions that is oppressive and who seeks to change what she does in response to their concerns is a model of critical reflection. Such a teacher is one who truly is trustworthy' (1995a: 26).

The emphasis in reflective practice is to treat lecturers and students as academic equals. 'Education' is defined as a dialogue among equals and: 'Through this dialogue, students are helped to name, honor, and understand their own experiences. They do this using categories of analysis that they have evolved themselves rather than those that have been externally imposed on them by the dominant culture' (1995a: 208–9).

This overturns what is normally thought of as education which involves submission to learning a culture, namely to come to learn and know the best that is known and thought. Love of subject is replaced by the love of individuals and true equality in the search for truth is replaced by a purely subjective valuing of experience. This may well build up student self-esteem as they no longer have to study to understand the best that is known and thought, but we argue that it is a profoundly destructive experience for academics.

Engaging in critical reflection might, at least initially, make us feel worse as teachers, through being 'more doubt ridden, puzzled, sadder perhaps. After all sadness and wisdom are not incompatible' (Jackson quoted in Brookfield 1995a: 239). Brookfield's own experience has been one of 'sustained epistemological demolition, as my certitudes are constantly crashing to the ground' (Brookfield 1995a: 239–40).

This therapeutic undermining of academic confidence is held to be a defence of collaboration in the face of rampant individualism in the university, where the culture is individualist and the model is the 'Lone Ranger'. Not surprisingly resisted by the Lone Rangers, a key step forward would be an institutional reward system to encourage critical reflection as a 'normal and desirable professional habit' (1995a: 252). This belief is becoming the norm, even if formal reward systems are absent. Interestingly, it is unlikely to be challenged by institutions since the therapeutic impulse locates discussions of power solely at the level of tutor/student relationships.

Such a re-location of power is entirely to the advantage of those who hold the real power to hire and fire and who can intervene in any conflicts at this level in a seemingly neutral and supportive way. However, this would not be a cynical move on the part of any institution. All institutions are susceptible to the therapeutic impulse since it allows them to develop new forms of legitimisation when old values no longer connect with a disenchanted public (Nolan 1998: 40–5).

Identity therapy

Many of us involved in teacher training for all the sectors of education seek ways of subverting, if not openly challenging, the government supported HEA model of teaching that reduces it to technical skills, 'competencies' and 'standards' and thereby 'refuses to acknowledge the passion for knowledge which is at the heart of learning and teaching' (Rowland in Rowland *et al.* 1998: 140). Rowland's solution is to advocate a therapeutic approach: 'My argument is … that university teaching in general, and educational enquiry on the part of university teachers in particular, can usefully draw on therapeutic insights' (2000: 107).

However this is done, we argue that it takes us away from the business of developing subject knowledge. Rowland argues that many 'experts' in teaching and learning have expertise in no subject and are like 'experts in love who have no lover' (Rowland *et al.*

Sarah learns to become a therapeutic lecturer

On the second week of her compulsory certificate in teaching in higher education, Sarah is required to develop her empathy for students' feelings of exclusion so that she can promote one of the course's core values: 'commitment to encouraging participation in higher education, acknowledging diversity and promoting equality of opportunity'.

> We had to get into 3s and each 'share' an educational experience where we felt included and excluded and then tell them to the whole group. The first was easy and we all chose one where we had got excited about a topic, and where even people in the group without English as a first language could join in. But the second example, being excluded, was more emotional. All of us had experienced not being selected for sports activities at school. Afterwards, the woman giving feedback for our group said, sort of humorously, 'we went deep in our group' and everyone laughed.

> But I was thinking I can't believe I just disclosed all that to strangers. It wasn't what I wanted to do – I'm happy saying that stuff to friends – and I wished I hadn't done it. The thing was, you felt you had to say something disclosing; it's all done on the hoof, 'get into 3s, you have five minutes, report back to the group' and so there's no space or time to think and so you're lulled into doing it. And you don't want to feel like you're repressed or unfriendly and so you go along with it.
>
> It's just the same with the reflective statement we have to do; I've got 2,500 words to write, I've left it till the last minute and it's being assessed. It's the way they write the questions: it's a horrible mix of NVQ-style competences, develop a portfolio of evidence, and questions about that invite you to write about how you feel not what you think or believe. It's really insidious.

1998: 135). Brookfield goes further in suggesting that there is a need to 'demystify, debunk and deconstruct the notion of the expert (1995a: 260). However, amateur teacher/therapists are experts and part of their expertise is precisely this denial of the role of the 'expert', meaning any subject expert confident in their knowledge and abilities. Again, we saw this attack on expertise in the secondary school chapter.

Therapists are, however, much more powerful because they exercise their trade by sleight of hand. It would be naïve to see therapists as any different from Rowland's 'experts'. The consequences are as bad for the love of one's subject. Stretching his analogy with a lover, his proposals are a form of teasing and, like Marvell's 'coy mistress', they declare love, but keep us from satisfying our desire. This is even clearer when Rowland suggests a further therapeutic activity that requires our personal commitment to examining the 'multiple selves' that constitute identity: 'One of the aims of enquiry into our teaching is to come to know these different identities, to bring ourselves into a closer harmony with our selves and thus into more authentic relationships with our students. This is a personal as well as a professional project' (Rowland 2000: 114).

Implications

The prospect of undergoing therapeutic forms of training might lead anyone to embrace competence-based training. In fact, the two alternatives are not contradictory but complementary. Competencies can be defined and imposed centrally, whether by the HEA or not, but this direction can co-exist with a local freedom of delivery through more humanistic or therapeutic methods. As we showed in Chapter 4, this is commonplace in teacher training and other assessment systems in further education where the addition of humanistic notions is precisely what gives 'competencies' their seductive power (Usher and Edwards 1994: 110).

Ultimately, these seemingly radical and liberating therapeutic alternatives will come to dominate teacher training for the university sector. Precisely because they adopt a radical and liberating rhetoric, they will be attractive to many new university lecturers because they seem to be 'oppositional' or subversive. However, that 'opposition' is entirely destructive of the project of the university. In attacking individualism and academic authority (expertise), acknowledging the value of subjective experience, accepting failing and frailties, bringing in uncertainty and doubt, they undermine the central ethical value of the university, namely, the disinterested pursuit of knowledge. Prioritising any other values diminishes this value precisely because the pursuit of knowledge then becomes 'interested'. If we set conditions to the pursuit of knowledge, we, in part, predetermine the outcome of inquiry.

The type of inquiry which therapeutic universities engage in are determined by therapeutic values. These are far from oppositional and liberating. Instead, they incorporate the orthodoxies of the therapeutic culture.

Conclusion

The university once produced academics who were natural critics because of an independence of mind brought about by their expertise in a subject area. In contrast, new and experienced lecturers are routinely offered counselling and therapeutic interventions such as induction and teacher-training programmes ... to help them function as academic workers. An academic life which requires self-denial and disinterested inquiry is being undermined by the promotion of vulnerable 'identities' and an obsession with feelings.

The therapeutic university discourages academics from becoming practised in the denial of self in the pursuit of knowledge. In the end, they may well love and respect their students and colleagues, but they will be diminished figures compared with the traditional academic who sought to be a determined and public critic of societal trends. This diminished academic self will also be reflected in the graduates of the therapeutic university who are future employees and citizens. They will enter civic life but the political consequence of a therapeutic education, from the early years curriculum to the postgraduate course, will be social passivity because a diminished and uncertain self can pose no questions and offer no challenge to anyone.

Chapter 6

The therapeutic workplace

Introduction

At the beginning of the twenty-first century, Phil Mullan suggested that new management trends would 'come together to crystallise in the emergence of the *therapeutic company* with its emphasis on self-help and self-improvement, on the importance of how workers feel and the pursuit of emotional literacy' (Mullan 2000: 9). In a remarkably short time since that prediction, the therapeutic company seems to be a reality. A survey undertaken in 2004 showed that 50 per cent of women and 38 per cent of men feel emotionally supported by their employer. Despite this, almost 1 in 2, some 45 per cent of the work force, would like confidential counselling or coaching from their employer (BACP/Future Foundation 2004: 24).

Similarly, trade unions increasingly offer counselling and advice lines to support vulnerable workers. Union officials and officers find more and more of their time taken up with problems such as stress and bullying. The workplace is no longer the battleground between 'capital' and 'labour': indeed, it is more accurate to say that the class war has become the 'couch war' with both sides trying to help employees onto the therapy couch. At a theoretical level, sociologists have noted the rise in importance or of 'emotional' or 'aesthetic' labour. And, as we have shown in earlier chapters, economists are looking seriously at measures of happiness and well being as indicators of prosperity, with schools as a key site for fostering them (Layard 2006; www.happinesspolicy.com).

Young people progressing to work from their experiences in schools, colleges and universities will be well prepared for many of the practices and assumptions they encounter at work. Circle time in staff development sessions, one-to-one reviews or progress, setting and monitoring personal targets, writing reflective accounts of progress in preparation for personal development reviews, completing staff evaluations of how you feel about work – all these staples of therapeutic education in schools colleges and universities are to be found in the workplace.

In this chapter, we show the ways in which a therapeutic turn in politics and culture has invaded the industrial, business and public sector workplace. We argue that workers who, less than 25 years ago, styled themselves as 'the enemy within' now find that they have an 'enemy within', namely an enemy constituted by consciousness of their own vulnerability. First, we outline the rise of diminished workers and managers, and offer examples of activities and images that create it. Second, we show why presenteeism has come to be seen as a problem and the social and personal functions that it reflects. Third, we explore examples of how workplaces provide therapeutic interventions for fractious workers who feel stressed and bullied. Fourth, we summarise how education in the form of credentialism pervades the workplace. Fifth, we show how the development, monitoring and the sacking of workers provide myriad opportunities for therapeutic activity. Finally, we highlight implications for the future of therapeutic workplaces.

Diminished workers and diminished managers

Workers' consciousness of vulnerability is not merely a matter of becoming stressed out, or of bullying or being bullied. Instead, it is a much deeper consciousness of yourself as a diminished worker, someone who feels they lack the skills and qualifications, personal abilities, attitudes, emotional qualities and understanding to do their job properly in the new workplace. We do not see the diminished worker as someone created solely by management in order to control or exploit them.

A diminished sense of oneself is not confined to workers: management have the same sense of themselves as diminished. As one executive director of a large and successful IT company told us, the biggest problem he had was that his managers were 'afraid to manage'. The rise in the number of away days and management training sessions is a result of the rise of the diminished manager. We do not see them in a cynical way as 'jollies', although they are undoubtedly indulgent and certainly expensive!

Going round and round in the counselling game ...

One academic team leader in a university told us the story of trying to deal with a difficult member of staff, who complained endlessly and made everyone's life a misery. Management were approached but seemed incapable of giving the simple instruction that such behaviour had to stop. They were all distinguished male academics. After much indecision they resorted to the suggestion that the team should take up the option of counselling.

The decision to go for counselling let management off the hook. They had done their bit.

But it did not end there. The team leader did not want the time consuming process they recommended but straightforward management action. The problem was a failure to manage, she said.

Management subsequently concluded that this was an instance of denial and that, as the team leader did not want the counselling service that might help *all* the team, she was obviously the cause of the problems in the department.

Management could feel very comfortable with themselves as there was no failure to manage, just one woman who had difficulties dealing with people, and particularly with male management!

Management training and development often have a childish and playful element to them which is always a sound indicator that the real subject of the training is not the stated objective but a therapeutic process of dealing with a diminished manager. Overtly childish activities such as outdoor pursuits and 'paintball' war games are about team building and developing trust, cooperation and supportive relationships. More traditional training for managers often takes the form of facilitated 'workshop' activities involving the ubiquitous flip charts, post-it stickers and practical but 'fun' activities such as selecting, or drawing pictures that reflect where the company or organisation is going.

As we showed in Chapter 4, these activities are also a staple ingredient of teaching in further education colleges. One manager described how enthusiastically teams from his company competed to see who could build the highest tower from Lego bricks! A similar activity was used to teach children about volcanoes as a 'learning power' activity in school (Claxton 2002). But the apparent infantilisation of adults through their involvement in these training or 'staff development' activities is not the point. Any manager that refused to participate would soon be left behind in the new therapeutic corporate world. These activities are done to engage emotions rather than minds in the therapeutic way we have discussed in relation to schools, colleges and universities. They also flatter participants by presenting their existing knowledge and insights as 'learning' or as more important than that of experts, another belief they are likely to have gained from college and university experiences with their emphasis on facilitating the construction of your own knowledge.

Yet, business would not waste time with such things, and the army of management training consultants promoting them would not be so large, if there was not a market imperative behind such training. That imperative is the 'soft skills' now sought for managers and employees to enable them to work creatively at problem solving in teams and to build up customer levels and loyalty by being more responsive, and critically, more emotionally engaged with them (see Chapter 4). Developing 'soft skills' requires an emotional re-education, almost a return to childhood, in order to engage with feelings that are neglected and suppressed in the rational and functional machinery of twentieth- century business. To survive in the twenty-first century, the therapeutic corporation requires not just a requirement to be 'ethical' or 'green' but to be emotionally engaged.

We could leave the matter there and suggest that the market is determining the need for therapeutic training. Happy employees and happy customers mean happy shareholders! This attractive argument is too simplistic. A more substantial cultural change has affected the world of work and created the therapeutic company. This change is experienced at an individual level through the phenomenon of 'presenteeism' and related issues such as reducing stress and the need for 'work-life' balance but the socio-cultural changes are profound.

The paradox of presenteeism

A decade ago Cary Cooper identified the phenomenon of 'presenteeism' or the 'long hours' culture (Culley *et al.* 1999). He pointed to the fact that we are all staying on at work for longer and longer. The situation in the intervening ten years has become much worse than the documented and dubiously productive practice of spending long hours in the workplace. We take more work home and on holiday, thanks to the mobile phone, laptop and the Internet.

It seems that we are all both oppressed and obsessed by work. To tackle the obsession with being at work, whether because of employer demands, increased workloads, new management practices or the 'macho' culture of the workplace, 'work–life balance' has become a major theme with the unions and employers. Ironically, though, trying to achieve 'work-life' balance becomes another workplace demand. We become more obsessed by work than ever as we try to 'balance' our lives and work.

The obsession with work

We are all obsessed by work seen in the growing popularity of work-as-entertainment. There are three sets of examples:

Television serials such as 'Ugly Betty', 'Drop Dead Gorgeous', 'Ally McBeal', 'Teachers, Waterloo Road', 'E.R.', 'Casualty', 'Scrubs', 'Holby City', 'Mile High'.

A seemingly endless stream of 'fly on the wall' documentaries about ordinary work such as 'Holiday Airport', 'Airline', 'Street Wars', 'Street Crime Live', 'Road Wars', 'The Enforcers' and 'A Life of Grime'.

The 'can you hack it' programmes showing how useless people are even at management level, such as 'Kitchen Nightmares' and 'The Apprentice'.

All the above and more are evidence of how life at work dominates the popular consciousness. We find such programmes entertaining when you would think that, once at home, we would want to escape from office politics, and the tedium and petty problems of work. But we don't switch off, we switch on.

The concept of 'work–life balance' is a useful key to explain a deep sociological misunderstanding by many of those who write about the contemporary workplace. The example of popular TV dramas, faction and 'reality TV' shows about work are revealing because they are least successful as drama when they concentrate on the details of work. In fact, these programmes are not primarily about work at all but about people, their personal relationships that are developing in the workplace and the social life that revolves around work. What they exemplify, and 'Ally McBeal' was the best illustration of this, is the fusion of the professional and the personal in the workplace. The workplace has become the location of what no longer exists in wider society and is often described as the end of tradition or the collapse of community (Giddens 2000; Hayes and Hudson 2001; Sennett 1998).

Economist Phil Mullan offers an alternative explanation along these lines that we feel contradicts the simplistic market or exploitative view of presenteeism. Work, he says, has become more important for reasons that derive from outside the workplace:

> ... work is being made to perform or fulfil additional social roles which have got nothing to do with the previous prime function of work as the place for value creation. Work has become more important because of the way the other parts of social life are not working as well as they used to: everything from the family and personal relationships to politics.
>
> (Mullan 2000: 1)

Mullan sets his study of the changing workplace in the wider sociological context of the last quarter of the twentieth century and comments that because marriages and other relationships are much more fragile and ephemeral '... it is more rational for people seeking happiness to invest their time and energy in their jobs than in their relationships ... the absence of much of a sense of fulfilment from the non-work aspects of life means that people invest more in their work' (2000: 2).

We must recognise that this is a paradoxical repositioning of the personal. Work is often blamed because overwork and increased working hours seem to threaten family life, to damage personal relationships and leave little time for active social and political involvement. At the same time, it is the relocation of personal and social concerns into the workplace that accentuates the feeling of a loss of a personal, family or community life.

In reality, there is no paradox here, merely an inversion of the truth. Work is not the cause of these problems at all: it is the social space that personal and social concerns now occupy. Presenteeism is one result of this and the counter-call for work-life balance is another, but both are examples of how working life now suffers the strain of trying to be the focus of the whole of civic life. It is in such potentially fractious circumstances that the management and unions both step towards adopting therapeutic methods and the therapeutic company becomes a reality.

Therapeutic interventions for the fractious worker

Workers in the therapeutic company are not fractious in the traditional sense of demanding pay rises, better working conditions and shorter hours. Fractious demands are still made but are now utterly outweighed by demands for better treatment of individual workers. These new fractious workers are diminished, exemplified by the nature of the things that bother them. Major fractious incidents arise daily but these are usually personal and often involve injuries to feelings rather than demands for objective improvements in pay, working conditions or resistance to restructuring and redundancy. The explanation is that, as the workplace becomes more important to people because it is carrying more of civic life, personal interests and relationships in the workplace carry more meaning and have more effect on people than they did in the past.

The inexorable rise of concerns with 'stress' and 'bullying' in the workplace over the last decade are two clearest examples of how the overburdening of work has created the conditions for the therapeutic company. Because they are so familiar it is hard to remember that they are very new individualised concerns. One major survey of 1,000 workers undertaken in the 1990s recognised there was a new concern with 'stress', particularly amongst younger workers. When questioned they related their feelings to increased workload and other objective factors. Bullying was not even considered a problem to be raised in the survey (Hudson *et al.* 1996: 38–9).

Stress at work

The term 'stress' is so widely used that it has no meaning outside engineering and there is a free for all in attempts to define it. The concept is free floating and is now routinely applied to anything that people feel is unpleasant, or unwelcome. Angela Patmore has analysed the meaninglessness of the concept and there are other critiques of the construction of an imaginary problem (Patmore 2006; Wainwright and Caplan 2002).

Despite these critiques, 'stress' continues to grow as a concern, particularly for workplace unions who enquire and report on stress at work year after year. A pamphlet produced by Unison for its health and safety reps in 2002 cites the Confederation of British Industry estimate that 'stress' illness costs the economy of £5 billion a year, compared with the Institute of Management's estimate of 270,000 working days lost per calendar day because of 'stress', producing a total bill of £7 billion if you include sick pay, lost production and NHS costs (Unison 2002).

Obsession with stress from the worker's side has lead to many reports of this sort. A support agency for college lecturers claims that 31 per cent of calls concern anxiety, stress and depression (CUSN 2006). Sixteen per cent of lecturers do not think their employers are doing enough to deal with stress. The major beneficiary is the stress industry which gathers support from the diminished worker who diagnoses him or herself as 'stressed'. Putting aside the fact that unions have found a new role as workplace counsellors and discovered a way of increasing membership through offering support to their stressed members, this undermines their ability for fight in traditional collective ways against overwork, and this, in turn, increases concern with 'stress'. As Patmore says:

In terms of industrial action over workers' rights, stress management ideology, taken to its logical conclusion, may sound the death knell. If workers en masse are taught to fear hard work and made afraid of their own bodily mechanisms, they will all need soothing and comforting. They will be far too sick to strike.

(2006: 222)

While this is a purely logical consequence of 'stress' creation, and may not happen in such an extreme way, Patmore argues that the 'stress' label disables workers who go in to see a doctor about their back pain and come out permanently ill with stress.

The irony is that unions, as well as management, create a more serious problem of what we call a diminished employee and what Patmore calls the 'can't cope worker'. The sort of employee that 'can't cope' is no use as a unionised worker or as a useful, never mind *creative* employee. If this is an act of the 'iron hand' of the market, then the hand has rusted up.

In Patmore's account of what people call 'stress', by far the biggest group of states or attitudes in her list refer directly to people's 'feelings'. The list could be doubled by adding less direct mentions of emotion:

Feelings

feeling abandoned; feeling appalled; feeling brow-beaten; feeling crestfallen; feeling cut up; feeling demeaned; feeling disheartened; feeling disrespected; feeling downtrodden; feeling driven; feeling frantic; feeling hell-bent; feeling ill-used; feeling insulted; feeling neglected; feeling nerve-racked; feeling overwhelmed; feeling overwrought; feeling paralysed; feeling petrified; feeling rattled; feeling scorned; feeling sickened; feeling stricken; feeling stunned; feeling suicidal; feeling tainted; feeling threatened; feeling thwarted; feeling trigger-happy; feeling troubled; feeling unlucky; feeling unmanned; feeling unnerved; feeling useless; feeling victimised ; feeling worthless; feeling wounded

(Thirty-eight of 277 'internal' states and conditions
to which the term 'stress' has been applied:
Angela Patmore, *The Truth About* Stress, 2006: 392)

Our explanation is that such heightened sensitivity to these states results not from the artificial creation of an illness, as Wainwright *et al.* think, although the stress industry is a reality. We argue, instead, that such sensitivity could not be there if there was not some foundation for it. That foundation is the collapse of traditional forms of civil life and the relocation of the personal and social demands they make into the workplace within a broader therapeutic culture. Where there is no outlet in the terms of traditional social activities for people's passions, the result is 'stress' and the diminished worker.

Bullying

Whereas 'stress' is an individual emotional response to almost any situation, the related use of the term 'bullying' refers to almost any relationship in the workplace that people dislike. In the education system, everyday activities, from playground rough and tumble to lecturing in universities, anything that is forceful or demanding, is increasingly labelled 'bullying'. We noted in Chapter 1 that giving harsh feedback on programmes such as 'The X Factor' and 'Strictly Come Dancing', is seen by the growing number of anti-bullying campaigns as 'media-condoned bullying'. While there is a minor literature in the press that is critical of bullying as a concept, like 'stress', it has become rife (see Hayes 2004, 2005; Kirwan-Taylor 2007). On the other hand, unlike 'stress', bullying has a more social purchase where any criticism of the notion is held to leave people more vulnerable to victimisation and even possible death.

From calling the G7 'Trade Bullies' or the Western leaders 'Blair! Bush! – Bullies', as we saw on postcards and placards respectively, any apparent power relationship is potentially a bullying one. Fighting against the bullies has become the new form of struggle in the workplace. It has the benefit of being a simple, mono-conceptual view of the world without any of the conceptual and linguistic demands of 'exploitative', 'oppressive' or 'authoritarian'. It is the cry from the playground. The workaday world has been divided into those who are, or potentially could be, bullied (being 'at risk' of bullying) and those who bully. Since there are fewer managers and peer bullying has not had much success as a sub-concept, the majority are always potential or actual victims. Like 'stress', the term is now so loosely applied as to have no meaning. We may as well say 'You are bullied if you *feel* bullied'.

Don't bully me! I'm a lecturer!

The slogan above was a suggestion to produce stickers for lecturers in a new university to wear. The lessons of the playground had clearly not been learnt in that institution or it would be common knowledge that such things would get you tied to the whiteboard!

The sorry tale of what gets called 'bullying' in Higher Education is told on a blog: Bulliedacademics.com.

But not only on this blog. Here is a list of some of the things we've recently seen or heard labelled as 'bullying': not getting your own way in a difficult series of academic meetings; changing someone's lecturing schedule; making academics redundant; asking someone to do extra work; undergoing a negative appraisal; having a line manger telling you firmly what he want you to do; having to re-apply for a post; suddenly being moved with all your books and papers to another office; not being respected or even liked by colleagues; not being recognised or valued for teaching or research; having someone raise their voice, be rude, or even 'shout' at a colleague; feeling too intimidated to speak up in a staff meeting; not being given a pay rise; not getting a promoted post for a second time; strongly encouraging academics to join a union; campaigning to get people to vote for you. We've even heard of 'bullying' e-mails!

To top all this, we have heard the forceful expression of opinions, ideas and argument called 'soft bullying'.

The catch-all nature of 'bullying' in the workplace shows both the infantilisation of life and the absence of serious organisations, such as political parties and unions, to tackle the inequities of civic life. There are no 'adult' routes to dealing with problems at work. The 'everybody out' whistle-blowing caricatures of the trade union official or the campaigning political activist have gone and unions and management now work to tackle a problem that simply does not exist outside the playground. By doing so, they further the creation of the diminished worker. One anecdote will illustrate this. A group of security guards in a university came to see a union official since they felt they were being 'bullied'. It turned out that their manager kept changing timetables without consultation, and for one of them in particular, this was causing domestic problems. The union official was rather old-fashioned and decided to go to see the manager and point out the error of his ways. At this point the guard who was most affected demurred: 'But what I want to know' he said, 'is *why* he doesn't like me?'

'Stress' and 'bullying' help define the diminished worker at almost every level. The response of unions and management alike is to produce policies to help workers cope with stress and deal with bullies. Both 'sides' offer personal counselling, counselling and training courses and buy in consultants to deal with these issues. In accepting both problem and solution, they foster the therapeutic workplace. What was once class collaboration is now couch collaboration.

The educationalising of work

The vocationalising of education is a well-known phenomenon and one that is opposed by many to a greater or lesser degree. Preparation for employment is now required on degree courses and increasingly demanded throughout the secondary curriculum. Adult education has been priced out of the market if it is not vocational and the proposed removal of funding for study towards equivalent or lower qualification (ELQs) is the latest step in the attack on knowledge for its own sake and on the adult education institutions with great prestige, Birkbeck College and The Open University.

The educationalising of work, on the other hand, is barely recognised except in relation to the training offered particularly to younger employees. The government announced in November 2007 that it would provide 7.5 million new training places including 120,000 new apprenticeships for younger workers and 30,000 for those over 25 as well as 3.5 million training places for those in need of help with English and maths. In further education, the new Train to Gain (T2G) programme and the Leitch review of skills all encourage employer involvement and delivery of training. Unions bemoan the lack of corporate investment in training, and denounce the one in three companies who refuse to train their workers (Mackney 2006).

The demand for training is not restricted to government, pressure groups and unions. The prioritisation of training by workers as the way to get on in life was the 'single most striking' result of some studies of attitudes to work among employees and led the authors to claim that the 'era of lifelong' learning was a reality (Hudson *et al.* 1996; Hayes and Hudson 2001).

What is generally called 'credentialism', the offering of qualifications for every job and management role, has become a distinct feature of the workplace over the last 50 years. This is only a part of what we mean by the 'educationalising of work'. We argue that the general emphasis given to education in the workplace is unique and is not restricted to narrow skills training as it is traditionally thought of. Nor is it restricted to narrow skills training with an hour or two of liberal education. The 'educationalising' of work involves the transformation of workplace relationships into quasi-educational ones, hence the emphasis on 'lifelong' learning and the 'learning organisation'. Whatever their intention in terms of efficiency and profitability, these workplace relationships reflect the new sociological role of the therapeutic company and must take therapeutic forms.

Since the introduction of training for 'employability' in the 1980s and 1990s there has been an emphasis on people's personal attitudes and behaviours (see Armitage *et al.* 1999 [2003]: Chapter 1; Hayes *et al.* 2007: 3–7). This is particularly the case with work preparation. The demise of the careers service and its replacement, as we discussed in Chapter 4, with the Connexions service offering a 'personal advisor' for every young person by advertising this as someone 'who knows about me!' is strong evidence of a major shift. Work training for adults is now also seen as conditional on them having the right 'communication', 'problem solving' and 'team working' skills. This is straightforward attitudinal and affective training, but the latest innovative programmes argue that even basic skills training cannot get going until the unemployed are in the right emotional state. At 'Come All Ye – A Scottish Festival of Learning' in 2007, a 'well-being' project was promoted as aiming to bring just this sort of confidence-building to the local community *before* they could develop basic and workplace skills. This is a far cry from radical liberating adult education, even if it still presents itself as such.

In the beginning, there was therapy!

Even 'hard' training takes a therapeutic turn ...

Engineering

A new engineering student on an MSC course at a Russell Group university told us of how in the first session of his course the tutor asked each of them to reflect on their feelings and expectations about engineering and what it was to be an engineer and share them with the group.

Police training

A tutor recalls sitting in on a session at a police training centre with trainee police officers sitting in a circle, out of uniform, discussing what it meant to be a police officer and exploring their attitudes, anxieties and feelings.

The importance of these examples is that whatever follows, and however technical it is, it is set within a therapeutic framework that emphasises the importance of feelings.

Of course, once young people or the unemployed are on skill training programmes, their learning may still have a more technical or instrumental focus than the therapeutic experiences offered to workers suffering from 'stress' or 'bullying'. Nevertheless, we argue that the emotional aspects of the training are the important ones, not only for training bodies but for companies themselves. They want skills but, above all, they want the right attitudes.

The examples and arguments we have put forward in previous chapters about the dangerous rise of therapeutic education have shown the ubiquity of therapeutic assumptions as children and young people navigate a widening array of therapeutic activities. This makes it very unlikely that training offered in or out of the workplace would be entirely different, especially in a context of an increasing need for customer-centred 'emotional' or 'aesthetic' labour. When we talk of therapeutic education and training, we are referring to something more pervasive than this specialist training for work in call centres and retail outlets.

Our argument has been disputed by Terry Hyland, who says that without further research, we cannot be sure that vocational education has taken what we call a therapeutic turn (Hyland 2006). We return to this criticism in Chapter 8, but the examples of skill training as therapy indicate that something has changed and the inexorable rise of therapeutic training at work will not be slowed or stopped by research.

One reason why training seems unproblematic, thereby suggesting that we are making a fuss about nothing, is that everyone supports education and training. It is therefore difficult to see the dangers in it and to recognise what has changed: the emphasis is increasingly on educating people's hearts rather than their hands and minds. We discuss in the next section how the educationalising of work has a more ubiquitous influence on working relationships and has led to employers adopting therapeutic forms of education as everyday workplace practice.

Developing, monitoring and sacking workers as therapeutic activities

The therapeutic workplace is not only characterised by the pyschologisation of traditional workplace roles and relationships. Employers turn to therapy as a matter of course since they are told that this is best practice. Putting aside obvious 'counselling' activities, consider these four broad areas of therapeutic activity in the workplace.

Staff development

It is the form of staff development rather than its obvious content that makes it a therapeutic activity. Much staff development is held in comfortable hotels and conference centres and is led by dynamic and enthusiastic management and other consultants who use group work and facilitation to create a democratic open 'space' in which workers and managers are 'enabled' to think outside normal work hierarchies. The intention is to use humour, playful activities and even music: one course we know of offered rhythmic hand clapping with a partner along to strumming as a prelude to discussing how you worked with others.

Fun it may be but, of course, you cannot refuse to play. Sometimes this is made absolutely clear even when management are not involved. On one occasion, a workplace consultant leading a workshop with unions, human resources and management in a university put up a list of 'values' that included being open, honest, non-confrontational and so on. He then declared that the participants in the workshop had to agree to these values, apparently without discussion, since 'they are your values not mine!' If there was argument about adopting them, he announced that the day could not work. The message was. You will have these values and you will play!

These activities that people are made to take part in may feel demeaning or tedious. 'Death by Flip Chart' has become a common expression from people forced through endless brainstorming, 'thought shower' sessions that seem to go nowhere and wandering round a room placing post-its of feelings and thoughts on flipcharts. Engagement in such activities is not meant to be intellectual but emotional. This explains both the deep resistance to such activities and the intolerance towards those who will not play. It also explains the energy which people end up putting into them once they are engaged: after they resist, they do it enthusiastically.

The slide from the engagement of the intellectual to the engagement of the emotional is extremely powerful. Staff development rarely has any real consequences but people enjoy it feel and even feel they are having a break – 'Two days in a posh hotel, that's alright by me'. Staff developers may try to chart the impact of their activities on the company, but in doing this they miss the point. These sessions are therapeutic for employees and management alike and, in the therapeutic company, such approaches are a way of dealing with the personal relationships that have become more emotionally charged than in the traditional firm. These activities are not always instrumental or ways of dealing with specific problems. In the therapeutic company as in therapeutic culture, therapeutic activities are an end in itself. They are just what you do.

Appraisal

Some proponents of appraisal see it as all about self development and management while others see it as all about performance management and targets. Others argue that the two are not incompatible. There are many books for employees on 'How to get the most out of your appraisal' and guides for managers about how to do it. Training to do appraisal and be appraised is now a standard requirement in schools, colleges, universities and many organisations. Whether appraisal is of any real value to business, given the time it takes, is doubtful and one study by the OECD suggested that appraisal like most individual performance-related pay initiatives is under researched and has clear risks (OECD 2003: 7). However, appraisal, and the language used in appraisal show it to be the most therapeutic of workplace activities. This therapeutic focus can exist alongside the instrumental setting of performance targets in the way that, as we showed in Chapters 4 and 5, meeting teaching 'competencies' and 'standards' can co-exist with humanistic teacher training, and where disciplinary forms of assessment are overlaid with humanist principles.

Whether appraisal is the much-vaunted '360-degree' approach that involves all the work force and even customers (students), self appraisal or traditional annual appraisal by a line manager, there will always be a focus on attitudes and personal

From therapeutic staff development to surveillance and monitoring

On a course to train staff in a local authority about customer care, participants had to sit in a circle, share their frustrations about customer care and then brainstorm ways they could improve it. Problems or negative points were only permitted if they were within the remit of workers and not the fault of the local authority and were allowed only if participants could offer a solution.

At the end, each person had to fill in a carbon duplicate sheet with 3 pledges of 'what I will do to improve customer care', keeping one sheet for themselves and giving one to the organiser from HR. After reading them out in turn, the organiser said cheerfully that everyone would receive individual weekly emails to ask them how their pledges were going!

'issues'. In one popular self-assessment sheet for use in appraisal systems, we found a list and a suggestion that you scored yourself out of ten for 'striving for personal development', 'understanding the way people feel', 'developing positive relationships', 'managing stress and conflict', 'contributing positively', 'having compassion and care for others' and so on (www.business.balls.com).

Even if they are not explicitly assessed, these emotional aspects of appraisal are part of the 'hidden appraisal'. More often than not, appraisals, frequently renamed as 'personal development reviews', are approached in friendly, and if not warm, at least emotionally engaged ways: appraisers often use high levels of emotional labour! As Mullan argued, the lines are blurred and we forget we are at work. Some managers adopt the role of amateur therapist and ask about whether the 'appraisee' is 'feeling comfortable' and 'unthreatened' or will ask, at the end 'How did that feel from your point of view?' A recent performance development review for a colleague working in a university opened with 'So, how has being here felt for you since you started with us?' These emotional openers and closures invite people immediately to shift from what they have done and achieved, to how relationships and activities have felt for them personally and emotionally.

Of course, meeting your manager-therapist is something you cannot opt out of doing, even if you are old-fashioned enough to dislike a hierarchy at work and do not want managers intruding into internal matters or your personal thoughts and feelings. Instead, contemporary appraisal requires a drama or role play of friendship and is both a response to the blurring of the line between work and private life and a practice that encourages it.

Open doors

The offer of 'open door' time by managers to whom you can talk to about anything that concerns you in confidence is another piece of therapeutic practice. Sometimes almost a religious 'confessional', these sessions can be seen as 'troubleshooting' or part of an 'early warning system' that allows managers to predict stresses and tensions, failure and mismanagement as well as to identify 'excellence' and 'good practice'. One newly appointed manager in a company invited all employees to come and talk about their experience and feelings about the business. Many managers offer short slots of time each week and staff make appointments.

The idea of managing director-as-therapist might easily be thought of as a step too far but the loss of a sense of being at work, particularly in the public sector, means that workers avail themselves of these opportunities and talk to senior staff about work and their private lives. While these activities are voluntary, we feel decorum is needed. There is, however, a sense in which all such activities are compulsory. If people do not avail themselves of such facilities, the therapeutic orthodoxy that they must be 'in denial' about their problems and difficulties comes into play. A consequence of these therapeutic processes of developments and monitoring is that, by the time restructuring and sackings come into play, we are all 'on the wrong foot'. In all too many restructurings, even where compulsory redundancies are involved, the charge is that people have not been consulted and that the management 'don't care about people or their feelings'.

Exit interviews

The 'debriefing' or 'exit interview' has a military origin. Leaving a powerful organisation, like the army, often left people feeling vulnerable and it was therefore felt that they needed debriefing so they could adapt to civilian life. Now the military assumption is that people are simply vulnerable and need debriefing. There is much debate about whether debriefing works, particularly when it is a one-off event. There is also a view that traumatic events require counselling and although it is now routine for counsellors to be brought into schools and workplaces when local traumatic incidents happen, the evidence does not support this view (Rose *et al.* 2003; Wessely 2005, 2007).

Yet, just as there is no evidence for the underlying assumptions and effects of the therapeutic interventions in schools, discussed in earlier chapters, there is no evidence here. But lack of evidence is utterly irrelevant to the inexorable rise of therapeutic interventions. This means that pointing out whether something works or does not, as Simon Wessely does, has little impact. The same problem applies to research that shows that concern with 'self-esteem' or 'happiness' has no evidence-base. As we have shown throughout the book, therapeutic activities arise from a broader therapeutic turn in culture and, in turn, policy makers have appropriated it. Evidence is not a concern for those who promote them.

The therapeutic company did not therefore arise out of any research base but from politics. The clearest example of this is that it was the Conservative government of the 1980s that introduced counselling for those about to be thrown out of work (Furedi 2004a: 92–5). To suggest that workers need counselling rather than leaving them alone to talk to friends, workmates, or the union, is premised on the assumption of their vulnerability. This replacement for normal civic life, organised by the state, further undermines normal social life by making a 'traumatic' experience the business of the employer. In many ways this government-sponsored intervention was the first step in the creation of the therapeutic company.

Less than 30 years after redundancy counselling was introduced, the ending of a job, whether through redundancy or by choice, is treated as a 'traumatic' event that needs debriefing. These sessions do more harm than good. It is not that they are uncomfortable or painful: they may or may not be. Rather, the serious problem is that such sessions, and the therapeutic orthodoxies that lie behind them, undermine the normal practice of talking with friends and workmates.

One university recently went to great lengths to ensure that a restructuring and redundancy situation was handled in an informal unthreatening way. This is possibly the first ever 'therapeutic sacking'. The staff involved were clearly confused by what was happening to them and a harsh redundancy situation might have been easier to cope with. They might have been able to oppose it but instead they had their hands held until their P45s arrived. But the process was not for them. The real beneficiaries of the therapeutic sacking are management. The therapeutic supportive process helps them feel better about themselves. The company needs these processes because it is composed of diminished workers and diminished managers who can no longer act out their traditional roles. In another example of a voluntary redundancy situation, management worked hard at 'consultation' and expressed a desire to ensure that their workers were 'respected in the process' and that they 'felt very comfortable' with their actions. In particular, they wanted to guard against 'negative effects' in case workers felt that they were chosen for redundancy because they were 'weak' or 'couldn't cope'. The therapeutic company now offers therapeutic sacking, but it is management that benefit.

Implications: the vulnerable worker

The TUC in 2007 carried the slogan 'Supporting Britain's vulnerable workers'. For us, that carried a much wider and more significant meaning than the TUC's concern with the 'millions of workers in 'unsafe, low paid, insecure employment' (www.vulnerableworkers.org.uk). Instead, just as 'vunerable' is applied increasingly to more and more students in further education, the slogan can apply to all workers. Unions are at the forefront in promoting counselling initiatives, help lines and reports that show how ever rising numbers of workers are stressed or bullied at work. All workers are vulnerable. This is how they see themselves and this is how the unions present their members to employers and to the public.

'Collective vulnerability' is partly a response to the collapse of the labour movement and workers starting to see their problems, and the solutions to them, as personal problems. Trade unions have responded to this perception by 'professionalising' their services, which means adopting support mechanisms to deal with increasing 'case work' that are largely therapeutic. And, of course, management agree. No managers defend bullying or encourage stressful work. They actively support counselling and other support services.

For what is actually a relatively short period, the therapeutic company seems not only to be a reality but to be successful. Does it have a future? There are three possible 'future scenarios' that tempt us.

The first is that the profit-driven exploitative nature of capitalism will create a period of crisis in which workers will be forced off the therapy couch into action. Second, it is very tempting for us to conclude that this situation will continue because, if stress and bullying, rather than capitalism, are the new problems for workers, then counselling not communism is the solution. Following this argument, the therapy couch is here to stay. However, the argument of this chapter suggests a different scenario.

The third scenario takes us outside the therapeutic workplace. We have argued that the therapeutic company comes into being because of the collapse of meaningful relationships and social structures outside work and the consequent over-emphasis on work and workplace relationships in people's lives. These fractured, damaged and diminished relationships and structures in wider society are the basis on which workplace therapy is built. Our belief is that a wider understanding and rejection of the therapeutic culture outside the world of work is the only way to stop work filling up with personal needs and problems that engender therapeutic responses.

Conclusion

Reflecting on his studies of workers in the new capitalism over almost 40 years, Richard Sennett concludes that 'What they need is mental and emotional anchor; they need values which assess whether changes whether changes in work, privilege, and power are worthwhile. They need, in short, a culture' (2006: 183). We argue that they have that culture already. It is provided by the therapeutic workplace and its therapeutic culture will undermine any proposals to reconstruct the dignity of work and workers.

Workers will not spontaneously arise from the therapy couch that they, together with their unions and managers, have created. Unless there is a challenge to the construction of the idea of human beings as vulnerable and diminished that is being strengthened through therapeutic education, it will be impossible for workers to confront and resist the therapeutic workplace.

That is why we have concentrated in earlier chapters on the rise of therapeutic education through school, college and on to university. We chose to explore therapeutic activities in the workplace to show that personal counselling and educational and training activities now extend across more and more workplaces and that the educationalising of work goes far beyond what is traditionally thought of as 'education'. The result is the creation and maintenance of a diminished rather than a skilled and confident worker. The rise of the therapeutic company shows that there is nothing special about the workplace in therapy culture. It is no longer the place where the exploitative conditions of capitalism will cause workers to resist their exploiters. It is not the class struggle but the struggle to resist therapeutic education in the classroom that will stop the reproduction of the diminished human being.

Chapter 7

Explaining the emotional state

Introduction

The rise of therapeutic education reflects a political and social orthodoxy about how to deal with what is variously seen as 'emotional vulnerability', 'low self-esteem', and a 'fragile sense of self or identity'. This orthodoxy both creates and exaggerates popular concerns and, in turn, it legitimises and reinforces rapidly growing political and professional interest in the emotional well-being of whole communities and groups of pupils and students at all levels of the education system. We have argued that therapeutic education prepares workers for the therapeutic workplace.

In the last six chapters, we have shown that diverse perspectives promote therapeutic education. Some supporters welcome a focus on emotional dimensions of pupils' and students' lives and their learning experiences as a relief from an over-cognitive and demotivating treadmill of targets and tests. Some aim to erode divisions between physical, emotional and intellectual dimensions of life and learning. Others hope that emotional interventions will counter bullying, mental health problems, behavioural problems and disaffection, and encourage inclusion, diversity, tolerance and empathy as part of citizenship. Some believe that attention to emotional well-being and emotional literacy creates a 'better' society. There are instrumental hopes that therapeutic education will raise attainment and encourage better 'engagement' in formal education and lifelong learning. Others see emotional literacy and well-being as outcomes that equip people for the labour market or as essential 'soft' personal and social outcomes.

Support from these very different perspectives has led to a wholesale adoption of therapeutic concepts, assumptions and practices across the education system and in the workplace. Self-awareness, self-esteem, emotional literacy and emotional well-being are, simultaneously, pre-conditions for learning and outcomes of participating in it. Such outcomes are increasingly regarded as the most important that the education system can produce: profound disillusionment with traditional subject disciplines runs in parallel with growing fears of undisciplined, emotionally dysfunctional children and young people and concerns about social problems.

This book is the first analysis of therapeutic education, highlighting its myriad manifestations and sources of support. Yet, such analysis on its own does not explain why therapeutic education and its underpinning assumptions, claims and practices have become so prominent in culture and policy. Something much more significant is going on. This chapter aims to show that we are living at a time when ideas about what it means to be human, and political responses to those ideas, are no longer defined ideologically or politically but culturally. The response by British policy makers to popular orthodoxies about emotional vulnerability, expressed through the rapid rise of therapeutic education since 1997, is a stark illustration of the way in which the political adapts itself to the cultural.

Of course, the processes and stages through which political ideas adapt to popular concerns are not explicit, linear or straightforward. Nor do they easily map across to changes in material or structural conditions. We argue that therapeutic education is the latest, most overt phase of the appropriation by policy makers of cultural preoccupation with therapy. This has been evolving over the past 40 years and is the latest phase in a series of political attempts to make the education system produce instrumental processes and outcomes integral to the social engineering of 'better' citizens.

In this chapter, we locate our arguments in Anglo-American philosophical, cultural and sociological analysis of the shift from an 'aesthetic' to a 'therapy culture'. We argue that it is impossible to over-estimate the epochal nature of this shift, its significance in both reflecting and shaping particular images of what it means to be human, and, therefore, its implications for educational goals and practices. We identify five distinct phases in the development of a theoretical understanding of 'therapy culture', associating each of the first four phases with a major theoretical work. In presenting them chronologically, we are trying make distinctive phases in the development of therapy culture explicit.

First, we offer a chronological survey to indicate why the shift to a therapeutic culture *is* epochal and we outline the beginning of what we see as a new, fifth phase. Second, we relate the manifestation of a therapeutic ethos in therapy culture to a pessimistic, 'diminished' image of the human subject prevalent in Anglo-American culture, psychology and politics. Third, we summarise three theories that seek to explain why a diminished human subject has evolved, and we outline implications for humanist education. Finally, we reiterate our thesis that therapeutic education is dangerous for everyone since it not merely reflects but promotes a diminished account of what it means to be human.

The evolution of the 'therapeutic' to 'therapy culture' 1966–2004

Transition: the loss of religion (1966)

Before the 1960s, the idea of 'therapy' or the 'therapeutic' was associated with the specialist ideas and practices of psychoanalysis. Sociologist Philip Rieff's *The Triumph of the Therapeutic: Uses of Faith after Freud*, published in 1966, was the first to analyse the shift from therapy as a professional specialism into wider culture and to show that a significant cultural shift in ideas about the self was underway. The main title almost says it all, but the subtitle sets it in a particular historical context. The book was both prescient and backward-looking, describing an epochal moment that Rieff calls 'the closing time of the ascetic culture ...' (Rieff [1966] 1987: 244).

Rieff attempted to produce a new theory of a culture that was well in advance of its time, admitting that he presented a 'tentative prospect of the revolution' he discerned ([1966] 1987: 242). It was to be over 40 years before the therapeutic culture he foresaw was at its zenith but his recognition of the 'closing time' of previous culture remains seminal because he analysed the epochal nature of a nascent 'therapeutic' culture and its creation of a new type of 'psychological' or 'therapeutic' personality.

In order to understand the new 'psychological' or 'therapeutic' person, Rieff offers a complex and very detailed analysis of Freud's influence on culture and ideas about the nature of humanity. Rieff argued that Freud used analysis to free people from their enslavement to the demands of an external, self-denying morality and to reconcile themselves to a tension between that and their self interest. The self-renunciatory character of a cultural personality from earlier epochs was replaced by one whose self interest dominated and who sought 'self-realisation' rather than external goals. Rieff shows Freud's contempt for communal values by reminding us of how, in therapeutic culture, each sees the other as 'trash' – a term Freud uses to summarise his 'general opinion of people' ([1966] 1987: 61).

Rieff's work was a sociological wake-up call in advance of its time, but it is essentially a statement of loss, of the ending of a certain type of moral personality where people 'in cultures past ... sacrificed themselves to heroic and cruel deceptions and suffered for glories' ([1966] 1987: 22). He characterises contemporary morality as involving little renunciation in the old religious and moral sense: 'Men already feel freer to live their lives with a minimum of pretence to anything more grand than sweetening the time' ([1966] 1987: 22). The affluence of the postwar boom provides the material context for this but the crucial point here is that the main focus is on a *cultural* shift ([1966] 1987: 27; 253).

In contrast to his analysis of the 'therapeutic', Rieff provides a historical overview of the pre-therapeutic American self:

> Americans no longer model themselves after the Christians or the Greeks. Nor are they such economic men as Europeans believe them to be. The political man of the Greeks, the religious man of the Hebrews and Christians, the enlightened economic man of eighteenth-century Europe (the original of that mythical present-day character, the 'good European'), has been superseded by a new model for the conduct of life. Psychological man is, I suggest, more native to American culture than the Puritan sources of that culture would indicate.

The therapeutic as an American type had therefore 'outgrown his immediate ancestor ...' ([1966] 1987: 58). The 'therapeutic' as a personality type, looks inward rather than outward and while the therapeutic has to engage in the world, he or she is conscious that there are no ethical heights to scale. The therapeutic is tolerant but indifferent to the Other so that external engagement or attachment is instrumental to the internal therapeutic effort: 'the ascetic ideal, shorn of any informing goal or principle; thus divested of the need for compulsive attachments, the ascetic becomes the therapeutic' ([1966] 1987: 60).

This survey of personality types confirms a shift; any lingering doubt is because of the nature of the shift. Since previous personalities were ascetic, we would expect an ascetic or violent shift to end an epoch: according to Rieff this is a mistake because '… what apocalypse has ever been so kindly?'([1966] 1987: 27). It is its kindliness that masks that the epochal nature of the shift, and it hard to see though the illusion:

> 'In its reasonableness, the triumph of the therapeutic cannot be viewed simply as a break with the established order of moral demand, but rather as a profound effort to end the tyranny of primary group moral passion (operating first through the family) as the inner dynamic of social order.
>
> ([1966] 1987: 243)

So what was distinctive about the therapeutic culture that Rieff foresaw? It was clearly anti-political in rejecting any communal striving for goals other than those concerned with the 'self'. This is unique enough. Rieff makes the point that even the traditional injunction to 'know yourself' was not about becoming inward-looking, never mind self-obsessed, but to find out what you really wanted to achieve in the wider world.

Rieff says little about the 'self' since he is describing a new culture in which the struggle to achieve communal ends, including the revolutionary will to change society, was disappearing. Instead, there were no longer any external ends or goals to strive for and human 'commitment was to the therapeutic effort itself' ([1966] 1987: 261). The new therapeutic personality lacked commitment to any form of morality and this lack of commitment to ends defined the epochal nature of the shift to a therapeutic culture:

> That a sense of well-being has become the end, rather than a by-product of striving after some superior communal end, announces a fundamental change of focus in the entire cast of our culture-towards a human condition about which there will be nothing further to say in terms of the old style of despair and hope.
>
> ([1966] 1987: 261)

Consolidation: the lonely self (1979)

Rieff acknowledged that his work may seem like it contained 'parodies of an apocalypse' ([1966] 1987: 27) but the apocalyptic note is salutary. In any case, Rieff could hardly envisage how the pre-occupation with the 'self' that he discerned was the first step on a road that would allow the political construction of the diminished self in a shift from 'the therapeutic' to 'therapy culture' over the next 40 years.

Within 15 years, and again relating changes in psychoanalytical thinking to broader shifts in American culture, Christopher Lasch described the individual personality type that that had developed in therapeutic America. As old certainties, sources of support and self-help declined, a narcissistic culture, described in *The Culture of Narcissism* in 1979, is made up of isolated individuals seeking essentially ephemeral moments of satisfaction and well-being:

> The contemporary climate is therapeutic, not religious. People today hunger not for personal salvation, let alone for the restoration of an earlier golden age, but for the feeling, the momentary illusion, of personal well-being, health, and psychic security.
>
> (Lasch [1979] 1991: 7)

Lasch analysed the first impact of a broader cultural turn towards the therapeutic on the practices and assumptions of individual psychology. In many ways it followed Rieff's analysis, but the individualism he described was not the individualism of the past: 'For the narcissist, the world is a mirror, whereas the rugged individualist saw it as an empty wilderness to be shaped to his own design' ([1979] 1991: 10).

Therapy was therefore moving from specialist study and practices into mainstream thinking, not least because therapists began to exert more influence on increasing numbers of individuals: 'therapists, not priests or popular preachers of self-help or models of success like captains of industry, become [the individual's] principal allies in the struggle for composure; he turns to them in the hope of achieving the modern equivalent of salvation, "mental health"'' ([1979] 1991: 13). By 1979, Lasch identified that the previous 25 years had seen a huge rise in 'borderline' patients with 'diffuse dissatisfactions ... subtly experienced yet pervasive feelings of emptiness and depression ... violent oscillations of self-esteem ... a general inability to get along' ([1979] 1991: 37).

Of course, it is possible to dismiss the characteristics of this period as a reflection of the self-obsession of affluent, middle-class people with too much time and affluence, as well as a sign that traditional forms of support and faith had declined. For our purposes, it was Lasch who began to identify the diminished expectations and obsession with the self, the 'self-absorption [that] defines the moral climate of contemporary society' ([1979] 1991: 25). Yet, as he noted, even this is unsatisfying and staring at the void within becomes so all consuming that it creates a desire to escape self-awareness.

Crucially, Lasch identified another cultural change that has become more and more significant, namely the 'emergence of a therapeutic ideology that upholds a normative schedule of psychosocial development and thus gives further encouragement to anxious self-scrutiny' ([1979] 1991: 48). He identified the beginning of the tension, so strong in current manifestations of popular therapy, between 'the ideology of personal growth, superficially optimistic [but which] radiates profound despair and resignation' ([1979] 1991: 51).

Uncertainty: the development of a therapeutic politics (1992)

Universal individual self-absorption does appear to replace the loss of religion but every culture has the possibility within it of political exploitation and, as Lasch observed in a later study, 'It did not take people long to see that a therapeutic point of view could be put to social and political uses' (Lasch 1995: 218).

In the 1990s, and specifically from the Democratic Party Convention of 1992, politicians latched on to the therapeutic personality of their constituency and began spontaneously to incorporate it into their political approach. The convention itself was compared by many with 'group therapy', and one *New York Times* article carried the title 'I'm in therapy, you're in therapy: a much-analyzed candidate offers a twelve-step plan to Democrats anonymous' (Nolan 1998 276). Talks after his election would soon parody Bill 'I'm in pain' Clinton. The satire was apposite since Clinton was a genuine master of therapeutic dialogue and thinking: in the 1992 campaign, for example, he told AIDS activists 'I feel your pain, I feel your pain … I understand you're hurting, but you won't stop hurting by trying to hurt other people' (Nolan 1998: 236). Clinton was the most famous expert in the discourse but the underlying therapeutic vocabulary and assumptions became ubiquitous.

It was this political exploitation of therapeutic culture that led us, and others, including James Nolan and Frank Furedi, whose work we discuss below, to talk of a 'therapeutic ethos' dominating political life. Analysis of how the American state promoted a therapeutic ethos is the subject of James L. Nolan's *The Therapeutic Sate: Justifying Government at Century's End* (1998). His central question was whether the therapeutic cultural ethos had '… begun to institutionalise itself into the various functions of the political order?' (Nolan: 1998: 1).

We drew on Nolan's work in the preface to define a therapeutic ethos as comprising the extension of activities such as counselling, psychoanalysis and psychology into more areas of social activity, policy and professional practice, but, crucially, as offering a particular way of thinking about ourselves and others. The exponential growth of such activities is relatively easy to chart, evident in the huge rise of therapeutic interventions in Britain and America: from the thousands of counsellors on the streets of Manhattan after the bombings in 2001 to everyday counselling, there has been an exponential rise of dependence on counselling, psychotherapy and psychology to deal with aspects of life once seen as private or dealt with informally by communities, workplaces or families. Nolan observes that 'there are more therapists than librarians, firefighters or mail carriers in the United States, and twice as many therapists as dentists or pharmacists. Only police and lawyers outnumber counsellors but only by a ratio of less than two to one in both instances' (Nolan 1998: 8).

There is a parallel development in Britain. The British Association for Counselling and Psycothterapy (BACP) issued a self-congratulatory press release in 2003 announcing a 160 per cent increase in membership in 12 years, from 7,713 in 1991 to over 20,000 in 2003. It gloated that there were only 10,500 parishes and merely 11,000 practising ordinands in the Church of England, adding an insightful comment to this declaration of how the therapeutic had triumphed over the ascetic:

> 'Talking Treatment' or 'Therapy' is becoming a normal part of the British way of life. As for the therapists – what used to be an informal activity or part-time voluntary career is turning into an everyday profession.
>
> (BACP 19 February 2003)

The BACP is keen to regulate the 'talking therapies' and the fringe practitioners, while well-known psychoanalysts such as Drs Pamela Stephenson Connolly and Derek Draper, resident columnists for *Psychologies* magazine and presenters of television programmes about psychotherapy, advocate a huge expansion of trained psychotherapists in the National Health Service (see www.campaignfortherapy. co.uk). In October 2007, the government announced funding for 1,000,000 extra people to receive therapeutic treatment from the National Health Service.

Yet, while numbers of quasi-therapists are growing alongside those who are professionally qualified, overall numbers are uncertain. Hansard (6/12/06) records a request to identify counsellors in the National Health Service with the aim of regulating their activities. Although the numbers of qualified psychotherapy workers were known and had increased, from 745 in 2000 to 1,087 in 2005, more detailed figures were not available. This is also true of many areas of public sector work: for example, social workers attend training courses to learn 'therapeutic skills' without being qualified or listed as therapists.

Overall, we estimate that there are more than a quarter of a million therapeutic workers including guidance workers, mediators, personal advisers and counsellors in Britain (Heartfield 2002; Hayes 2003a). These figures do not include the burgeoning industry of teachers trained in therapeutic techniques and skills, life coaches, workplace coaches and peer mentors, all of whom are integral to therapeutic education. If we add these, the number of therapeutic workers increases dramatically. Nor is it an exaggeration to claim that almost everyone in education now has some counselling or therapeutic aspect to their work. We also showed in Chapter 1 that magazines like *Psychologies*, weekend supplements such as *The Times 'Body and Soul'* and guides for people to diagnose their own mental health encourage people to begin their own therapeutic diagnosis before seeking 'professional help'.

The extension of therapeutic interventions is therefore central to a therapeutic ethos. Yet, its real significance and power is to offer a new sensibility, a form of cultural script, a set of explanations, underlying assumptions about appropriate feelings and responses to events, and a set of associated practices and rituals, through which people make sense of themselves and others. Cultural and political preoccupation with emotion and its effects on all aspects of life is expressed through the subtle ways in which therapeutic language, symbols and processes have moved into everyday thinking. As we have shown in Chapter 1 and in subsequent examples of therapeutic education, the language and images of a therapeutic ethos permeate our consciousness and interpretations of behaviour, inside and outside educational settings.

In his account of a therapeutic ethos in American politics and culture, Nolan shows how emotion and vulnerability emerged through powerful cultural symbols such as ex- President Clinton whose appeal rested in large part on an unprecedented political ability to project empathy and to use the emotions and language of therapy. The elision of political and cultural symbols in Clinton illustrates another central theme in a therapeutic ethos, namely his appeal to the popular idea that we are all flawed because we are 'only human'. He used this to good effect in maintaining public popularity during political attempts to make him take responsibility for his affair with Monica Lewinsky (see Fevre 2002).

The ability to acknowledge the flaws and weaknesses of being only human resonates both with our everyday perception that we are 'far from perfect' and with the therapeutic orthodoxy of 'love yourself as you are'. Yet, despite its apparent tolerance, powerful and relentless cultural narratives of emotional vulnerability and dysfunction signify a shift from responsible agency and leads to negative images of people at a deeper cultural level. Nolan relates Clinton's potent appeal to the rise of subtle but profound changes in American popular and political understanding of behaviour. He points to numerous indicators. For example, a huge increase in lawsuits to redress emotional and psychological damage and the pathologising of a widening range of everyday behaviours as 'illnesses', 'disorders' and 'syndromes' suggest that literally millions of Americans are dysfunctional, either mentally, emotionally or physically, and that, in turn, many physical symptoms have emotional causes. These trends are reinforced by the American Psychological Society which lists over 800 psychological syndromes that cause physical symptoms or behaviours.

Both individually and collectively, a therapeutic ethos casts people and their behaviours in pseudo-scientific terms, where past experiences and dysfunctional traits explain a growing number of behaviours, from the most extreme or rare to the most commonplace and banal. American trends signify a profound change in cultural understanding of behaviours and emotions, displacing responsibility for behaviour to merely understanding its roots and psychological causes. As the previous chapters have shown, the incursion of cultural accounts of vulnerability into educational contexts creates more informal and formal assessments of emotional causes and effects where an empathetic understanding of possible sources for emotional and social problems is never far from judgemental labels to justify particular interventions.

A therapeutic ethos therefore emerges from cultural images about the sorry state of human emotions and the inexorable rise of therapeutic interventions initiated by individuals and offered by state agencies. This has led to a professionalising of private and individual life that would have been unthinkable only ten years ago, not only through formal therapeutic interventions but also in the examples from popular culture that we used at the beginning of the book.

Nolan's work shows in detail that a therapeutic ethos was indeed becoming prevalent in all American state institutions throughout the 1990s but, recognising the reciprocal impact this would have on culture, he concluded that it was too early to identify what these effects might be. The processes Nolan identified in American politics were soon to transfer to British politics in an accelerated form. The specific form of the acceleration is the explicit adoption by New Labour of the politics of the 'third way'.

The climax of therapy culture: a new system of meaning (2004)

Despite its potency, though, a therapeutic ethos cannot account for the broader cultural interest in emotions and vulnerability outlined above. By the time that the British sociologist Frank Furedi described the full flowering of the therapeutic culture in the first comprehensive review of developments in Britain and America, in *Therapy Culture: Cultivating Vulnerability in an Uncertain Age*, published in 2004, the political promotion of a therapeutic ethos was at its zenith. In his account of the rise of therapeutic culture, mainly in the UK but also in America, Furedi argues that what distinguishes today's therapeutic turn from previous therapeutic regimes is that it is not confined to a distinct, functionally specific role.

Instead, in contrast to past therapeutic regimes, the contemporary manifestation of a therapeutic ethos has merged with wider cultural institutions and has an impact on all institutions of society. Therapy culture is a key influence on people's perception of their ability to cope with the problems of life, and is shaped, in turn, by the account their culture offers of what it means to be human and about the nature of human potential (Furedi 2004). According to both Furedi and Lasch, individuals make sense of their experience through reflection on their individual circumstances and in line with the expectations transmitted through prevailing cultural norms. As Lasch argued 'Every society reproduces its culture – its norms, its underlying assumptions, its modes of organising experience – in the individual, in the form of personality' ([1979] 1991: 34).

In this way, therapy has become a cultural phenomenon – a system of meaning – that informs life:

> a culture becomes therapeutic when this form of thinking expands from informing the role between the individual and therapist to shaping public perceptions about a range of issues. At that point, it ceases to be a clinical technique and becomes an instrument for the management of subjectivity.
>
> (Furedi 2004: 413)

As we have argued throughout the book, education and work are key sites for this reproduction and its management of subjectivity. Furedi's description of the fully-fledged therapeutic individual as 'the diminished self' was a crucial contribution to understanding therapy in politics as a cultural phenomenon, revealing not the success of the adoption of the therapeutic ethos but its futility.

The evolution of a therapeutic culture in America took place over a longer period than here. The parallel process in Britain was slower but accelerated rapidly under the New Labour government led by Tony Blair between 1997–2007. We showed in Chapter 1 that Blair's government saw emotional vulnerability as both a cause and outcome of social deprivation, where the state's role is to respond to people's emotional state. The popular and cultural conditions were also clearly evident but our contention is that the accelerated take up of the therapeutic ethos in Britain was primarily a result of the state of British politics.

The most symbolic moment was on 31 August 1997, only a few months after New Labour's landslide election victory, when Princess Diana died in a road accident in Paris and became, within a few days, the spiritual embodiment of victim culture and a new era of emotionalism. This new era was described by one journalist as a new 'AD' or 'After Diana', characterised not by political correctness (PC) but by an oppressive 'emotional correctness' (EC) (Hume 1998). Politicians exploited the urge to be EC in order to make an emotional connection with people. While hardly as sophisticated as Clinton's approach, Blair tapped into a therapeutic ethos with his declaration that Diana was 'the people's princess' and her appeal to victim status was crucial to her popularity. Although the media encouraged post-Diana emotionalism, it could not have affected so many without particular social cultural and political conditions in which it could take root.

Our analysis of the political background to the accelerated rise of therapy culture in Britain is set in the context of policy making in the latter half of the twentieth century and the first few years of the new century. The best way of understanding how a therapeutic ethos come to dominate contemporary politics is to remember the popular description of New Labour politics in Britain and, to some extent, that politics of the American Democratic Party under Clinton, as the politics of the 'third way' and to ask the simple question: if this is the period of 'third way' politics, what were the 'second' and 'first' ways? (for a fuller discussion see Blair 1997; Giddens 1998; Hayes 2003a).

The 'first way' from postwar reconstruction until the mid-1970s was a period of relative political consensus about the 'welfare state'. This period was unique because the postwar boom, the most dramatic expansion of capitalist production, allowed, among many other developments in welfare and public provision, the expansion of education even if this never quite amounted to a 'golden age'. This boom was over by 1972, marked by oil crises and a huge increase in unemployment. For educationalists, the key date marking the end of the 'first way' is 18 October 1976, when Prime Minister Callaghan's Ruskin College speech launched his 'great debate' about education that culminated in giving business a greater say in the content and process of education. This began the end of consensus, starting a process of turning the education system into the producer of social, personal and economic outcomes.

In a sense, the 'second way' of Conservative governments from 1989 to 1997 began then. It set out to destroy what the Conservatives saw as 'socialism', namely trade unions and communities developed through the period of welfare consensus. However, Thatcherism left nothing in their place, only 'individuals and their families' and illusory 'market mechanisms' imposed on public sector institutions. Under the Thatcher government, state-sponsored therapy was introduced on a large scale through counselling and associated teaching interventions for the unemployed in further education colleges and employment training schemes, discussed in Chapters 4 and 6.

And so to the 'third way', in which no return to the welfare consensus seems possible, and the free rein of market forces is equally unacceptable. Often represented as a period in which creativity could be unleashed alongside the promise of experimentation with new ideas, the reality is the opposite. The new freedom is not positive but leads, instead, to uncertainty and constant change.

'Third way' policy making becomes uncertain because policies are not aimed at any stable or traditional communities since the destructive period of the 'second way' erased traditional communities, including strong professions with links to politicians and policy makers. In these circumstances, the third way is characterised by the artificiality and *fragility* of all policies and practices.

This explains the phenomenon of 'policy churn', namely the production of policy after policy. In education, Alan Smithers explains this as a consequence of the New Labour government's desperation to be 'seen to be doing good things', to the extent that 'Everyday without a new education headline was regarded as a day wasted ...'. Smithers asked: 'What are we to make of all this activity? Has the Blair government really had 'a big picture', with the many initiatives necessitated by numerous faults in the system? Or has it tended to dissipate its political capital by failing to focus sufficiently on the main issues, rushing off in all directions?' (Smithers 2001: 425). He inclines to the latter suggestion.

In contrast, we argue that this is not directionless behaviour but a necessary artificiality in 'third way' politics. The demise of traditional communities and politics and the need to establish a link with a society made up of isolated individuals produces policy churn. It explains not only why policies are constantly produced but also why they are quickly abandoned as they fail to engage with anyone, particularly professionals.

We argue that such fragile policy making is an expression of a political vacuum into which aspects of the therapeutic culture gains purchase. The political climate of the 'third way' is fundamentally about the uncertainties of a political elite anxious about the emotional state of ordinary people. Lacking traditional organisations that represent, and also discipline people, including trades unions, the political elite can only, in an entirely spontaneous way, encourage low horizons and low expectations. To gain reassurance for themselves about their own precarious role, they promote ideas and policies of self-limitation and self-regulation. This would, however, be impossible outside a culture in which people saw themselves as vulnerable.

Governments always have to work hard for their legitimacy, and to find new ways to secure a commitment to goals of public policy amongst practitioners and the public. Policy makers are all too aware of growing scepticism about the value of their ideas, about the effectiveness of public spending on education and the roles of local and central government. In the political period of the 'third way' the situation is worse than ever and policy making constantly faces the problem of public 'disconnection'. For example, the MORI Foundation has been working with the Number 10 Policy Unit and the DfES to survey the scale of this dissatisfaction and to find ways to 'engage' more effectively with the public. As we showed in Chapter 3, personalised public services', and their educational version 'personalised learning', are one such outcome. As Nolan and Furedi both show, by slowly coming to adopt a therapeutic ethos, state agencies can reinvent themselves in more relevant ways to the prevailing tone and concerns of the media, and cultural debates.

In this fragile policy making world, the therapeutic turn becomes a general, if spontaneous tendency. A therapeutic ethos is easily established since there is no alternative to the dominant culture. James Woudhuysen has described New Labour politics as 'T2V: therapy to victims' (Woudhuysen 2002). Clever as this labelling is, its clarity carries a danger because the politics are not worked out in such a structured, complete and coherent form. Instead, as we have argued, they are a fragile response to a political vacuum. This means that the rise of therapeutic education is not a strategy or a conspiracy by the state to control people. Nor, on the other hand, is it naïve or accidental. We have tried to show, instead, that education is the key site for working out a new, diminished concept of what it is to be a person to be worked out.

Beyond therapy to victims: coaching happiness and well-being (2007)

In a section on 'final thoughts' at the end of his book, Furedi notes that: 'The institutionalisation of therapeutics endows it with a potentially coercive dimension' (2004: 197). The numerous examples of therapeutic interventions and assumptions that he charted through different areas of social policy contained a strong element of 'we'll help you whether you like it or not'. He noted too that therapy culture reflected a shift towards a view by governments under New Labour that the state needed to 'confer' esteem on a fragile public through depictions of people as marginalised, excluded and vulnerable, something we also discussed in Chapter 1. Yet, as Furedi argues, a rhetoric of encouraging civic engagement is belied by the ways in which calls for recognition and affirmation are abstracted from the social and cultural contexts that generate people's *own* aspirations for recognition. The need for recognition in this cultural context means that people come to seek recognition as victims. There is even a website where people can register as victims (www.victims.org.uk and www.victimsvoice.co.uk). Yet voluntary self-recognition and acknowledgement of victim status is increasingly unsatisfactory, simply because an anxious political class still finds it leaves too much to chance and to the will of individuals.

Further signs of authoritarian tendencies lie beneath therapeutic advocacy of an empathetic, 'non-didactic' approach based on 'mutual exploration' and 'problem solving' and the idea that 'we are all vulnerable'. In the crudest instances, contempt for people is blatant. For example, Richard Sennett argues that empathy from public sector workers for their clients often becomes condescending and then contemptuous. Far from being the basis for the sort of respect that enables professionals to help people build genuine skills and knowledge as ways out of deprivation, he argues that expectations of professional empathy and disclosure in order to bond with clients offer affirmation and esteem but undermine respect and belief in capacity for agency (Sennett 2003). And, as Helen Colley has shown, pity, contempt and strong judgements often accompany the empowering ideals of schemes to mentor disaffected young people (Colley 2003a). Therapeutic interventions such as parenting classes, anger management classes and counselling are also compulsory conditions in many cases for welfare benefits or court sentencing and therefore belie an ethos of voluntary participation (cf. Nolan 1998).

We agree that the institutionalisation of a therapeutic ethos has always had a distinctly authoritarian aspect. Yet, while overt authoritarianism is relatively easy to discern, its subtle manifestations are difficult to trace without an understanding of therapy culture. We therefore argue that in the few years since Furedi studied the rise of therapy culture, current developments are moving rapidly beyond it. This might seem an invalid argument because, while therapy was always potentially coercive, it still focused on a process which left open the potential for the opposite, for someone to reject being taught to feel and respond in certain 'appropriate' or 'effective' ways. Adoption of humanistic and life enhancing methods rooted in positive images of the self-actualising human subject with potential for agency, both individually and collectively, leaves open a possibility for agency that rejects a therapeutic diagnosis and prognosis.

In what we see as the start of a new, fifth phase, the humanist possibility that therapeutic processes have uncertain outcomes can be dealt with through two approaches that we have demonstrated in earlier chapters. First, by changing humanistic techniques of therapeutic education and, second, by introducing a new positive content to counter manifestations of a therapeutic ethos that aimed to address vulnerability and perceived emotional dysfunction or illiteracy.

The first change replaces humanistic principles and practices with the more directive technique of 'coaching' the emotions, evident in some of the examples we described in primary schools. Coaching is rapidly becoming a popular subject across the educational system, through peer mentoring in schools, universities and workplaces, and in induction courses, and particularly in management and leadership training. For example, there is a British Educational Research Association (BERA) Special Interest Group on mentoring and coaching and coaching and mentoring are promoted by professional bodies for teachers as a powerful form of professional development.

We suggest that coaching emerges because therapeutic process and techniques leave opportunities for people to choose independently and do not aim to foster a particular emotional response. The 'right' emotional response (or in current emotional well-being and literacy orthodoxy) an 'appropriate' or 'effective' response, is unpredictable: individuals faced with crude forms of coercion can reject therapeutic authority, while less coercive approaches cannot guarantee that individuals' emotional response will be the right one.

The second approach links to the first, and is what Layard calls the 'new science' of 'happiness' that draws academic credibility from the rapidly growing discipline of 'positive psychology'. Happiness teaching initiatives, courses and articles in the media have sprung up since we first started to write this book but in less then a year there has been a significant shift towards a new content for therapeutic education and a curriculum based on happiness and well-being. As we showed in Chapter 1, this adopts overt notions of 'building emotional resilience' and making people feel 'emotionally positive' and teaching them techniques that have measurable outcomes of well-being.

While, as Furedi argued, building a happier society was always a traditional therapeutic goal, this was overtaken by a focus on victimhood in a response to cultural images of the diminished self. In the shift to this focus, therapy culture also constructed the diminished self. Yet, in a curious inversion, the goal of building a 'happy society' now looks set to be imposed. This raises the distinct possibility that therapeutic education as we have depicted it throughout this book will be replaced, not merely by hoping that emotionally-based interventions will foster well-being, but by coercing people's behaviour through coaching them in the means to be happy.

This is too new a subject to analyse in detail here and we introduce it as a thesis that has emerged for us through the process of writing this book. Yet, even at this early stage of what we see as a new phase in therapy culture, it is clear that there is a paradox in 'coaching' people to be 'happy'. Happiness' is a goal seemingly shared by all, and not merely the vulnerable. It may, therefore, seem to offer a more positive content to education than remedial work with diminished selves, even if this remedial work has an inclusive goal to destigmatise mental illness or emotional 'unwellness'. Happiness, like therapeutic goals for the diminished self, such as getting in touch with your emotional side, building self-esteem and confidence, are the by-products of striving for other things. Once this positive by-product becomes a central focus for a coercive education, the outcome will be much more uncertain, for although it can only foster more absorption with the self, the cry 'Why am I not happy?' will have an external object to blame, namely the coach.

The rise of the diminished human subject

Being 'only human'

Embedded within the evolution of a therapeutic ethos over the past 40 years are three transitions in views of the self and of what it means to be human: the first, shown in the shift to the 'therapeutic' discussed by Rieff and Lasch, is from the repressed, adaptive self of Freudian psychoanalysis to the espoused optimism of the self-actualising, self-aware and potentially liberated self of liberal humanist therapy, epitomised by Alfred Maslow and Carl Rogers. The humanistic idea that people are potentially able to take charge of their lives, and that individual enlightenment leads to personal and social action, was at the heart of therapeutic practices, particularly through the popularisation of individual and group counselling. The second shift, noted by Nolan, is from the liberal self-actualising, narcissistic self to a more critical, corrosive view of the dysfunctional self. The third, noted by Nolan and Furedi, is towards the fragile, vulnerable, 'merely human' self that needs emotional support. As we have noted, the fourth shift is to align the vulnerable and emotionally dysfunctional self with the self that the state can make happy, emotionally well and emotionally literate.

As we have shown throughout the book, images of the self in therapeutic education show a constant tension. On one hand, are humanist notions of empowerment, authenticity and all the trappings of 'be your true self' and 'realise your dreams' embedded in popular images of therapy. On the other, are deterministic images of vulnerable, dysfunctional people who need formal support because they are trapped emotionally by their past and by current circumstances. The evolution of therapy culture shows the extent to which preoccupation with explanations of the self has moved over 40 years from the realms of specialist psychoanalysis into mainstream counselling, popular culture and now into therapeutic education.

A permanent consciousness of vulnerability

Whatever well-meaning rhetoric is used, political sponsorship of therapeutic education institutionalises a profoundly diminished account of human potential and behaviour. The research we have reviewed in this chapter shows that a diminished view of the human subject pervades Anglo-American culture and politics. It erodes the idea of humans as conscious agents who realise their potential for individual and social change through projects to transform themselves and their world and replaces it with a narrow, introspective view of what it means to be human.

A therapeutic ethos encourages an emotional form of introspective individualism that treats problems as both individual and psychological. Old forms of support such as family, lovers, friends, unions and political groups are no longer reliable sources of help in understanding or affirming one's identity (Lasch 1979; Furedi 2004). Indeed, in the popular orthodoxies of contemporary therapy, sources of external help, particularly families and lovers, are frequently regarded as the sources and causes of dysfunction and emotional difficulty.

Diminished images offer a further elision by singling out, simultaneously, the emotional vulnerability of particular groups whilst normalising similar feelings in the general population. The idea that our confident public facades belie our fragile self-esteem and emotional vulnerability promotes feelings of inclusion based on the shared belief that we are all damaged, to a greater or lesser extent, by life events. Yet, the diminished self is not merely emotionally vulnerable, insecure and fearful, or individualistic and introspective. Instead, therapeutic education encourage us all to respond first and foremost to events and experiences emotionally rather than intellectually. The three Rs of the diminished self are that it responds, regards and relates to the world, and its place in it, emotionally.

Studies of therapeutic interventions by state and other agencies through the work of British and American agencies in aid interventions, truth commissions and postwar rebuilding programmes, show how therapeutic activities are inserted into cultures that draw on very different forms of support and coping strategies. According to Vanessa Pupavac, these interventions exemplify a cultural retreat from positive individualism to a view that crises and life events lead people to manifest signs of 'post-traumatic stress'. Old humanist ideas that psychological problems and symptoms of stress or low self-esteem are exceptional cases within an otherwise normal population are therefore giving way to the view that stress and low self-esteem are normal, even universal. Such trends widen the definition of trauma, crisis and dysfunction caused through life crises, mundane personal events and horrendous social catastrophes (see Pupavac 2001, 2003).

In the light of these arguments, it is a diminished view of the self that invokes our empathy and interest in others because someone's vulnerability and damage supposedly illuminates our own. A sense of our individual uniqueness is not, therefore, based on aspirations for us to strive individually and collectively for change and achievement, and through these, affirmation. Instead, claims for recognition are increasingly made on the basis of vulnerability and fragility as part of a new identity.

Explaining the diminished human subject

In this section we summarise three explanations for the appearance of the diminished subject at the end of the twentieth century, namely ethical, philosophical and political. Each has some validity but we argue that the political is the most potent analysis.

Ethical demoralisation

The incursion of therapeutic ethos into new areas of culture and politics cannot wholly explain the rise of interest in emotion and the language of emotional subjectivity. A deeper cultural demoralisation in ideas about the nature of self and what it means to be human is evident. This argument draws on two meanings of 'de-moralisation': one is a general everyday depiction of demoralisation as a loss of morale. As Ralph Fevre notes, this is a relatively recent meaning. The other is de-moralisation as a deeper process of stripping out morality from our lives that leads to a loss of purpose in Western culture and our sense of human potential. Fevre argues that nervousness about putting debates about policy and practice onto a moral terrain is reinforced by liberal, individualist dislike of being 'preached at' or 'moralised' to. A therapeutic ethos and images of the diminished subject reinforce this because, as emotions and psychological causes of behaviour and events gain salience, notions of responsibility, guilt, right and wrong lose it (Fevre 2002).

De-moralisation undermines debates about pressing social and individual problems while demoralisation leads to a loss of political and public motivation and confidence for dealing with genuine moral dilemmas. According to Fevre, public debate is increasingly about ethics and value preferences rather than about confrontation with moral dilemmas. For him, such trends explain public interest in famous people's transgressions and emotional difficulties as a vicarious but vacuous source of moral interest. He argues that, too often, technical rationality and common sense inform moral debate when emotion, trust and faith would be better foundations. Conversely, the tendency to resort to emotional explanations when rational debate is needed, also causes de-moralisation.

Both meanings of demoralisation can be detected in calls for educators and policy makers to develop emotional well-being and to confer recognition and esteem on people deemed to be unable to call for their own. This is, in part, a sign of the way in which the left has lost its optimism that political struggle enabled people to fight for recognition rather than having it conferred on them by a benign state. De-moralistion as loss of belief in what might be possible is also implicated in avoidance of a robust analysis of the fundamental purpose of education and the prognosis for social change. A focus on people's emotional well-being, rather than their potential for individual and social agency, reflects de-moralisation and creates lower educational aspirations.

Philosophical doubts about human progress

Sometimes, we have wondered if the notion of a diminished human being is a figment of our imagination and we have often been told by our critics that it is. After all, policy documents and educators do not appear advocating the diminished self. Then along comes a best-selling book by Professor of European Thought, John Gray, and so, thankfully, we did not have to invent him to prove a point!

If anything, Gray does not even have the low horizons of a diminished sense of humanity: instead, his writings celebrate humanity's *irrelevance*. His book sets out 'to present a view of things in which humans are not central' by explicitly attacking human rationality (2002: ix). Gray declares that 'Humanists like to think they have a rational view of the world; but their core belief in progress is a superstition, further from the truth about the human animal than any of the world's religions' (xi). His argument is one of despair that advocates giving up trying to remake the world because 'most humans who have ever lived have not believed this – and a great many have had happy lives' (xiv). Essentially his message amounts to 'do not be human beings dissatisfied; be pigs satisfied'. At one point Gray makes his bestial account of humanity explicit: 'We do not speak of a time when whales or gorillas will be masters of their destinies. Why then humans? ((2002: 3)

Gray's ideas, like many pessimists who promote anti-human philosophies, abound in simple pieces of sophistry, usually about science. For example, he defines humanism as a belief in progress, observing that 'Outside of science, progress is simply a myth' (xi). The sleight of hand would be obvious outside the context in which it is made, namely a cultural crisis of confidence. Putting aside a desire to defend achievements in literature and the arts, that phrase '*outside* of science' ignores the fact that science is at the heart of every aspect of modern society and that the most significant human achievements are scientific.

According to Kenan Malik, one cause of cultural de-moralisation and demoralisation is that cultural pessimism and uncertainty reinforce doubts about human agency and the ability of humans to deal with moral problems. Gray's misanthropic diatribe is a crude but clear statement of this standpoint. In his recent writings, Malik provides an historical analysis of changing ideas about human nature and their dialectic relationship with structural and cultural trends. He illuminates how science and philosophy construct what it means to be human and how, in turn, culture and education make ideas about human nature and science meaningful to us (Institute of Ideas 2002; Malik 2001). In recent history, liberal, conservative and Marxist visions of humanism each offer different ideas about what conditions create human agency and offer different views about who is capable of such agency.

Notwithstanding fundamental differences about conditions and who has capacity for agency, all three visions were optimistic about personal development, social and scientific progress and human emancipation. Malik argues that the 'dignity of man' and our desire to determine the future are crucial to a belief in human agency, arguing that in the past, all three visions of humanism

> held to the idea of humans as conscious agents, who realise themselves only through projects to transform themselves and the worlds they inhabit. At the heart of humanism, therefore, is a belief in emancipation, the faith that mankind could achieve freedom, both from the constraints of nature and the tyranny of Man.
>
> (Malik 2001: 6)

Since discourses of humanism are culturally and historically specific, they offer different languages for understanding what it means to be human. For Malik, humanism links our inner and outer worlds and depicts humans optimistically as agents in transforming both worlds. In contrast, the rise of evolutionary psychology, postmodern philosophy and risk consciousness, together with the decline of civic engagement with politics, reveal growing disillusionment with transforming the outer world, together with a melancholy view of mind and nature in cultural and scientific arenas. Malik argues that these trends offer an increasingly narrow, introspective view of humanness and encourage the idea that attempts to dominate nature are dangerous (see also Beck 1992).

One of the strongest manifestations of a diminished view of humanity is profound disillusionment with science, exemplified by writers like Gray but also evident in popular culture and politics (see Beck 1992; Furedi 1999). Malik argues that even within science itself, views of the mind and human nature are becoming increasingly mechanistic and deterministic. For example, the rise of evolutionary psychology has promoted neo-Darwinism as a social theory, while new ideas in cognitive science, neuro-psychology and artificial intelligence encourage determinism. According to Malik, these influential trends produce a 'triumph of mechanistic explanations of human nature [which] is as much the consequence of our culture's loss of nerve as it is of scientific advance (2001: 13–14).

A profound crisis of confidence in intellectual values, in reason, science and progress, and the promotion of a diminished humanity that is essentially bestial, is therefore integral to the cultural context in which educational policies and innovations are produced. Educationalists may not have read books like Gray's but their influence is profound and profoundly pessimistic.

Political erosion of the subject

Although ethics and philosophy have contributed much to the understanding of a diminished self, they are reflections on major political change. Demoralisation many be the result of a lost sense of human agency, but that loss of belief in human agency reflects a historically specific end to any idea of the possibility of political change. Again, we can approach this by understanding the significance of the philosophical attack on the human subject. James Heartfield's aptly titled *The 'Death of the Subject' Explained* (2002) argues that the postmodern attack on the subject has two prongs. Postmodernists attack objective knowledge (the subject), but also attack the Enlightenment concept of the human subject, mankind, that can have that knowledge and use it in rational ways to advance society.

This two-fold attack undermines both the subject and object of knowledge. Attacks on science and knowledge have parallels in the attack on the *knowing subject*. For example, postmodernists and others talk not about knowledge but 'knowledges' or mere stories or narratives and subjective accounts in the form of 'discourses'. In this parallel discussion, the self becomes our 'multiple selves', or identity becomes 'multiple identities' or, worse, 'fractured' or 'fragmented' identities. Understanding one's identity, multiple or fragmented identities and learning to live with them, induce anxiety and endless introspective 'deconstruction': this encourages a therapeutic approach to education. But the deconstruction of the human or knowing subject is not a lesson from postmodernism or any other philosophy. Postmodern deconstructions of knowledge have appeal because they seem to offer a philosophy that matches a contemporary political mood.

What these deconstructionists never recognise, as some critics clearly point out, is that they express a philosophical response to a political problem, namely the collapse of the human subject that occurred as a result of the end of the collective forms of working class organisation, in the form of the labour and trade union movement, as well as of more radical projects (Callinicos 1989; Eagleton 1996). The working class, as the 'subject' or subjective factor pushing society forward, disappeared as a political force after the collapse of communism in 1989.

The demise of the political subject inevitably meant the demise of the human or knowing subject since, without that progressive force, there was little reason to want to know anything that might lead you to want to control your life when control had no purpose. Why not let some other force, even nature, dominate your life? This is a feeling that John Gray has expressed in his misanthropic account of people as animals. Heartfield tracks the political defeat of working class parties and struggles and their reflection in radical theorising that culminated in the 'death of the subject' and left the human agent, the working class powerless.

The mass democracies of the twentieth century enjoined the greater part of society to understand its own ambitions through the prism of the politics of left and right. As the political machines have been demobilised, participation of the greater mass of people in questions that shape their lives has been cut off. The effect is to set the mass of working people back to a state something like eighteenth century, when politics was largely the preserve of the upper classes. For the working classes, public life looks the modern equivalent of following court gossip and watching public hangings. Our relationship to power is largely tangential and voyeuristic, as we follow the celebrity powerful (2002: 187).

From a political perspective, then, the working class is not even constituted by atomised individuals: instead, it is made up of atomised diminished subjects. Rebuilding politics, as Heartfield says, must start with the recognition that this diminished subject is our starting point (2002: 205–6).

We argue, therefore, that it is the absence of politics that allows therapeutic culture its strongest fulfilment. This was not something that Reiff or Lash could have foreseen. It is therefore a unique historical period, barely reflected in Nolan but crucial to the analysis of academics such as Furedi, Pupavac, and ourselves. It is too crude to say that the demise of working class struggles or the collapse of communism caused the therapeutic ethos to become the focus of contemporary politics, but in the absence of any sense of alternative, the self becomes the political.

A diminished education

Our thesis that therapeutic education embeds and legitimises a diminished notion of human beings at the heart of the state's activities has serious implications for educational values and purposes. This marks a new turn in long-running conflict about what these should be. For over 2,000 years, debates about what to teach children took the form of a clash of values, usually between those who emphasised *education* and those who favoured *training*, namely between those who treated the child as the 'heir of all the ages', and those who treated the child as 'job fodder' (Anderson 1980: 156).

Once what we can refer to in shorthand as 'education for its own sake' is lost, there is a vacuum. The language of skills and narrow job training fill the void, but cannot displace the sense that something needful is missing. This is not because there has been an intellectual victory for the philistines, but a gradual abandonment of the pursuit of education for its own sake. The contemporary rush to produce new policies and practices that reflect an endless series of fads and fashions, is a consequence of the end of the belief in education.

The appeal of fads, including those that comprise therapeutic education, might seem to restore balance or expand education creatively by covering neglected areas of personal development such as the emotions. Yet, the question here is not one of balance between the intellectual and the emotional aspects of a rounded personality. In his *Autobiography* John Stuart Mill gives an account of a stage in his intellectual development when he had a breakdown. This mental crisis led him to see that there were gaps in his personal education and he says that thereafter: 'The cultivation of the feelings became one of the cardinal points in my ethical and philosophical creed' (Mill [1873] 1989: 118). Taken out of any context, this might seem like a defence of something like the current fad for emotional education. However, earlier in the paragraph from which the sentence is taken, he says that despite this change: 'I never turned recreant to intellectual culture'.

In contrast, interest in therapeutic education takes place in a climate where most educationalists are recreant to intellectual culture. The emphasis on faddish innovations takes place not as an additional or supplementary aspect of education but replaces it with something much more insubstantial and fragile. For example, many policy texts from the New Labour government have no subject: Every Child Matters talks about 'enjoying' and 'achieving' and there are 'enjoying' and 'achieving' co-ordinators in schools! In schools, as we showed in Chapter 3, the subject curriculum is being eroded rapidly.

The loss of the subject obscures the fact that intellectual culture is central to our concept of what it was to be human. This is something that is no longer obvious or to be taken for granted. We need to remind ourselves of Michael Oakeshott's crucial observation that: 'Every Human being is born an heir to an inheritance' and to enter this common inheritance of human achievements through education is 'the only way of becoming a human being, and to inhabit it is to be a human being' ([1967] 1973: 158). Not to inhabit it is to be less than human.

The early grammar schools embodied a humanist ideal of education that persisted for over five centuries. In the 1960s Paul Hirst articulated liberal education as embodying initiation into what he called the distinctive 'forms of knowledge' with their own particular concepts, logical structures, and ways of being tested against experience. They are: mathematics, physical sciences, human sciences, history, religion, literature and art, moral knowledge and philosophy (Hirst [1965] 1973). He differentiates them from 'fields of knowledge', such as geography, which draw on the various forms. His proposal for a school curriculum, with its subjects and the separate nature of his 'forms of knowledge', is contested (O'Hear 1981; Cooper 1993). In recent years, Hirst has revisited his work and criticised his earlier approach as too 'rationalistic' (Hirst 1993). This debate is worth remembering, not to resolve the contested questions but because, whatever view of the 'forms of knowledge' you have, this was at least a debate about the nature of *education*.

Similarly, the desire for comprehensive education, before it became a project of social engineering to promote notions such as social justice, inclusion and citizenship, was the culmination of the idea, embodied in the traditional grammar school, that all children are capable of becoming fully human by gaining knowledge of the range of subjects that constituted a liberal education. The idea of a comprehensive education embodied the humanist ideal that everyone could benefit through acquiring knowledge.

Such ideals made it impossible to win an argument that the working class, or women, or black and ethic minority groups were not capable of being educated to the highest levels. Whatever social, genetic, cultural or psychological arguments were devised to show failings and barriers to the acquisition of knowledge, they were mostly thinly disguised exercises in prejudice. They made little headway against the idea that every human being had such potential that its frustration was the result of social or psychological prejudice and discrimination. The comprehensive ideal was perhaps most potent in workers' education and adult education from the turn of the century to the 1980s.

This manifestation of liberal education is genuinely modern, rather than 'traditional', 'old' or 'elitist'. Part of the reason for its loss is that many educationalists and teachers see children as incapable of education because they are no longer seen as truly human: there is no point offering an education you do not believe in to children you believe cannot benefit from it. Of course, this philosophy embodies such a diminished view of human potential that it cannot be expressed in this way. Policy makers and politicians cannot argue for a philosophy of education that celebrates a diminished human being.

Yet, as we showed in Chapter 3, a diminished view pervades proposals to dismantle the subject-based curriculum, where children and young people are presented all too frequently as hopeless and hapless victims of their situation, at risk of serious social and individual problems, 'vulnerable' and 'at risk'. Crucially, they are presented as people who 'are what they are', and who are therefore only motivated to learn what is immediately relevant to their personal lives and interests.

We argue that such views are both dehumanising and false. Policy making based on this view rejects a defining feature of education – its *disinterestedness*. Education has knowledge and understanding, *clarity*, as its aim in order to move beyond narrow personal and social concerns and problems. The emotional initiatives that comprise therapeutic education are concerned not with education but with 'learning', a much more general activity that does not require a teacher. A teacher is needed to teach subjects: therapeutic education merely requires teachers trained in therapeutic approaches and an array of support workers, including peer mentors for children, young people and adults.

Examples of the diverse initiatives that comprise therapeutic education reveal a decline in what we think children and young people are capable of, refracted through the prism of what policy makers and the emotional well-being industry think they need. From education to learning, from learning to learning to learn, and from learning to learn to learning to feel and respond 'appropriately', the collapse of belief in human potential is palpable.

A broader social phenomenon of a loss of confidence in human potential lies behind the collapse of the idea of education: Bookchin identified the problem over a decade ago when he suggested that society was suffering from a

> sweeping failure of nerve ... a deep-seated cultural malaise that reflects a waning belief in our species' creative abilities. In a very real sense, we seem to be afraid of ourselves – of our uniquely human attributes. We seem to be suffering from a decline in human self-confidence and our ability to create ethically meaningful lives that enrich humanity and the non-human world.
>
> (Bookchin 1995: 1)

Conclusion

We have related the rise of therapeutic education in British educational policy and practice to five distinct phases of political and cultural change. We accept that some writers may mark the development in other ways, query the phases we identify or suggest other works than the ones we associate with them. Notwithstanding possible disagreements, we believe that the broad sweep of the changes identified here is correct and explains the recent and fullest development of therapeutic culture. Not least, it enables us to offer a prognosis for the form that therapeutic education is likely to take, arguing that distinctly authoritarian tendencies are emerging in a turn away from conferring recognition and esteem on people deemed to be victims, towards imposing happiness and well-being and coaching people in the right ways to achieve them. Time will tell if we are right.

We have also aimed to show that different phases of therapy culture reflect changing beliefs about the human subject, culminating in a profoundly demoralised and diminished account in contemporary politics and culture. This means that, whatever humanistic and empowering notions are to promote therapeutic education, its practices and orthodoxies reveal the opposite. This is why, despite claims for success and benefits, therapeutic education cannot be liberating.

Our analysis, arguments and polemics have already been the subject of denunciations, counter arguments and counter polemics: we respond to some of these in the last chapter. At this point, we do not seek to do more than get the careful reader to decide if we are convincing and to offer a simple question that might assist in deciding whether we are or not: 'What sort of child, young person, adult, what sort of *human being,* is presupposed in this policy or initiative?' We argue that the answer will invariably be someone vulnerable and diminished who needs an emotionally engaging, personally relevant 'education' and a lot of emotional support. We suggest that everyone concerned about education should denounce and reject such images in policy and practice.

Chapter 8

The therapeutic turn in education

A response to our critics

Introduction

The rise of therapeutic education takes different forms in different sectors of the education system and reflects changing ideas of what problems it is trying to address. In primary schools, the development of emotional literacy and the 'skills' associated with emotional well-being begins children's preoccupation with themselves, introduces the idea that life makes us vulnerable and offer prescriptive rituals, scripts and 'appropriate' ways of behaving emotionally. In secondary school, interest shifts from responding to vulnerability towards the seemingly positive idea that we can teach young people the means to be happy citizens. There is a shift from images of children as anxious, at risk, and emotionally fragile towards a new language of resilience, optimism, happiness and well-being. The overall effect of therapeutic education in primary and secondary schools is to dismantle subject disciplines and to use them as vehicles for the latest manifestation of social engineering.

Further education repairs the damage to self-esteem, identity and sense of self supposedly wreaked by schooling for those too old to have experienced the new curriculum of the self. Universities both fuel and reproduce uncertainty and pessimism about knowledge, truth and reason and encourage therapeutic approaches to knowledge. They instil the idea that the pursuit of knowledge, once a liberating ideal, is inherently emotionally unsettling and even damaging. Universities have produced a distinguished voice, in Richard Layard, and numerous research centres in positive psychology, to promote the 'new science of happiness'. Workplaces foster the idea of vulnerable workers, who feel increasingly harassed, stressed, and bullied, allowing management to offer face-saving therapy to cover the continuing ruthlessness of business. And, behind the rise of therapeutic education in these contexts, are apocryphal depictions of extreme levels of physical and emotional deprivation and social breakdown. Deep cultural shifts in ideas of what it means to be human have been incorporated into political ideology and practice: the cultural has, we argue, become the site of contemporary political contestation.

We stated at the outset of the book that our critique is controversial. In this concluding chapter, we respond to key criticisms made about our ideas, either as comments in seminars, conference plenaries and private correspondence, or in print. We use these to bring together the key arguments of our thesis from earlier chapters and to draw out its implications for educational goals, practices and outcomes. Finally, given that we are critical of the impoverished vision of education offered by those who promote the therapeutic turn in education, it is obviously important to articulate a vision of our own. The last section of the chapter therefore responds to our critics' injunction to make it clear where we stand on questions raised by the book.

You have no concrete evidence to prove your case

A common objection to what we have called the rise of 'therapeutic education', or the 'therapeutic turn' in education, is that, without 'appropriate research surveys and case studies', our case has 'not been proven' (Hyland 2005: 17; see also Hyland, 2006). The notion of 'proof' is used here very loosely. It is more of a charge that we need to undertake empirical studies before we can make assertions about the state of education rather than a demand that we apply a mathematical notion of 'proof' to our arguments. Our first response is, therefore, that it is just as true that our case is *not unproven*.

Our second response to Hyland's charge is that it is otiose. We are pointing to *examples* of a strong cultural change in society towards belief in the diminished self. We argue that therapeutic education and its underlying claims and assumptions reflect a corresponding rise in beliefs and images of the diminished self. We have aimed to show that this change is very dangerous: the examples we have drawn on from popular culture, politics and practices in different educational contexts have become widespread across the education system and they erode a robust and confident sense of human possibility. A deeply pessimistic and instrumental view of education has emerged in its place.

We are pointing to a trend, or a change that, when we first wrote and spoke about it in 2002, was not at all obvious. It was coming out in the use of therapeutic techniques in teacher training, and in the adoption of 'circle time' and similar approaches across the school and college curriculum. It was emerging rapidly in widespread enthusiasm for emotional literacy and emotional intelligence. More than anything else, it was coming out in the ubiquitous concern amongst various professions, including trades unions, with low self-esteem, together with an obsession with bullying and emotional well-being in all sectors of education.

Our third response, therefore, is that Hyland's charge is simply false. This book catalogues numerous examples of the rise of therapeutic education. A few years ago, it may have been easy to avoid seeing the cultural shift and to duck our claims with charges of 'where's the evidence?', but it is increasingly there and we have drawn together diverse examples that have not been brought together before. We have each been charting the rise of therapeutic education for five years, alongside other academics here and the United States, discussed in Chapter 7, who have charted the broader rise of therapeutic culture and politics, and accompanying demoralisation, over the past 30 years.

Yet, we did not predict the extent to which the government would seize on emotional well-being as a central focus for education policy. Nor did we predict its recent and rapid shift from remedying emotional vulnerability towards calls that the education system can teach people to be happy. Although claims that 'no education professional is against the refocus on the meaning of education which to lead our young people to flourishing and well-being' (Sharples 2007) seem to be intensifying, it is significant that in recent seminar and conference presentations of our ideas, we receive more confirmations that our concerns are valid than we did a few years ago.

We recognise the need for empirical study of the effects of therapeutic education on teachers' and students' attitudes to learning and education (Ecclestone and Quinn 2008; Ecclestone and Hayes 2008). Nevertheless, we defend our approach to induction or 'proof' in this book because presenting examples from diverse areas is the most appropriate way to identify cultural shifts as they are happening. In the preface, we argued that it is from *examples* as well as from the rhetoric of policy documents or texts for teachers and parents that we can extract the unarticulated vision of children and young people offered by governing elites, advisers to government, researchers in think tanks and all those working in the emotional well-being industry. We addressed our contention that therapeutic education expresses a profoundly diminished sense of what it is to be human, in Chapter 7 and we return to it in the final section of this chapter.

Although we have no interest in calling for evidence that therapeutic education 'works', it is salutary that there has been no strong challenge for 'proof' directed towards the UK government. Policy makers have sponsored therapeutic education, and many support it evangelically without any robust evidence that it works even on the terms set by its advocates, and without any systematic, independent evaluations of the various interventions that comprise it. We simply do not know if therapeutic education will create emotionally literate, empathetic, happier, more tolerant people.

However, while it is important to challenge a serious lack of evidence for the claims made by advocates of therapeutic education, this is irrelevant in the light of our fundamental disagreement with therapeutic education. Although emotional intelligence, emotional literacy and emotional well-being have not been shown to be valid, reliable and beneficial, a more serious problem is that they are not educational activities. Children who are emotionally damaged need therapy from mental health specialists outside the classroom. Playing with children's feelings is personally damaging and profoundly anti-educational and we have offered reasons for our view throughout the book.

There are a lot of damaged people out there

We have received numerous comments that we underestimate the extent of emotional suffering: as James Park and John Field have both said 'there are a lot of damaged people out there' (Park *et al.* 2006, in conversation, and Hunt and West 2006). These educationalists see therapeutic pedagogies as a useful way of overcoming emotional problems as if they were traditional 'barriers to learning' like poverty.

This is a widespread view. In America, estimates of emotional disorder extend to 77 per cent of the population (Sommers and Satel 2005b). We put this to a test with British teachers at a conference of the Standing Committee for the Education and Training of Teachers (SCETT) in 2006: the participants, all experienced educationalists, guessed that anything from 20 to 60 per cent of children and young people were in the socially and emotionally vulnerable category.

There have also been attempts to theorise this view and, in the light of assumptions about new and intractable problems of mental health, some of our critics regard therapeutic education as the latest manifestation of critical pedagogy, a way of fighting for social justice,

> re-visioned as a war for health – the health of individuals, of the nation, of the earth itself … far from deploring the links between education and therapy, between the provision of adult learning and the improvement of mental and physical health in the population, perhaps we should be doing everything we can to make such links stronger and more explicit.
>
> (Parrott 2005: 15)

Supporters of this view regard therapeutic education as a counter to the emotional problems of 'damaged' people in two closely connected ways. The first aims to de-stigmatise problems for a minority by suggesting that everyone has emotional problems and should be included in therapeutic interventions. The second resonates with the therapeutic orthodoxy that we are all, to a greater or lesser extent, 'damaged' and would, therefore, all benefit from developing our emotional resources and, in turn, that this is crucial for the health of society, not merely individuals. The example in Chapter 1 of marshalling the 'concealed' neuroses, maladies and disorders of children's fictional characters in order to de-stigmatise mental ill-health and to promote the benefits of therapy as normal, show how far these goals have extended.

As we showed in that chapter, it is widely accepted that levels of depression and mental ill-health are rising and that schools, colleges, universities and workplaces should offer interventions that might prevent or counter these problems. Yet, we also showed that estimates vary greatly, as do definitions of mental or emotional 'disorders', 'difficulties', 'syndromes' and 'problems', 'support from the caring professions' and 'treatment'. This does not mean that emotional problems are merely suggestible or imagined but there are many critiques about how concepts like 'stress' are manufactured and how even everyday feelings such as 'shyness' become pathologised (see Wainwright and Caplan 2002; Patmore 2006; Lane 2007). We believe that we have shown the therapeutic turn in education which has pathologised 'emotions' in the same way, advancing the idea of children and young people as vulnerable beings. The paradox then emerges where a non-problem becomes a problem and more and more people describe normal states as ones that cause difficulty and distress.

Cultural accounts of problems and the therapeutic industry that reinforces them expand definitions of damage, dysfunction and emotional problems and inflate the numbers of those suffering from them. Felicia Huppert, Professor of Psychiatry at the University of Cambridge's Centre for Well-Being, argues that the proportion of the population who have a common condition is related to the underlying level of symptoms in the population as a whole: the higher the symptoms in the general population, the higher the number with a mental disorder (Huppert 2007). Not only does the emotional well-being and popular therapy industry encourage the self-diagnosis of emotional problems but it easier than ever to be diagnosed medically with depression while lively, energetic, or disruptive children are diagnosed with ADHD or ODD. In addition, the shift from 'mental health' to 'emotional well-being' extends the spectrum of feelings, behaviours and responses to life situations that might be defined as mental ill-health or emotional unwell-being. In colleges and universities, the loosening of what counts as a 'clinically well-recognised disability' and the legal requirement for institutions to support disabilities, has led to an exponential rise in the self-reporting of low level mental and emotional disorders that create barriers to learning.

Yet, accounts of distress and responses to them are historically and culturally situated. For example, Furedi shows how the resilience, stoicism and community support systems that got people through the horrors of the Aberfan coal tip disaster of 1966 are now being reinterpreted by psychologists as signs of dysfunction and the repression of emotion: counselling and therapy are being offered 40 years later to remedy the damage done by not offering them at the time (2004). Vanessa Pupavac's studies of aid interventions, truth commissions and postwar re-building by Western governments in developing countries show that the imposition of counselling and therapeutic interventions inserts a vocabulary of dysfunction and damage into societies unfamiliar with the assumptions and orthodoxies that underpin them (2001, 2003).

Our caveats about definitions and the self-fulfilling prophecy of cultural accounts about vulnerability mean that we question both the nature and extent of the problem that therapeutic education is supposed to address. Focusing on everyone's emotional well-being blurs the line between those few children, young people and adults who have serious problems, and everyone else. 'Inclusion' universalises emotional vulnerability and the parallel idea that we all have 'special emotional needs'. This pessimistic, diminished view of what we have in common enables the emotional well-being industry to castigate characteristics of resilience and optimism as signs of repressed vulnerability and then to offer the teaching of the same characteristics as part of 'the means to be happy'.

Many children and young people are so disaffected from traditional subjects and education that we need an alternative to engage them

This is a modern shibboleth. Policy makers, teachers and teacher unions all believe that 'relevance' is all when it comes to engaging young people. We offered numerous examples in Chapter 3 of policy-focused papers and publications advocating the dismantling of an elitist, outdated curriculum because (a) young people do not want it and (b) most are not up to old-fashioned intellectual endeavour.

Talking about young people in FE, for example, Joe Harkin, well known for his work on learner voice in 14–19 education, has put this point to us:

> The kids you taught in FE in the 1980s are not the same now. They have fragmented lives, less optimism and aren't sure why they are in college. They're alienated from education. Most of all, they want humane, respectful relationships where teachers treat them like adults and that's what they don't get from many teachers.
>
> (Harkin 2007 – in conversation)

We are frequently told that we are living in the past, that not only has society 'changed' but, children and young people have 'changed' and that they are more 'disaffected' from education than ever. The range of concerns that have contributed to the rise of therapeutic education, summarised in Chapter 1, is overwhelming: materialism and the desire for consumer goods; depravity; spiritual breakdown; testing, targets and an arid school curriculum; too much emphasis on rational, cognitive learning; emotional damage on an unprecedented scale in the form of low self-esteem, fragility, vulnerability and mental health problems; disaffected, unruly boys who do not achieve, are disruptive and socially excluded and who do not conform to New Labour's idea of caring masculinity; emotionally illiterate parents; too much freedom; not enough freedom; too much risk adverse parenting; technology, advertising and the media.

And so the list goes on. The strength of such concerns is that they include standpoints that, politically, go beyond out-dated divisions of 'left' and 'right'. This enables any government to respond on an emotional level and to depict schools, colleges and universities as able to solve an ever-widening range of social, economic and private problems. Such responses encourage the authoritarian fallacy that we can be taught emotional literacy and emotional well-being, and that, if we fail, despite all the support on offer, we are either emotionally unwell, emotionally incompetent or emotionally illiterate.

Whether presented as a problem of damaged vulnerable people, or, increasingly commonly as a problem of anti-social behaviour by 'scary' children, there is a moral crisis about childhood and the lives of young people and a profound demoralisation about how to deal with it (Waiton 2001, 2007). More potently, adults' own guilt about this state of fears is palpable in many of the accounts we have cited. Such fears lead to claims that emotional well-being is the most important outcome for schools to develop. Presenting emotion as a 'subject' in a more 'personally relevant curriculum' that will engage learners denotes much more than notions of 'motivation' and 'participation'. They signal, instead, the state's intention to find an emotional basis for making its citizens engage with its activities.

To this end, traditional subjects are co-opted as vehicles for citizenship, personal development and emotional literacy. As we showed in Chapter 3, subjects such as English, PE, biology, drama and Art become 'opportunities' to understand the physiology of emotion and its effects on the body and behaviours, or to develop empathy, rehearse anti-bullying strategies and practise assertiveness techniques. In same vein, the idea that everyday life activities are 'therapeutic' emerges in extra-curricular activities cited in Chapter 2, such as 'circus skills', which are sold to parents as an 'opportunity to build self-esteem' while everyday activities in schools, such as chatting to children in the bus queue, enable teachers to 'model' empathy. The debasing of education in such examples is extreme.

Subjects such as 'philosophy for children' use therapeutic rituals to train children in empathy, respect, 'appropriate' ways of listening, tolerating diverse views and responding in particular ways in order to be emotionally literate, tolerant citizens. We also showed that notions such as 'learning to learn' or 'learning power' indicate a shift towards thinking about what it feels to do science, history or geography, to empathise with the role of scientist, historian or geographer, and to explore the risks and emotions associated with 'doing' a subject rather than learning its substantive content.

Therapeutic education is therefore the latest onslaught in an ongoing denigration of notions of subject, curriculum and education. Supporters present it as something that is seemingly less 'political' than cruder manipulations of education to achieve social engineering goals (see, for example, Whelan 2007). Adults' own demoralisation has led them to abandon their belief in education and in the teaching of subjects: we argue that doing almost anything to 'engage' young people who are supposedly disaffected, rather than tackling the arid nature of schooling and testing, is a betrayal of education.

Therapeutic insights and practices are integral to good teaching

For numerous critics, focusing on emotional aspects of learning is integral to good teaching. Michael Rustin, who has written of the implications of psychoanalysis for social life, politics and education for over 20 years, declares that 'Learning ... has an essential dimension of feeling or emotion. Most of our implicit theories of learning which underpin our educational practice take little account of this, focusing for preference on the various cognitive dimensions of the learning task' (2001: 201) But he complains that students in higher education need to have a say and that they find issues that are relevant to them more interesting. This is another contradiction. The diminished self obviously finds its diminution interesting. Education cannot he built on the diminished self.

'Obviously not' say some critics of our work, making a move that we can only characterise as the 'therapeutic fallacy'. They argue that they do not advocate crude applications of what Sommers and Satel call 'therapism' but something more complex, subtle and specialist (Sommers and Satel 2005a, 2005b). However complex, subtle or specialist, this is still a defence of the therapy culture. Since the therapeutic culture is so elastic, critics will never find the 'right' approach.

For the most part, appeals to the 'emotional' in learning when it is seen to support the 'whole person' over the intellectual or cognitive (what we would argue is the *essence* of the person) and claims that emphasising other things diminishes the person, are mere assertion. In her criticisms of our ideas, Sue Clegg asserts just this and then seeks to find the evidence for her assertions: 'The development of critical facilities in students is fundamental to university education. But we do ourselves and out students no favours by refusing to recognise the role of emotion on the mistaken grounds that to do so would entail wallowing in 'relativism, subjectivity and feelings'' (Clegg 2005).

The intellect, of course, is dispassionate: the self may be interested. Clegg simply confuses the two. It is rather like confusing the subject of a sentence with the proposition it asserts. For example in the statement 'I know that Socrates was given hemlock' the statement of what is known, 'Socrates was given hemlock', has nothing to do with the knower or their subjective states, whether joy, depression of fear of a similar death. To confuse the subject of the known proposition with the knower of that proposition is to make communication impossible (Anderson 1980; Hayes 2003) Anything can be claimed about subjective states and this is useful for the proponents of emotionality. But confusion is no basis for an education and Clegg and her associates go on to assert claims like:

> The significance of the break with rationalist or linguistic accounts of the self is that it opens up the theoretical space to properly explore the ways in which students engage as fully functioning selves in their learning. We are, therefore, able to consider the affective dimensions of learning in ways which do not reduce to individual psychology, but instead preserve the idea of human beings with their full range of emergent.
>
> (Beard *et al.* 2007: 235–6)

This clear shift away from rationality to something supposedly more 'emergent' is actually more diminished and shows that these authors are 'in denial'. Our aim is not to offer a therapeutic view of the pedagogic encounter that some recent critics have suggested is prevalent in work critical of the logocentrism of enlightenment thought (Furedi 2004; Ecclestone 2004a, 2004b), but rather to offer a more fully articulated model of students as persons which 'transcends the cognitive focus of most discussions of learning' … (Beard *et al.* 2007: 236).

It is the rationality and the logocentrism that make us fully human. Such confusion and obfuscation is then followed up by simplistic claims:

Our argument is, therefore, both theoretical and sociological: theoretical in that accounts of the university as a place of learning which dwell solely on the rational are analytically impoverished, and sociological in that accounts in the literature point to the fact that student success is heavily dependent on aspects of social integration which involve the affective dimensions of their engagement with higher education ... Both arguments are based on a rejection of higher education's tendency to work with a model of the student and theorisations of pedagogy that downgrade the affective dimensions of learning.

(Beard *et al.* 2007: 236)

Here there is a sudden shift to 'student success' which is entirely different and relatively banal compared with the holistic, diminishing critique of the enlightenment project. The idea that student success in therapy culture, and an educational system that adapts to and fosters it, are related to emotionality or 'affective dimensions' could quite easily be the case but proves nothing except that emotionality is needed for success in therapy culture. This is a truly self validating proposition and it is not surprising that a string of academics can be found to refer to it, in order to support this obvious point.

There is, though, a subjective appeal in all this that the best therapists express, but which those promoting therapeutic education appear blind to. Therapy is deeply rewarding for practitioners who look at their diminished pupils and students through the eyes of therapy. Here is an extract from Irvin D. Yalom's reflections on being a therapist in *The Gift of Therapy*:

When I turn to others with the knowledge that we are all (therapist and patient alike) burdened with painful secrets – guilt for acts committed, shame for actions not taken, yearnings to be loved and cherished, deep vulnerabilities, insecurities and fears – I draw closer to them. Being a cradler of secrets has, as the years have passed, made me gentler and more accepting. When I encounter individuals inflated with vanity or self-importance, or distracted by a myriad of consuming passions, I intuit the pain of their underlying secrets and feel not judgement but compassion, and above all, connectedness.

(Yalom 2002: 257–8)

We have both known, and still know, colleagues in FE and other parts of the education system who have this quiet superiority and feelings of power.

For us, it is stating the obvious that emotions are involved in teaching but primarily with the intention and not with the content of what is transmitted. Knowledge can be taught passionately or indifferently by and to people who may be distraught, upset, happy or content. It does not matter. Knowledge, as it were, conquers all.

What we are teaching is not touched by the emotions. We argue that there is room for emotion in education only as the passionate pursuit of truth in the sciences and the study of beauty and human emotions in the arts. Emotion itself is a study for biologists, social scientists, psychologists and others but it is not a subject, in the sense of an intellectual discipline.

Obsession with emotional aspects of the *processes* of 'good teaching' reinforces an avoidance of questions about *what* we are teaching. The claims and assumptions of therapeutic education subjugate the teaching of subjects to the supposed emotional effects of processes and go much further than merely requiring teachers to be 'sensitive to feelings' and to 'take emotions into account'. Therapeutic education is no longer confined to remedial approaches for a minority of young people and adults deemed to need a more supportive approach. Instead, the principle in liberal humanist approaches to teaching and counselling that damage is the exception, requiring specific remedies, has given way to the idea that all children from early years' education onwards need therapeutic interventions. The other Rogerian principle, that humans have innate potential to learn has given way to a much more diminished sense of permanent vulnerability and being 'at risk'.

Therapeutic education also leads to unethical assessments. Despite serious doubts about the validity and reliability of constructs and measures of emotional literacy, emotional intelligence and self-esteem, there is growing interest in developing measures of happiness and well-being. Routine labels of 'low self-esteem', 'poor emotional literacy', 'repressed feelings of vulnerability' and 'being at emotional risk' are already meted out to individuals and whole groups, particularly those deemed to be disaffected or disruptive. The study of nurture groups discussed in Chapter 2 shows that children made to take part in therapeutic interventions internalize a vocabulary of 'dysfunction' and psychological syndromes to explain their social and educational difficulties (Bailey 2007).

We showed in Chapter 1 that strong images of emotional deficiency are prevalent amongst policy makers and parts of the emotional well-being industry. We have also heard numerous casual observations of this kind from teachers, support workers and friends who are parents, based on the idea that the emotional lives of certain families are dangerous, abusive and dysfunctional for many more children than is assumed.

We argue that the empowering rhetoric of therapeutic education belies fears of anti-social, disruptive and divisive behaviour and masks the discipline and social training of citizens. The spectre of emotionally dysfunctional children and young people goes hand in hand with the scary and recalcitrant 'buggers' promoted in books for teachers such as 'get the buggers to behave/do maths, etc.': get the buggers to be emotionally literate and happy is the new refrain.

Emotions are integral to successful learning and have been overlooked in education for too long

In parallel to criticisms that we do not recognise the benefits of therapeutic interventions and insights for teaching, we are accused of overlooking the benefits of a more emotionally-tuned awareness for learning. Critics argue that many of the interventions we have challenged in this book 'work'; they are motivating, enjoyable and they help learners achieve better than they would without them:

> Good learning that fosters positive feelings about oneself is more likely to empower than disempower learners ... and there is substantial evidence that learners value the raised self-esteem and confidence they acquire ... way above outcomes such as qualifications.
>
> (Ecclestone and McGiveney 2005: 8)

In a similar vein, Alan Parrott wrote about his experience of adult education:

> I would defy Kathryn or any other adult educator not to be moved ... by some of the oral testimony and by some of the portfolios ... I was privileged to read. For these adults, the concept of increased self-esteem was definitely not an abstract or empirically dubious concept. It was an actual event in their life brought about by a well-designed educational intervention.
>
> (Parrott 2005:15)

And, as Guy Claxton argued in a debate at the Battle of Ideas festival in 2005, many of his suggested interventions for developing learning power are simply part of 'good teaching' and, far from being therapeutic, eliciting students' feelings about what they are learning and how they are learning it enhances the teaching of subjects. 'What', he asked, ' can possibly be wrong with that?' (Claxton 2005).

We have aimed to show throughout the book that therapeutic education goes far beyond being tuned into learners' feelings. Instead, children are learning from an early age that life, with all its trivial and serious tribulations, mundane and difficult low moments, 'sucks' and requires an array of 'therapeutic support workers' in the form of peer buddies, theatre educators, teachers trained in various therapeutic approaches, life coaches and mentors, or specialist counsellors. Therapeutic education elevates everyday feelings of uncertainty, vulnerability, discomfort or lack of confidence and depicts them as 'treatable'.

Children and young people learn that some of their peers are assessed as being more emotionally literate or having better emotional well-being and given the status of angels, peer mediators and 'bully counsellors'. They learn that the emotional effects of life experiences are not only a subject in their own right but they can be explained through therapeutic orthodoxies. The activities that lead to these insights are compulsory and prescriptive.

Our presentations to staff in colleges and universities attract numerous examples from teachers who are required to raise the spectre of emotional 'barriers to learning' with students during an induction to a new course, and where growing numbers of students pressurise teachers to take account of their emotions in time-consuming and debilitating ways. In Chapters 4 and 5, we showed how colleges and universities provide rising levels of support for emotional difficulties, encompassing growing numbers of students reporting 'low level' stress and anxiety as well as clinically diagnosed problems. Workers in learning support services say they offer emotional support that 'busy' teachers or lecturers do not have time for or that lecturers are too focused on rational aspects of learning and inflict threatening forms of assessment on students (see Loads 2007). This undermines education and teachers' authority.

Some advocates of therapeutic education concede the danger of suggestibility and introspection. Carol Craig quotes a warning from Katherine Weare that 'an overload of emotional awareness can lead to paralysing introspection, self-centredness and/or dwelling or getting stuck in a difficult mood rather than trying to deal with it' (Weare quoted by Craig 2007: 27). Craig also shows that such cautions were not quoted in Weare's report for the DfES, despite saying explicitly that the report would list drawbacks to the introduction of emotional literacy in all schools. Instead, the final report lists strong recommendations for extensive work in this area. Despite these warnings, the point here suggests that more evidence is needed rather than suggesting emotional literacy should not be taught at all.

We oppose this view, and argue that teachers and students should resist therapeutic education. Presenting learning as emotionally difficult and suggesting that emotions create barriers to achievement undermines teachers' authority as subject experts who can teach, assess and challenge their students. The converse is also true: the more that students are embroiled in therapeutic education, the less they want to be taught, assessed and challenged. Therapeutic education draws students towards easy, unchallenging preoccupation of everyday concerns and feelings and away from a desire to rise to the challenging of pursuing truth, mastering a difficult subject or learning craft skills.

You have set up a straw man of reductionist 'pop' therapy

We have been criticised often for representing therapy, therapy culture and psychodynamic ideas in caricatured and reductionist ways, and for using this straw man to construct a false thesis that therapeutic education offers a diminished view of learners. For example, Celia Hunt and Linden West allege that we homogenise 'diverse and even discordant practices: the Oprah Winfrey approach to public disclosure and sharing of trauma is elided with diverse schools of psychotherapy and psychoanalysis ... we need a more discriminating level of analysis' (Hunt and West 2006: 142).

A parallel criticism contrasts our false depiction of therapeutic interventions as safe, comforting and victim-focused with their depiction as challenging, empowering and life-changing. For example, Veronica McGiveney, Principal Research Officer for the National Institute of Adult and Continuing Education argues that, far from being 'diminished',

> Most adult educators seek to [focus on self-esteem] as a matter of course as part of the learning process ... this does not imply a view of learners as emotionally frail, weak or vulnerable: it implies a recognition that, in order to progress, some individuals need to change their self-image and raise their estimation of their talents and potential ...
>
> (Ecclestone and McGiveney 2005: 8)

Hunt and West suggest that teachers of adults should 'focus less on reported meanings and motivations and more on what is happening under the surface of human encounters' in educational relationships and contexts (Fenwick quoted in Hunt and West 2006: 153).

In their claims that adult education can be

> a deeply reflexive, sustained, meaning making engagement with experience and emotional complexity, and the muddle, messiness and pain that can surround our lives … It can help us understand how we often contribute, unconsciously, to our own oppression and suffering by perpetuating particular forms of behaviour, by resisting new possibilities and relationships … We never fully transcend earlier dimensions of ourselves … and these aspects of who we are can find expression in new situations and need to be attended to.
>
> (Hunt and West 2006: 152)

The popular orthodoxy that we are all, to a greater or lesser extent, doomed by our past, is evident. From this pessimistic perspective, teachers need much better 'psychosocial, more holistic understanding of why apparently similar people differ in responding to similar experience, including in educational settings' (Hunt and West 2006: 153).

Criticisms that our straw man overlooks important distinctions between the ideas and practices of counselling, different approaches to psychology, therapy and psychoanalysis, resonate with a criticism that we do not understand how a better knowledge of psychology and its practical application enables teachers to understand the emotional effects of social problems, and, through this, to help people to deal with them. In other words, as Brahm Norwich, Professor of Educational Psychology at the University of Exeter, pointed out, 'science and practice [of psychology] have advanced and you are out of date' (Norwich 2005).

We recognise that specialist branches of therapy, psychoanalysis and counselling are not synonymous with therapeutic education and we are not anti-therapy per se. Yet, even if we were to accept that better understanding of therapeutic approaches will solve perceived emotional problems, even teachers trained properly in cognitive behavioural therapy, transactional analysis or other well-known approaches, cannot understand or deal with the complexities of psychology, poverty and social conditions and translate these sensitively into their emotional dealings with students. Conversely, courses that aim to train teachers to apply 'three basic principles' of humanist counselling or cognitive behaviour therapy, or to use transactional analysis to 'transform individuals and communities', pander to the sweeping claims and simplistic stereotypes of pop therapy.

Those who criticise our lack of interest in the respective merits of Jungian, Freudian or Rogerian approaches, transactional analysis or CBT, psychotherapy or psychodynamic approaches, or simply the benefits of emotionally-tuned teaching, miss completely our reasons for challenging the reductionist orthodoxies of popular therapy. It is precisely *because* popular, caricatured therapy resonates so powerfully with cultural explanations about emotional problems that policy makers and the emotional well-being industry have seized on it. 'Robust' evidence and better validity and reliability of constructs are not simply irrelevant but their absence is integral to the rise of therapeutic education because popular 'evidence' is all that government needs to legitimise it. In their clamour to have particular specialisms recognised in the flourishing industry surrounding therapeutic education, advocates legitimise an eclectic, popular approach and reinforce a lack of evidence.

You are anti-happiness miserabilists/what's wrong with promoting happiness?

There is a profound category mistake in pursuing happiness for its own sake that makes it self-defeating. But this challenge raises a question at the heart of the 'therapeutic turn' and of the shift to therapy culture. In Chapter 7, we supported the view of Rieff and Lasch that the therapeutic turn was epochal in that it put aside the self-denying goals of previous cultures and put the search for the illusion of self-fulfilment in its place. We also pointed out that this was a contradictory process since these 'fulfilled' states can only come as a by-product of working towards other altruistic or self-denying goals. As a consequence, the real commitment is not to self-denying goals or to their by-products, but a commitment to the therapeutic process itself. The search for happiness and emotional well being are the apogee not only of therapeutic education, but of therapy culture itself.

No one put this better than John Stuart Mill, who after his famous emotional crisis, reflected on the emphasis on being 'happy' in relation to what he discovered was Thomas Carlyle's 'anti-self-consciousness theory':

> I never, indeed, wavered in the conviction that happiness is the test of all rules of conduct, and the end of life. But I now thought that this end was only to be attained by not making it the direct end. Those only are happy (I thought) who have their minds fixed on some object other than their own happiness; on the happiness of others, on the improvement of mankind, even on some art or pursuit, followed not as a means, but as itself an ideal end. Aiming thus at something else, they find happiness by the way. The enjoyments of life (such was now my theory) are sufficient to make it a pleasant thing, when they are taken *en passant*, without being made a principal object. Once make them so, and they are immediately felt to be insufficient. They will not bear a scrutinizing examination. Ask yourself whether you are happy, and you cease to be so. The only chance is to treat, not happiness, but some end external to it, as the purpose of life. Let your self-consciousness, your scrutiny, your self-interrogation, exhaust themselves on that; and if other wise fortunately circumstanced you will inhale happiness with the air you breathe, without dwelling on it or thinking about it, without either forestalling it in the imagination, or putting it to flight by fatal questioning. This theory has now become the basis of my philosophy of life. And I still hold to it as the best

theory for all those who have but a moderate degree of sensibility and of capacity for enjoyment, that is, for the great majority of mankind.

(Mill [1873] 1989: 117–18)

Unlike the desire to be personally 'happy' or less 'miserable', the desire to remove misery and create human happiness is not self-defeating. The difference is whether the object of that consciousness is internal or external.

We believe that consciousness of human misery, personal discontent and unhappiness are more likely to motivate people to change the world. This does not mean we want people to be miserable. Instead, it is a reminder that old political traditions on the left advocated the autonomy and capacity of people to claim recognition on their own behalf as a way of liberating themselves from personal unhappiness, or suppressed aspirations. In older traditions of working class education, consciousness of discontent was a spur to individual or collective action. It was not a condition of vulnerability remedied by therapeutic affirmations of esteem and the development of 'skills' in expressing and dealing with feelings.

Our political and philosophical objections to therapeutic education are usually ignored. Rather, frequent accusations that we are 'uncaring', that we advocate the repression of feelings and a return to the days when children were 'seen and not heard', that we tell people to 'get over it, get a grip', are occasionally accompanied by a searching therapeutic question along the lines of 'what are your own "issues" around your preoccupation with emotional well-being'? We are sometimes directly criticised for denying or repressing our own emotional 'issues'. In the first draft of a response to an article by Kathryn for the June edition of *Psychologies* magazine (Ecclestone 2007), the magazine's resident psychotherapist, Derek Draper, alleged that her questioning of concepts such as emotional well-being and self-esteem either signified her own over-high self-esteem, or, conversely, the repression of low self-esteem: both problems made her incapable of empathising with others who have emotional problems. After a presentation at a seminar about therapeutic education at Roehampton University, a psychotherapist challenged her publicly to address her own 'obvious issues with esteem'.

It is telling that Kathryn has received more slights about her own 'esteem issues', alongside injunctions to 'be reflexive' about her emotional stance in relation to criticisms of therapeutic education, than Dennis who is simply dismissed as an uncaring 'alpha male'. This gendered response appears to assume that Kathryn cannot possibly be as uncaring as she comes across (or has her own repressed emotional 'issues' for seeming so) while Dennis, as a mere man, might be expected to be. Reflecting a common therapeutic (and feminist) orthodoxy, this is put more strongly by Peter Sharp who attacks critics by claiming: 'Emotions, and hence emotional literacy, is sometimes derided or rejected as too 'touchy-feely' or as 'psychobabble', usually by people (and mostly men) who are at the lower end of the emotional literacy spectrum themselves' (2003: 89).

While we find it amusing that our challenges lead us to be dismissed as emotionally illiterate or 'in denial' of our own 'issues' (and how we have come to loathe the term 'issues'!), the serious point is that such criticisms are not only emotive and anti-intellectual but they also exemplify the strength of the simplistic therapeutic orthodoxies we have analysed in the book. It is deeply ironic that critics of our focus on reductionism pop therapy resort to it in order to close down argument and debate about our analysis.

What is your alternative?

We argue that, however well-meant and uplifting, the goals and methods of those who are now encouraging schools to coach students in the mindset and attributes of happiness and well-being are authoritarian, normative and dangerous. Not surprisingly, we are frequently asked to offer a practical alternative to our criticisms of policy and practice. For example, Karen Willis, Director of Widening Access at the University of Chester, argues that

> The whole area [of your critique] is not entirely susceptible to reasoning, though, and there will always be those who feel, whilst recognising the hold which the rhetoric of this discourse has established, that it still represents the broad moral position and values of a 'civilised society' rather than being symptomatic of a weakening of the (bourgeois?) individual. The hardest bit, as we've discussed, will not be in deconstructing the prevailing position but in offering a clearly-expressed alternative that people can buy into i.e. what should be the case, if the current position won't do?
>
> (Willis 2007: e-mail communication)

We stated at the outset of the book that we hope to begin a battle of ideas for the hearts and minds of educators, parents and students about the fundamental purposes of education. We could offer some practical 'strategies' for resisting the rise of therapeutic education, such as 'avoid using its languages, assumptions and practices'. We could say 'don't use circle time' or 'don't talk about negative feelings with students', but that it is 'alright to use other techniques'. Yet, as we argued above, this misses the point that, however well-meaning, therapeutic techniques cannot be separated from a culture that promotes the diminished self.

We could, like the authors of the Nuffield Review of 14–19 Education who go further than most critics of policy by discussing the wider loss of educational purpose, call for a debate about the values of education. The authors argue that 'Government policy documents on 14–19 have largely failed to articulate underlying aims. There needs to be a constant appraisal of the values which are embedded in educational language and practice and which shape learning experience.' Their concern was that more needs to be said about educational aims because 'They reflect the kind of life that is thought to be worth living, the personal qualities worth developing and the sort of society worth creating' (Hayward *et al.* 2005: 24–5). What the report said of 14–19 education applies to all educational policies.

Despite its focus on values, the poverty of the review's critique is that it is made within a historical framework that no longer has any application. As we argued in Chapter 7, it is the ending of this historical framework that makes contemporary education fundamentally different. This means that practices which were innocuous ten years ago have a very different significance in the cultural and political context we have analysed in the book.

Instead, we face a much more serious problem. It has become clear during the writing of this book that the authoritarian tendencies of therapeutic education are taking root because many educators and policy makers have given up thinking about what state-funded education means because they no longer believe in it and they cannot articulate the diminished, dehumanising idea that lies behind this abandonment, namely that no child or young person is capable of education.

We believe that debates about our arguments need to focus not on the crisis *in* education but on the fact that we face a crisis *of* education, a crisis which comes from the disintegration of the idea of education and of loss of belief in human potential. The rise of the diminished subject, discussed in Chapter 8, and the corresponding loss of belief in education, means that calling for debate about values has no meaning. The battle of ideas we want to create is about the account that state education increasingly offers of what it means to be human. For us, 'what is at stake here cannot be overstated, for it involves the very survival of what it means to be human' (Smith 2005: x).

In this context, therapeutic education is a powerful instrument of social engineering and control because it encourages people to come to terms with being a feeble, vulnerable human subject and then to allow the state to coach the appropriate dispositions and attitudes of the emotionally well citizen. For us, the rapid, unchallenged rise of therapeutic education is evidence that the radical transformative aspect of 'liberal' education has been lost. Calling education 'transformative' is shorthand for the transformative power of human beings to try to change the world and, in doing so, to change themselves. In the present climate, the focus has shifted completely away from changing the world towards changing yourself in order to accept your vulnerability and human frailty and then to be coached to have 'appropriate' emotions associated with emotional well-being.

Unlike a tiny minority on the contemporary left, we are not hoping for some resurrection of political action based on consciousness of dissatisfaction or waiting for the resurgence of some vague 'politics of hope'. And nor, like a large number on the left and liberal left, do we see the need to offer therapeutic repair to the large numbers assumed to be so emotionally 'damaged' by capitalism that they need therapeutic support in every educational institution and workplace: this particular distortion of left wing politics is itself a sign of despair and pessimism. And nor do we adopt the safe form of verbal radicalism of liberals who cite the emancipatory rhetoric and beliefs of educators such as Paulo Freire without any recognition that the structural and material conditions that shaped it are starkly different from current conditions.

Instead, our counter to the dangerous rise of therapeutic education is to assert a purpose of education that emanates from what we term 'radical humanism'. In its widest sense, radical humanism stands for humanistic values associated with the enlightenment: reason, science and progress. Radical humanism is essentially a rational philosophy that focuses on the ability of humans to transform the world by making scientific and social progress through reason. We mean reason in all its aspects, the ability to think, argue, plan, design, create and manufacture. We hold that free speech is the driver that makes possible all scientific and social progress.

The philosophy of education associated with radical humanism reflects a strong belief in the importance, power and optimism of progress, particularly of technological and scientific progress. It promotes a vision that students of all ages, children, young people and adults, have the potential to understand and create if they are provided with a broad education that covers the arts and literature, science and mathematics, history, philosophy and languages. Many of those dismissing the value of a broad liberal education benefited from it themselves.

Yet, while a radical humanistic education has historical connections to what was once called a 'liberal education', notions of 'liberal' and 'broad' are now discredited and their meaning distorted. The aims of 'student-centred learning', 'personalisation', 'broadening' the curriculum to relate to the concerns of everyday life are being promoted rapidly as ways of making subject disciplines more relevant and less restrictive. Developing cross-curriculum topics that pick up everyday interests and then use a subject focus to explore them and making key subjects like geography, history and English 'vocational' or 'functional' reflects a huge shift away from subject disciplines.

Instead, we argue that if a 'subject' is to be educational, it must be based on the intellectual disciplines rather than a fashionable idea, a pressing professional concern or political interference. Indeed, the insertion of political imperatives in education amounts to social engineering of the most pernicious sort.

Finally, although arguments that you must change yourself and overcome emotional barriers before changing the world sound similar to a founding goal in traditions of critical and transformative education, we believe that many advocates of this radical-sounding rhetoric are divorced increasingly from political understanding and cultural shifts in images of the human subject. Conservative interest in the fragile aspects of self is the opposite of radical humanistic education. Instead, the rise of 'happiness', 'emotional literacy' or 'emotional well-being' as goals and outcomes of the education system indicates the extent to which passionate belief in the pursuit of knowledge, craft skills and understanding no longer underpins state education for the majority of its students.

Restoring confidence by example

The next step towards re-humanising education would be for educationalists to defend radical humanist education for all children and young people in subjects such as literature and the arts, science, history and mathematics and to re-establish proper craft skills and high quality training. The trouble is that educationalists do not have the confidence for this defence because, deep down, they no longer believe children and young people are capable of education of the sort we have defined here. Our response to this lack of belief is to ask them to look at their pupils and students and see if they conform to the diminished images prevalent through the system, or to a picture of a young person who we can call 'Alex':

Anyone who is involved with the Institute of Ideas and Pfizer 'Debating Matters Competition' will recognise many young people like Alex, who describe themselves in such inspirational ways. Educationalists have a duty to humanity to offer all children the possibility of achieving what Alex had achieved by 15.

Alex

Alex is 15. She wants to study Maths, Physics, History and English Literature in the sixth-form. She is a voracious reader and wants to know everything about every subject. She is an accomplished musician and speaks French and Italian fluently. She writes short stories and has had one published. She is unsure whether she wants an academic career or to go into politics. Whichever she chooses in the end, she wants to go to the top, to be a Professor at Oxford or Cambridge or to be Prime Minister. She admires Mrs Thatcher! Her parents have no post-school education. Her mother works as a classroom assistant and her father works in a vehicle repair workshop.

Conclusion: don't change the subject

Therapeutic education exposes children from the ages of 3 to 18, and older people, to intrusive interventions that probe, elicit and assess their emotions, and make them accountable for them. This reinforces a view that they are vulnerable and at risk. The elision of citizenship, participation, personal and social health education, behaviour management and inclusion is equated with the development of emotional well-being through attributes and 'values' associated with not offending anyone, tolerating difference, eradicating anti-social behaviour. We argue that therapeutic education is social engineering of the feeble, passive subject on an unprecedented scale. This argument highlights stark and uncomfortable questions about the outcomes of what seem like positive, benign and empowering interventions.

Our thesis is novel and we have expected, and received, numerous challenges to it. What runs through these criticisms is a three-fold attempt to change the 'subject'. First, our critics do not want to address the issues we raise but to talk about something else. They literally want to change the subject we are talking about. Presented with our critique of therapeutic education they reply that they don't want to talk about what we call therapy but something else that is 'real' therapy or really efficacious therapy. We do not agree and argue that, except in a few cases where children and young people need therapy because they are emotionally ill, it amounts to the same emotional training for damaged individuals – however empoweringly it is dressed up. The majority of children and young people are not damaged, but the training will damage them. It is no accident that children reporting anxiety in unprecedented numbers have experienced the interventions we discuss in the book: therapeutic education inserts vulnerability and anxiety, children express it and then get more therapeutic interventions.

Second, our critics want to change the subject or subjects that make up the curriculum by adding more emotional or relevant 'subjects'. Making subjects more relevant invariably means adding something that is more related to the problems of everyday life, to the personal and emotional. Even when skills are identified, they are invariably about communication, understanding and relating. In other words, changing the curriculum subject is to take a therapeutic turn. It offers a diminished curriculum for diminished individuals.

Third, and most dangerous of all, they want to change the human subject. The celebration of the emotional over the intellectual fundamentally alters the historical idea of what it is to be human. Far from creating a more balanced and rounded personality, therapeutic education promotes the emotionally diminished human subject and promote a life focused on the self and self-fulfilment rather than with understanding and changing the world. The paradox of therapeutic education, as we have argued, is that an obsession with the self means that you will not change the world, and nor will you change yourself: it is active engagement with the world that leads to confidence, self-esteem, fulfilment or, to use the latest piece of therapy-speak 'happiness and well-being'. The wish and the will to change the world characterises humanity: to turn humanity inwards is to diminish all our selves.

Our final message is: don't change the subject. Don't support changes in the education system which promote a therapeutic ethos which is central to the conscious political construction of the diminished self. Don't devise or adopt any innovative change to the curriculum that presumes many or most children and young people are damaged. Finally, don't proselytise a philo-psychology of the emotions that is misanthropic.

Radical educational humanists continue the Socratic tradition by believing that a life that is unreflective is not worth living. As John Stuart Mill put it: 'It is better to be a human being dissatisfied than a pig satisfied; better to be Socrates dissatisfied than a fool satisfied' (Mill 1863: 140).

What makes humanity is the intellectual and an education based on *cogito ergo sum* not *sentio ergo sum*.

Bibliography

Aaronovitch, D. (2003) 'Less therapy? What we need is more …', *Guardian*, 11 March.

Alexander, R. (2007) *Community Soundings: First Report of the Cambridge University Primary Review Group*, Cambridge: Cambridge University Press.

Anderson, J. (1980) 'Education and practicality', in *Education and Inquiry*, Oxford: Basil Blackwell: 153–8.

Antidote (2001) *Manifesto: Developing an Emotionally Literate Society*, London: Antidote.

Antidote (2007) www.antidote.org.uk (accesed 6 March 2008).

Armitage, A., Bryant, R., Dunnill, R., Flanagan, K., Hayes, D., Hudson, A., Kent, J., Lawes, S. and Renwick, M.([1999, 2003] 2007) *Teaching and Training in Post Compulsory Education*, 3rd edn, Maidenhead: Open University Press.

Arnold, M. ([1864] 2003) 'The function of criticism at the present time', in Collini, S. (ed.) *Culture and Anarchy and Other Writings*, Cambridge: Cambridge University Press: 26–51.

Arnot, C. (2006) 'Ode to joy', *Education Guardian*, 6 June.

Atkins, E. (2007) 'The impossible dreams of an invisible cohort: a case study exploring the hopes, aspirations and learning identities of three groups of level 1 students in two English further education colleges', Education Doctorate Thesis, Sheffield: University of Sheffield.

Avis, J. (2007) *Education, Policy and Social Justice: Learning and Skills*, London: Continuum.

Avis, J. and Bathmaker, A.-M. (2006) 'From trainee to lecturer: trials and tribulations', *Journal of Vocational Education and Training*, 58, 2, 171–89.

BACP/Future Foundation (2004) *The Age of Therapy: Exploring Attitudes Towards and Acceptance of Counselling and Psychotherapy in Modern Britain*, London: Future Foundation.

Bailey, S. (2007) 'So what's all the fuss about nurture groups?', paper presented to Annual Conference of British Educational Research Association, Institute of Education, London, 5–8 September.

Barnett, R. (2000) *Realizing the University in an Age of Supercomplexity*, Buckingham: SRHE/ Open University Press.

Barnett, R. (2007) *A Will to Learn: Being a Student in an Age of Uncertainty*, Maidenhead: SRHE/Open University Press.

Bates, I. (1991) 'Closely observed training: an exploration of links between social structures, training and identity', *International Studies in Sociology of Education*, 1, 2, 225–43.

Bawden, A. (2007) 'Walking back to happiness', *Education Guardian*, 20 March: 8.

Beadle, P. (2007) 'Children's happiness is the only thing worth aspiring to', *Education Guardian*, 20 February: 6.

Beard, C., Clegg, S. and Smith, K. (2007) 'Acknowledging the affective in higher education', *British Educational Research Journal*, 33, 2 (April), 235–52.

Beck, U. (1992) *Risk Society: Towards a New Modernity*, London and New York: Sage.

Bennett, C. (2005) 'The benefits of headline therapy', *G2 Supplement, The Guardian*, 31 May: 9.

Best, R. (2007) 'University students also self-harm: a case study'. Project funded by Sir Halley-Stewart Trust and Roehampton College, London: Roehampton University.

Biesta, G. and Tedder, M. (2007) 'Agency and learning in the lifecourse: towards an ecological perspective', *Studies in the Education of Adults, 39*, 2, 132–49.

Black, P. and Wiliam, D. (1998) 'Assessment and classroom learning', *Assessment in Education*, 5, 1, 7–70.

Black, P., Harrison, C., Lee, C., Marshall, M. and Wiliam, D. (2003) *Assessment for Learning: Putting it into Practice*, Buckingham: Open University Press.

Blair, T. (1997) Speech given to Stockwell Park School, London, December 1997.

Bliss, T. (2004) *Coming Round to Circle Time: A Training Video*, Bristol: Lucky Duck Publishing.

Bliss, T., Robinson, G. and Maines, B. (1995) *Coming Round to Circle Time: A Training Video*, London: Paul Chapman.

Bloom, A. (2007a) 'Lessons in handling the worries of the world', *Times Educational Supplement*, 11 May: 10.

Bloom, A. (2007b) 'The new stuff of nightmares', *Times Educational Supplement*, 11 May: 30.

Bookchin, M. (1995) *Re-Enchanting Humanity. A Defense of the Human Spirit Against Anti-Humanism, Misanthropy, Mysticism and Primitivism*, New York: Cassell.

Boxhall, M. (2002) *Nurture Groups in Schools: Principles and Practice*, London: Paul Chapman.

Brookfield, S.D. (1995a) *Becoming a Critically Reflective Teacher*, San Francisco, CA: Jossey-Bass Publishers.

Brookfield, S.D. (1995b) 'Changing the culture of scholarship to the culture of teaching', in Schuller, T. (ed.) *The Changing University?* Buckingham: SRHE/Open University Press: 128–38.

Broxtowe-Smith, N. (2007) 'Addressing the mental health needs of students', workshop session, Annual Staff Conference, Truro College, 10 July.

Callinicos, A. (1989) *Against Postmodernism: A Marxist Critique*, Cambridge: Polity Press.

Chipmunk Publishing, www.chipmunkpublishing.co.uk (accessed 7 July 2007).

Claxton, G. (2002) *Building Learning Power*, Bristol: TLO Ltd.

Claxton, G. (2005) 'It ain't what you do, it's the way that you do it: a debate about learning to learn', Battle of Ideas Annual Conference, Royal College of Art, London, 29 October.

Claxton, G. (2007) Presentation to the All-Party Parliamentary Group seminar, 'Well-being in the classroom', Portcullis House, London, 23 October.

Clegg, S. (2005) 'It's ok to think about feelings', *THES*, 11 November.

Coffield, F., Moseley, D., Hall, E. and Ecclestone, K. (2004) *Learning Styles in Post-sixteen Education: A Systematic and Critical Review*, London: Learning and Skills Research Centre.

Coffield, F., Hodgson, A., Spours, K., Finlay, I., Edward, S. and Steer, R. (2008) *Improving Learning, Skills and Inclusion: The Impast of Policy on Post-Compulsory Education*, London: Routledge.

Colley, H. (2003a) *Mentoring for Social Inclusion: A Critical Approach to Nurturing Mentor Relationships*, London: Routledge.

Colley, H. (2003b) 'The myth of mentor as a double regime of truth: producing docility and devotion in engagement mentoring with disaffected youth', in Satterthwaite, J.,

Atkinson, E., and Gale, K. (eds) *Discourse, Power, Resistance: Challenging the Rhetoric of Contemporary Education*, Stoke-on-Trent: Trentham Books.

Colley, H. (2006) 'Learning to labour with feeling: class, gender and emotion in childcare, education and training', *Contemporary Issues in Early Childhood*, 7, 1, 15–29.

Colley, H. and Hodkinson, P. (2001) 'Problems with "Bridging the Gap": the reversal of structure and agency in addressing social inclusion', *Critical Policy Review*, 21, 3, 337–61.

Collins, M. (2001) *Circle Time for the Very Young*, Bristol: Lucky Duck Publishing.

Cooper, D. (1993) 'Truth and liberal education', in Barrow, R. and White, P. (eds) *Beyond Liberal Education: Essays in Honour of Paul H. Hirst*, London and New York: Routledge: 30–48.

Cornwall, J. and Walter, C. (2006) *Therapeutic Education: Working Alongside Troubled and Troublesome Children*, London: Routledge.

Cowan, J. (1998) *On Becoming an Innovative University Teacher: Reflection in Action*, Buckingham: SRHE/Open University Press.

Cowie, H., Boardman, C., Barnsley, J. and Jennifer, D. (2004) *Emotional Health and Wellbeing: A Practical Guide for Schools*, London: Paul Chapman.

Craig, C. (2007) *The Potential Dangers of a Systematic, Explicit Approach to Teaching Social and Emotional Skills (SEAL)*, Glasgow: Centre for Confidence and Well-Being.

Crick, B. (1998) *Education for Citizenship and the Teaching of Democracy in Schools*, London: QCA.

Cully, M., Woodland, S., O'Reilly, A. and Dix, G. (1999) *Britain At Work. As Depicted by the 1998 Workplace Employee Relations Survey*, London and New York: Routledge. http://www.stressbusting.co.uk./news_present.htm.

Curphey, M. (2002) 'Talking about making a career out of helping others?', *Guardian*, 5 October.

CUSN (2007) CUSN reports 188 per cent growth in calls to help line: http://www.cusn.info/node/44 (accesed 6 March 2008).

Daugherty, R., Black, P., Ecclestone, K., James, M. and Newton, P. (2007) 'Assessing significant learning outcomes', paper presented to British Educational Association Annual Conference, Institute of Education, London, 5–8 September.

Davenport, N. (2007) 'The rise and rise of credentialism', in Hayes, D., Marshall, T. and Turner, A. (eds) *A Lecturer's Guide to Further Education*, Maidenhead: Open University Press: 126–43.

Davies, J. and Ecclestone, K. (2007) '"Straitjacket" or "springboard" for sustainable learning? The implications of formative assessment practices in vocational learning cultures', Paper presented to British Educational Research Association Annual Conference, Institute of Education, London, 5–8 September.

Deakin-Crick, R. (2007) 'Learning how to learn: the dynamic assessment of learning power', *The Curriculum Journal*, 18, 3, 135–53.

Delanty, G. (2001) *Challenging Knowledge: The University in the Knowledge Society*, Buckingham: SRHE/Open University Press.

DEMOS (2005) 'The adaptive state: putting people before policy in public service reform: an outline of current projects', www.demos.co.uk (accessed 6 March 2008).

Department for Education and Skills (2002a) 'Education: breaking the cycle of deprivation', DfES Research Conference, 12 November, London: DfES.

Department for Education and Skills (2002b) *Transforming Youth Work: Resourcing Excellent Youth Services*, London: DfES.

Department for Education and Skills (2003) *Every Child Matters: Change for Children*, London: DfES.

Department for Education and Skills (2004) 'Every Child Matters', DfES website, www.dfesf. gsi.gov.uk (accesed 6 March 2008).

Department for Education and Skills (2005a) *Youth Matters*, London: DfES.

Department for Education and Skills (2005b) 'Emotional, behavioural and social skills – guidance', www.dfes.gsi.gov.uk (accesed 6 March 2008).

Department for Education and Skills (2005c) *Social, Emotional Aspects of Learning – Guidance*, London: DfES.

Department for Education and Skills (2005d) *Personalised Learning*, London: Innovations Unit.

Department for Education and Skills (2005e) 'Personalised learning in the learning and skills sector', seminar, London, 13 January.

Department for Education and Skills (2006) 'The wider benefits of learning: a synthesis of findings from the Centre for Research on the Wider Benefits of Learning 1999–2006', Research Brief RCB05-06, October, London: DfES.

Department for Education and Skills (2007) *Early Years Foundation Stage Cards*, London: DfES: http://publications.everychildmatters.gov.uk/default.aspx?PageFunction=productetails &PageMode=publications&ProductId=DFES-00012-2007&.

Eagleton, T. (1996) *The Illusions of Postmodernism*, Oxford: Blackwell.

Ecclestone, K. (2002) *Learning Autonomy in Post-16 Education: The Politics and Practice of Formative Assessment*, London: RoutledgeFalmer.

Ecclestone, K. (2004) 'Learning or therapy? The demoralisation of education', *British Journal of Educational Studies*, 54, 3, 129–47.

Ecclestone, K. (2007a) 'Compliance, commitment and comfort zones: the impact of formative assessment on vocational students' learning careers', *Assessment in Education*, 14, 3, 315–33.

Ecclestone, K. (2007b) 'An identity crisis? Current concerns in research', editorial, *Studies in the Education of Adults*, 39, 2, 121–31.

Ecclestone, K. (2007c) 'Do we need more therapy?', *Psychologies*, June 2007.

Ecclestone, K. (2009) *Transforming Formative Assessment in Further and Vocaional Education*, Maidenhead: Open University Press.

Ecclestone, K. and Hayes, D. (2008) 'Exploring FE teachers' practices in the development of students' emotional well-being', Centre for Excellence in Teacher Training Research Project, Oxford Brookes University.

Ecclestone, K. and McGiveney, V. (2005) 'Are adult educators obsessed with developing self-esteem?', *Adults Learning*, 16, 5, 11–14.

Ecclestone, K. and Quinn, J. (2008) 'Evaluating images of the diminished self in interventions for emotional well-being', bid submitted to the ESRC, January 2008.

Ecclestone, K., Biesta, G. and Hughes, M. (eds) (2008) *Transitions Throug Education, Work and the Life Course*, London: Routledge.

Ecclestone, K., Hayes, D. and Furedi, F. (2005a) '"Knowing me, knowing you": legitimising diminished expectations in post-16 education', Studies in the Education of Adults, 37, 2, 182–200.

Ecclestone, K., Blackmore, T., Biesta, G., Colley, H. and Hughes, M. (2005b) 'Transitions through the lifecourse: political, professional and academic perspectives', paper presented at the Annual TLRP/ESRC Conference, University of Warwick.

Edwards, R. and Usher, R. (1991) 'Disciplining the subject: the power of competence', *Studies in the Education of Adults*, 26, 1, 1–14.

Eldred, J., Ward, K., Snowdon, K. and Dutton, Y. (2005) *Catching Confidence: Guidance for Tutors*, Leicester: NIACE.

Emler, N. (2001) *Self-Esteem: The Costs and Causes of Low Self-Worth*, York: Jospeph Rowntree Foundation.

Evans, J. and Martin, W. (2003) 'Widening participation and studentship in HE: learner perspectives and reflections: the impact of discourse', in Satterthwaite, J., Atkinson, E. and Gale, K. (eds) (2003) *Discourse, Power, Resistance: Challenging the Rhetoric of Contemporary Education*, Stoke-on-Trent: Trentham Books.

Feinstein, L. (2007) Response to presentations to the All-Party Parliamentary Group seminar 'well-being in the classroom', Portcullis House, London, 23 October.

Fevre, R. (2002) *The Demoralisation of Western Culture: Social Theory and the Dilemmas of Modern Living*, London: Continuum.

Fevre, R. (2003) *The New Sociology of Economic Behaviour*, London: Sage.

Field, J. (2000) *Lifelong Learning and the New Educational Order*, Stoke-on-Trent: Trentham Books.

Fielding, M. (2007) 'The human cost and intellectual poverty of high performance schooling: radical philosophy, John McMurray and the remaking of person-centred education', *Journal of Education Policy*, 22, 4, 383–411.

Francis, B. and Skelton, C. (2006) *Reassessing Gender and Achievement*, London: Routledge.

Frankel, H. (2007) 'Surviving the leap year', *Times Educational Supplement Magazine*, 15 June.

Furedi, F. (1999) *The Culture of Fear: Risk Taking and the Morality of Low Expectations*, London: Cassell.

Furedi, F. (2003a) *Culture of Fear: Risk taking and the Morality of Low Expectations*, 2nd edn, London: Continuum.

Furedi, F. (2003b) 'Making people feel good about themselves', inaugural lecture, University of Kent, 24 January.

Furedi, F. (2004) *Therapy Culture: Creating Vulnerability in an Uncertain Age*, London: Routledge.

Gardener, H. (1999) *Intelligence Reframed: Multiple Intelligences for the 21st Century*. New York: Basic Books.

Gardner, H. (2007) *Five Minds for the Future*, Harvard: Harvard Business School Press.

Giddens, A. (1991) *Modernity and Self-Identity: Self and Society in Late Modern Age*, Oxford: Polity Press.

Giddens, A. (1995) *The Transformation of Intimacy: Sexuality, Eroticism and Love in Modern Societies*, Oxford: Polity Press.

Giddens, A. (1998) *Third Way: The Renewal of Social Democracy*, Oxford: Polity Press.

Giddens, A. (2000) *Runaway World: How globalisation is Reshaping our Lives (The Reith Lectures)*, London: Routledge.

Gleeson, D., Davies, J. and Wheeler, E. (2005) 'On the making and taking of professionalism in the further education (FE) workplace', *British Journal of Sociology of Education*, 26, 4, 445–60.

Goleman, D. (1996) *Emotional Intelligence: Why it Can Matter more than IQ*, London: Bloomsbury.

Gray, J. (2002) *Straw Dogs: Thoughts on Humans and Other Animals*, London: Granta Books.

Guignon, A. (2004) *Being Authentic*, Lonodon and New York: Routledge

Hardy, R. (2007) 'The happiness workout', *G2 The Guardian*, 30 October: 16–17.

Hargreaves, E. (2007) 'The validity of collaborative assessment for learning', *Assessment in Education*, 14, 2, 185–99.

Harkin, J., Turner, G. and Dawn, T. (2001) *Teaching Young Adults: A Handbook for Teachers in Post-compulsory Education*, London: Routledge.

Harlen, W. and Deakin-Crick, R. (2002) *A Systematic Review of the Impact of Summative Tests on Students' Motivation*, Report for the EPPI Centre, London: Institute of Education.

Harrison, C. (2007) 'Assessment for learning and well-being in schools', Presentation to Happiness and Well-Being in Schools seminar, King Alfred School, London, 8 November.

Hatcher, R. (2005) *Personalised Learning as Social Selection*, London: Anti-Sats Alliance.

Hayes, D. (2003a) 'New Labour new professionalism', in Satterthwaite, J., Atkinson, E. and Gale, K. (eds) *Discourse, Power, Resistance: Challenging the Rhetoric of Contemporary Education*, Stoke-on-Trent: Trentham Books

Hayes, D. (2003b) 'The changing nexus between education and work', in Lea, J., Hayes D., Armitage, A., Lomas, L. and Markless, S. (eds) *Working in Post-Compulsory Education*, Maidenhead: Open University Press.

Hayes, D. (2004) 'Being bullied? Just grow up!', *FE Focus TES*, 13 August 2004.

Hayes, D. (2005) 'Why I believe we must stop using the b-word in the academy', *The Higher*, 11 March 2005.

Hayes, D. and Hudson, A. (2001) *Basildon: The Mood of the Nation*, London: DEMOS.

Hayes, D. and Wynyard, R. (2002a) 'Whimpering into the good night: resisting McUniversity', in Ritzer, G. (ed.) *The McDonaldization Reader*, Thousand Oaks CA: Sage: 116–25.

Hayes, D. and Wynyard, R. (2002b) 'Introduction', in Hayes, D. and Wynyard, R. (eds) *The McDonaldization of Higher Education*. Westport, CT: Bergin and Garvey: 1–18.

Hayes, D., Marshall, T. and Turner, A. (2007) *A Lecturer's Guide to Further Education*, Maidenhead: Open University Press.

Hayward, G., Hodgson, A., Johnson, J., Oancea, A., Pring, R., Spours, K., Wilde, S. and Wright, S. (2005) *The Nuffield Review of 14–19 Education and Training: Annual Report 2004–2005*, Oxford: Oxford University Press.

Heartfield, J. (2002) *The 'Death of the Subject' Explained*, Sheffield: Sheffield Hallam University Press.

Hegarty, S. (2006) 'Schooling for the future', paper for DfES Seminar 'Future Horizons', Moorfoot, Sheffield, January.

Hirst, P.H. ([1965]1973) 'Liberal education and the nature of knowledge', in Peters, R.S. (ed.) *The Philosophy of Education*, Oxford: Oxford University Press: 87–111.

Hirst, P.H. (1993) 'Education, knowledge and practices', in Barrow, R. and White, P. (eds) *Beyond Liberal Education: Essays in Honour of Paul H. Hirst*, London and New York: Routledge: 184–99.

Hoggett, P. (2000) *Emotional Life and the Politics of Welfare*, Basingstoke: Macmillan.

Hopson, B. and Scally, M. (1980) *Lifeskills Teaching Programme*, Leeds: Lifeskills Associates Ltd.

Hudson, A., Hayes D. and Andrew, T. (1996) *Working Lives in the 1990s*, London: Global Futures.

Hughes, J. (2005) 'Intelligent hearts: emotional intelligence, emotional labour and informalisation at work', a working paper, University of Leicester: Centre for Employment Studies.

Hughes, M., Pollard, A., Claxton, G., Johnson, D. and Winter, J. (2007) *Ready or Not? DVD on Transitions from Primary to Secondary School*, Home and School Knowledge Exchange Project, Teaching and Learning Research Programme, Bristol: University of Bristol.

Hume, M. (1998) *Televictims: Emotional Correctness in the Media AD (After Diana)*, London: LM Special.

Hunt, C. and West, L. (2006) 'Learning in a border country: using psychodynamic ideas in teaching and research', *Studies in the Education of Adults*, 38, 2, 141–59.

Huppert, F. (2007) Presentation to the All-Party Parliamentary Group seminar 'well-being in the classroom', Portcullis House, London, 23 October.

Hyland, T. (2005) 'Learning and therapy: oppositional or complementary processes?', *Adults Learning*, 16, 5, 16–17.

Hyland, T. (2006) 'Vocational education and training and the therapeutic turn', *Educational Studies*, 32, 3, 299–306.

Institute of Ideas (2001) *What is it to be Human?: Conversations in Print*. London: Institute of Ideas.

James, D. and Diment, K. (2003) '"Going underground"? Learning and assessment in an ambiguous space', *Journal of Vocational Education and Training*, 55, 4, 407–22.

James, D. and Biesta, G. (2007) *Improving Learning Cultures in Further Education*, London: Routledge.

James, K. (2004) *Winning Hearts and Minds: How to Promote Health and Well-being through Participation in Adult Learning*, Leicester: National Institute of Adult and Continuing Education.

James, K. and Nightingale, C. (2004) *Discovering Potential: A practitioner's Guide to Supporting Self-esteem and Well-being through Adult Learning*, Leicester: National Institute of Adult and Continuing Education.

James, L. (2007) *Tigger on the Couch: The Neuroses, Psychoses, Disorders and Maladies of our Favourite Childhood Characters*, London: Collins.

James, O. (2003) 'If only we graded mental well-being', *Times Educational Supplement*, 11 April.

James, O. (2007) *Affluenza: How to be Successful and Stay Sane*, London: Vermillion.

Johnson, M. (2004) 'Personalised learning: new directions for schools?', *New Economy*, 11, 4, 187–248.

Johnson, M., Ellis, N., Gotch, A., Ryan, A., Foster, C., Gillespie, J. and Lowe, M. (2007) *Subject to Change: New Thinking on the Curriculum*, London: ATL.

Journal of Vocational Education and Training (2007) 'Learning and inclusion in the learning and skills sector', Special Edition, 59, 2.

Kahr, B. (2006) 'Teaching emotional literacy in secondary schools', Woman's Hour, BBC Radio 4, 5 December.

Kant, I. ([1781] 1978) *Critique of Pure Reason* (trans. N. Kemp-Smith), London and Basingstoke: Macmillan.

Kirk, G. and Broadhead, P. (2007) 'Every child matters and teacher education: a position paper', London: Universities Council for the Education of Teachers.

Kirwan-Taylor, H. (2007) 'Beware the victim', *ES Magazine* 16 November.

Klein, R. (2006) 'The secret of happiness', *Times Educational Supplement*, 13 January: 29.

Kneen, J. (2007) 'Cute calves or just tasty steaks?', *Education Guardian*, 9 October: 9.

Kurlbaum, J (2007) 'Learning to learn: transferable skills for life', *Curriculum Briefing*, 5, 3, 43–9.

Lacewing, M. (2007) 'Is philosophy for children philosophy?', *Communities of Enquiry SAPERE Newsletter*, May: 5–7.

Lane, C. (2007) *Shyness: How Normal Behaviour Became a Sickness*. New Haven, CT: Yale University Press

Langston, V. (2005) 'Putting the psychological aspects of trauma management into an organisational context: a standardised approach', ACW Conference Report, *Counselling at Work*, Summer, 24–5.

Lasch, C. ([1979] 1991) The *Culture of Narcissism: American Life in an Age of Diminishing Expectations*, New York: W.W. Norton.

Lasch, C. (1984) *The Minimal Self: Psychic Survival in Troubled Times*, New York: W.W. Norton.

Lasch, C. (1995) *Haven in a Heartless World*, New York: W.W. Norton.

Lasch, C. (1996) *The Revolt of the Elites and the Betrayal of Democracy*, New York and London: W.W. Norton.

Layard, R. (2006) *Happiness: Lessons from a New Science*, London: Penguin.

Layard, R. (2007) Presentation to the All-Party Parliamentary Group seminar 'well-being in the classroom', Portcullis House, London, 23 October.

Lea, J., Hayes D., Armitage, A., Lomas, L. and Markless, S. (2003) *Working in Post-Compulsory Education*, Maidenhead: Open University Press.

Leadbetter, C. (2004) *Personalisation through Participation*, London: DEMOS.

Limb, A. (2002) 'After dinner speech', Sixth Annual Research Conference of Learning and Skills Research Network, 12 December, University of Cambridge, December.

Loads, D. (2007) 'Reply to Kathryn Ecclestone, Dennis Hayes and Frank Furedi: Knowing me, knowing you – the rise of therapeutic professionalism in the education of adults', *Studies in the Education of Adults*, 39, 1, 92–4.

Lowenthal, D. (2006) Introduction to 'Invited Seminar on Children, Well-being and Therapeutic Education', Roehampton University, 14 December.

Mackney, P. (2006) 'Leitch is in jeopardy without new measures requiring employers to train', Speech to the Labour Party Conference, 25 September 2006: http:www.ucu.org.uk/index. ctm?articleid=1830.

Malik, K. (2001) *Man, Beast or Zombie?*, London: Weidenfield.

Matthews, G., Ziedner, M. and Roberts, R. (2002) *Emotional Intelligence: Science and Myth*, Cambridge, MA: Massachusetts Institute of Technology Press.

Mill, J.S. ([1861] 1991) 'Utilitarianism', in Gray, J. (ed.) *On Liberty and Other Essays (World's Classics)*, Oxford and New York: Oxford University Press: 129–201.

Mill, J.S. (1863) *Utilitarianism*, London: Fontana.

Mill, J.S. ([1873] 1989) *Autobiography*, Harmondsworth: Penguin Classics.

Mortiboys, A. (2005) *Teaching with Emotional Intelligence*, London and New York: Routledge.

Mullan, P. (2000) 'The remodelling of work', paper presented at Mind the Gap: The Educationalising of Work conference, Institute of Ideas/Canterbury Christ Church University College, Canterbury, Kent, 17 June.

Newman, T. and Blackburn, S. (2002) *Transitions in the Lives of Children and Young People: Resilience Factors*, Edinburgh: Barnardo's Policy Research and Influencing Unit/Scottish Executive.

Noddings, N. (2002) *Educating Moral People*, New York: Teachers College Press.

Nolan, J. (1998) *The Therapeutic State: Justifying Government at Century's End*, New York: New York University Press.

Norman, M. and Hyland, T. (2003) 'The role of confidence in lifelong learning', *Educational Studies*, 29, 2/3, 261–72.

Norwich, B. (2005) 'Response to a presentation by Kathryn Ecclestone at a seminar on cultural studies in education', School of Education Seminar Programme, University of Exeter, 15 June.

Nuffield Review of 14–19 Education (2007) Symposium on 14–19 Assessment, Nuffield Foundation Bedford Square, London, 11 October.

Oakeshott, M. ([1967] 1973) 'Learning and teaching', in Peters, R.S. (ed.) *The Concept of Education*, London: Routledge & Kegan Paul: 156–76.

Oates, T (2007) 'Assessing soft outcomes of education', Presentation to the Fabian Fringe, Labour Party Annual Conference, 25–29 September.

O'Connor, W. and Lewis, J. (1999) *Experiences of Social Exclusion in Scotland*, Scottish Executive Central Research Unit, Research Programme Research Findings No. 73, Edinburgh: SEC.

Office for Standards in Education (2005) *Healthy Minds: Promoting Mental Health and Emotional Well-being*, London: OfSTED.

O'Hear, A. (1981) *Education, Society and Human Nature: An Introduction to the Philosophy of Education*, London and New York: Routledge.

Organisation for Economic Cooperation and Development (2001) *The Well-Being of Nations: The Role of Human and Social Capital*, Paris: CERI/OECD.

Organisation for Economic Cooperation and Development (2007) *Understanding the Social Outcomes of Learning*, Paris: CERI/OECD.

Page, B. (2005) 'Some social trends in the UK', presentation to DfES seminar Personalised Learning in the Learning and Skills Sector, 13 January.

Palmer, S. (2006) *Toxic Childhood*, London: Orion Publishers.

Park, J. and Tew, M. (2007) 'Emotional rollercoaster: calming nerves at times of transition', *Curriculum Briefing*, 5, 3, 21–8.

Parris, M. (1996) 'Dunblane and Philip Lawrence's murder should not lower the hurdles for changes in the law.' *The Times*, 28 October.

Parrott, A. (2005) 'Education for health', *Adults Learning*, 16, 5, 14–15.

Patmore, A. (2006) *The Truth about Stress*, London: Atlantic Books.

Pollard, A. and James, M. (eds) (2004) *Personalised Learning: A Commentary from the Teaching and Learning Research Programme*, London: Institute of Education.

Pollard, A., Triggs, P., Broadfoot, P., McNess, E. and Osborne, M. (2003) 'What pupils say: changing policy and practice in primary education', *Journal of Educational Change*, 4, 1, 94–6.

Preston, J. and Hammond, C. (2002) 'The wider benefits of further education: practitioner views', Research Report No. 1, London: Centre for Research on the Wider Benefits of Learning.

Pupavac, V. (2001) 'Therapeutic governance: psycho-social intervention and trauma risk management', *Disasters*, 25, 4, 358–72.

Pupavac, V. (2003) 'War and conflict: the internationalisation of therapy culture', paper presented to Institute of Ideas Conference, Therapy Culture, London, 22 November.

Qualifications and Curriculum Authority (2005) End of Key Stage statements for PSHE (including Citizenship at Key Stages 1 and 2) qca.org.uk (accessed 6 March 2008).

Quinn, J., Thomas, L., Slack, K., Casey, L., Thexton, W. and Noble, J. (2005) *From Life Crisis to Lifelong Learning: Re-thinking Working Class 'Drop-Out' from Higher Education*, York: Joseph Rowntree Foundation.

Rieff, P. ([1966] 1987) *The Triumph of the Therapeutic: Uses of Faith after Freud*, Chicago, IL and London: University of Chicago Press.

Rooney, K. (2004) 'Citizenship education: reflecting a political malaise', in Hayes, D. (ed.) *The RoutledgeFalmer Guide to Key Debates in Education*, London: Routledge.

Rose, N. (1990) *Governing the Soul: The Shaping of the Private Self*, London, Routledge.

Rose, S., Bisson, J. and Wessely, S. (2003) 'Psychological debriefing for preventing post-traumatic stress disorder (PSTD) (Cochrane Review)', *The Cochrane Library*, Issue 1, Oxford: Update Software.

Rowland, S. (2000) *The Enquiring University Teacher*, Buckingham: SRHE/Open University Press.

Rowland, S. (2006) *The Enquiring University: Compliance and Contestation in Higher Education*, Maidenhead: SRHE/Open University Press.

Rowland, S., Byron, C., Furedi, F., Padfield, N. and Smyth, T. (1998) 'Turning academics into teachers?', *Teaching in Higher Education*, 3, 2, 133–42.

Rustin, M. (2001) *Reason and Unreason: Psycholanalysis, Science and Politics*, London and New York: Continuum.

SAPERE (2007) Newsletter, May, Oxford: Oxford Brookes University.

Sennett, R. (1976) *The Fall of Public Man*, London: Penguin.

Sennett, R. (1998) *The Corrosion of Character: The Personal Consequences of Work in the New Capitalism*, New York and London: W.W. Norton and Company.

Sennett, R. (2003) *Respect: The Formation of Character in an Age of Inequality*, London: Allen Lane/Penguin.

Sennett, R. (2006) *The Culture of the New Capitalism*, New Haven, CT and London: Yale University Press.

Sharp, P. (2003) *Emotional Literacy: A Practical Guide for Teachers, Parents and Those in the Caring Professions*, London: Kogan Page.

Sharples, J. (2007) E-mail communication to participants of the All-Party Parliamentary Group seminar 'Well-being in the classroom', Portcullis House, London, 23 October.

Shore, C. and Wright, S. (eds) (2005) *Anthropology of Policy: Critical Perspectives on Governance and Power*, London: Routledge.

Smith, C. (2005) *Karl Marx and the Future of the Human*, Lanham, MD: Lexington Books.

Smithers, A. (2001) 'Education policy', in Seldon, A. (ed.) *The Blair Effect*, London: Little Brown & Company: 405–26.

Social Exclusion Unit (1999) *Bridging the Gap: New Opportunities for 16–19 Year Olds not in Education or Training*, London: SEU.

Social Exclusion Unit (2005) *Transitions for Young People with Complex Needs*, London: SEU.

Sommers, C.H. and Satel, S. (2005a) *One Nation Under Therapy: How the Helping Culture is Eroding Self-Reliance*, London: St Martin's Press.

Sommers, C.H. and Satel, S. (2005b) 'The tyranny of therapism', *spiked-essays*, 21 June: http://www.spiked-online.com/Printable/0000000CABF8.htm (accessed 6 March 2008)..

Spratt, J., Shucksmith, J., Philip, K. and Wilson, C. (2007) 'Embedded yet separate: tensions in voluntary sector working to support mental health in state-run schools', *Journal of Education Policy*, 22, 4, 411–29.

Stephenson Connolly, P. (2007) *Head Case: Treat Yourself to Better Mental Health*, London: Headline.

Stewart-Brown, S. and Edmunds, L. (2003) *Assessing Emotional and Social Competence in Early Years and Primary Settings: A Review of Approaches, Issues and Instruments*. London: DfES.

Stobart, G. (2008) *Testing Times: Uses and Abuses of Assessment*, London: RoutledgeFalmer.

Sutherland, M. (2006) 'Emotional well-being: lessons from neuroscience', presentation to Childhood and Well-being Seminar, Roehampton University, 14 December.

Teachernet (2003) 'Peer mentoring: a listener's experiences', article commissioned by Teachernet: www.teachernet.co.uk (visited 17 July 2007).

Tett, L. and Mclaughlan, K. (2007) 'Adult literacy and numeracy, social capital, learner identities and self-confidence', *Studies in the Education of Adults*, 32, 2, 150–68.

Tew, M. and Park, J. (2007) 'Emotional rollercoaster: calming nerves at times of transition', *Curriculum Briefing*, 5, 3, 21–8.

Torrance, H., Colley, H., Garratt, D., Jarvis, J., Piper, H., Ecclestone, K. and James, D. (2005) *The Impact of Different Modes of Assessment on Achievement and Progress in the Learning and*

Skills Sector, Learning and Skills Development Agency, available at https://www.lsda.org.uk/cims/order.aspx?code=052284&src=XOWEB.

Toynbee, P. (2005) 'They must be having a laugh: the battle for the heart of government', *The Guardian*, 19 April, 2005: 40–1.

Turner, P. (2007) 'The transition to work and adulthood', in Hayes, D., Marshall, T. and Turner, A. (eds) *A Lecturer's Guide to Further Education*, Maidenhead: Open University Press.

UNICEF (2000) *Annual Report*, New York: UNICEF.

UNICEF (2007) *A World Fit for Us: The Children's Statement from the United Nations*, New York: UNICEF.

Unison (2002) *Stress at Work: A Guide For Safety Reps*, London: Unison: http://www.unison.org.uk/acrobat/12879.pdf.

Usher, R. and Edwards, R. (1998) 'Confessing all? A postmodern guide to the guidance and counselling of adult learners', in Edwards, R., Harrison, R. and Tait, A. (eds) *Telling Tales: Perspectives on Guidance and Counselling in Learning*, London: Routledge.

Wainwright, D. and Caplan, M. (2002) *Work Stress: The Making of a Modern Epidemic*, Buckingham: Open University Press.

Waiton, S. (2001) *Scared of the Kids?*, Sheffield: Sheffield Hallam University Press.

Waiton, S. (2007) *The Politics of Antisocial Behaviour: Amoral Panics*, London: Routledge.

Weare, K. (2004) *Developing the Emotionally-Literate School*, London: Paul Chapman.

Weare, K. and Gray, G. (2003) *What Works in Developing Children's Emotional and Social Competence and Well-being?* London: DfES.

Wessely, S. (2005) 'The bombs made enough victims – let's not make more', *Spiked-Online*: http://www.spiked-online.com/index.php?/site/article/874 (accessed 6 March 2008)..

Wessely, S. (2007) Speech at the 'Battle of Ideas' festival, Royal College of Art, London 26 October.

West, L. (2004) 'The trouble with lifelong learning', in D. Hayes (ed.) *The RoutledgeFalmer Guide to Key Debates in Education*, London: Routledge.

Wetherall, M. (2006) 'Identities and transitions: insights from the ESRC "Identities" Research Programme', paper given to the ESRC Transitions through the Lifecourse Seminar Series, University of Nottingham, 11 November.

Whelan, R. (ed.) (2007) *The Corruption of the Curriculum*, London: Civitas.

White, J. (2007) 'What schools are for and why', IMPACT Pamphlet No 14: Philosophy of Education Society of Great Britain.

Willis, K. (2007) Private communication by email, 6 July.

Woodhead, C. (2003) 'Let off for bad behaviour', *The Sunday Times*, 16 November.

Woudhuysen, J. (2002) 'Organisational Innovation in public services: a kind of devolution', *BT Public Policy Forum, Insight paper*, http://www.egovernment.bt.com/ppf_open/insight_reports.html.

Wright, S. (2006) 'The struggle for moral education in English elementary schools 1879–1918', unpublished PhD thesis: Oxford Brookes University.

Wright, S. (2007) 'Into unfamiliar territory? The moral instruction curriculum in English elementary schools 1880–1914', *History of Education Researcher*, 79, 31–9.

Yalom, I.D. (2002) *The Gift of Therapy: Reflections on Being a Therapist*, London: Piatkus.

Zembylas, M. (2007) 'Emotional capital and education: theoretical insights from Bourdieu', *British Journal of Educational Studies*, 55, 4 (December): 443–63.

Index